VLADIMÍR
HRONSKÝ

SLOVAK
WINE
GUIDE

Palugyay sparkling wine made in Bratislava was also served to the first class passengers on the Titanic.

VLADIMÍR HRONSKÝ

SLOVAK WINE GUIDE

slovart

Copyright © Slovart Publishing Ltd 2016
Text © Vladimír Hronský 2016
Translators © Elena and Paul McCullough 2016
Design & Layout © Branislav Gajdoš 2016
Photos © Ondrej Korpás, Martin Krystýnek 2016
Maps © Daniel Gurňák 2016

The book was published thanks to the generous support of

First published in 2016 by Slovart Publishing Ltd, Bratislava.
Editor: Zita Ročkárová
Production: Dana Klimová
Typography & DTP: A21 – studio of fine graphic design, Bratislava
Printed in FINIDR, Český Těšín

All rights reserved. No part of this publication may be reproduced, photocopied or multiplied in any form without the prior written permission of the publisher.

ISBN 978-80-556-1340-6
10 9 8 7 6 5 4 3 2 1
www.slovart.sk

CONTENT

FOREWORD	7
ABOUT THE PUBLICATION	8
VITICULTURE AND WINEMAKING IN SLOVAKIA	10
Viticultural Region of the Small Carpathians	13
Viticultural Region of Southern Slovakia	14
Viticultural Region of Nitra	15
Viticultural Region of Central Slovakia	17
Viticultural Region of Eastern Slovakia	18
Viticultural Region of Tokaj	19
Vintage Quality Overview	21
GRAPEVINE VARIETIES IN SLOVAKIA	22
Traditional White Varieties	25
Traditional Red Varieties	33
Tokaj Varieties	37
New White Clones	39
New Red Clones	43
HOW WINE IS MADE IN OUR COUNTRY	48
White, Rosé and Red Wines	50
Sparkling Wines	53
Tokaj Wines	56
Innovative Methods in Wine Production	59
WHAT DO THE LABELS OF SLOVAK WINES REVEAL?	60
Labeling of Slovak Wines	62
Wine without Geographical Indication	63
Wine with Protected Geographical Indication	64
Wine with Protected Indication of Origin	65
Quality Wines with Attribute	67
Other Traditional Indications	69
OVERVIEW OF THE BEST WINES IN THE MARKET	70
Wines Made of Traditional White Varieties	73
Wines Made of Traditional Red Varieties	88
Wines Made of Tokaj Varieties	98
Wines Made of New White Clones	100
Wines Made of New Red Clones	106
Rosé Wines	111
Terroir-respecting Wines	113
Innovative Wines (Barrique / Kryo / Sur lie)	118
Cuvée / Blends	122
Classical Tokaj Wines	127
Bio Wines	129
Sparkling Wines	131
SLOVAK WINE AND CHEESE	134
SLOVAK WINERIES FROM A TO Z	142
INDEX	241

ACKNOWLEDGMENTS

I would like to thank my family for their tremendous patience and support, as well as Zita Ročkárová, my editor, translators Elena and Paul McCullough and Braňo Gajdoš and his team of graphic designers for their excellent work. I am also indebted to Ondrej Korpás and his son Ondrej for advice and the provision of beautiful photographs of grapevine varieties, Martin Krystýnek for photographing hundreds of bottles of Slovak wine, Juraj Heger for his universal help as a publisher; and the Slovak wine growers and winemakers for their cooperation.

FOREWORD

The passage of time is a strange phenomenon. It brings new incentives and new challenges as well as the opportunity to summarize and make use of experience from everyday life. It's hard to believe that fifteen years have passed since the publication of my first book. During this time, I travelled thousands of kilometers to seek out the best wines on this planet; I became acquainted with famous and completely unknown destinations of the Old and New World, while tasting thousands of wine samples representing hundreds of varieties and dozens of terroirs. I met many fanatics similar to me: winegrowers, winemakers, sommeliers, laymen and enthusiastic lovers of good wine.

Although I continue to travel for good wine, my journeys always lead back to my homeland – Slovakia. Our country, situated in the heart of Central Europe, has enchanted me by its proud winemaking temperament, winegrowing tradition, winemaking vitality passed down from generation to generation and the effort to bring them to perfection by understanding and applying current trends in winegrowing and winemaking.

Credit for the *Slovak Wine Guide* that you now hold in your hands goes out to many excellent teachers, winegrowers, breeders, winemakers, sommeliers and friends of quality wine whom I esteem tremendously. The book provides the objective view of a professional regarding the current quality, diversity and classification of Slovak wines. It reveals the mastery of winemakers and focuses on the essence of Slovak wines, which lies in our soil, the environment in which we grow the grapevines, as well as in the cellars where we make the wine. In our wine you will find our hearts, as well as our love and hard work without which Slovakia could not have entered the annals of viticultural history.

Slovak winegrowing and winemaking stand at the beginning of a new era. A young generation has emerged and is striving to make our wines more perfect, more complex, more attractive for everyone at home and abroad. We are a small, and for many people, undiscovered country of great wines. I believe that my overview of their quality will help you to find your favorite vintages, compare your own sensory experience and pick the wines which you think are best for you.

ABOUT THE PUBLICATION

Changes in the social system after 1989 also triggered a revolution in the development of Slovak viticulture and winemaking. Slovak wines begin to appear on the European wine market in the early 1990s; they competed for a place in regular restaurants and at special gastronomic events and scored points at prominent international competitions. Although the wine production of Slovakia amounts to 0.1 % of the world's wine production, many sommeliers, wine lovers and wine merchants have become interested in its attractive assortment. The many positive responses and the growing demand of international consumers gave me the idea to write an original, understandable and comprehensive guide for good Slovak wine and its producers. As a result, this publication, which provides useful information in English about Slovak wines and winemakers, fills a space that had long remained empty on the shelves of bookstores.

The introductory chapters are dedicated to winegrowing and winemaking in Slovakia, as well as the viticultural regions and grapevine varieties most frequently cultivated in our territory. Readers will find out how professionals make wine, how it is labelled and what the labels reveal about the wine.

The main section presents profiles of 50 Slovak wineries and their wines. I have selected winemakers which are interesting in terms of the quantity and quality of the wine they produce. Although I asked the winemakers to recommend a number of representative wines from their selection and to provide relevant information about their wineries, the making of this book did not in any way include their financial support.

However, I would like to thank the producers for the complimentary samples of the wines described in this guidebook. I tasted each wine twice: immediately after receiving delivery of the samples, and then two or three months later. Wines which showed shortcomings in their microbiological purity, lacked data in according to valid European legislation or for which the producer failed to indicate the origin of grapes used for their making were not included in this book. The same rule applied for companies that were not validly entered in the winemakers register.

Each wine profile features the following data: the name of the wine, vintage, varietal composition in the case of quality branded wines, classification according to origin and grape quality, classification according to residual sugar, and production volume in liters, bottle volume. Each profile also contains information about the retail price recommended by the producer, and the production batch number and alcohol content. My commentary on the taste and style of the wine, its potential for maturing in bottles and overall evaluation were complemented based on my own sensory analysis.

This guide features a selection of the 365 most interesting wines representing contemporary Slovak winemaking. Most wine guides classify wine in a chart according to quality based on total points acquired in evaluation; however I have decided to use a thematic arrangement. I present an overview of the best vintages from the most frequently cultivated traditional varieties and new clones according to color and the vinification method used for their production. Special collections feature wines respecting terroir, innovative wines, cuvée, classical Tokaj wines, bio wines and sparkling wines.

Gourmets, sommeliers, and winemakers can also draw inspiration from the chapter entitled Slovak Cheeses and Wines. We present here a selection of dairy products which I combined with optimal categories of wine as well as specific wines in a joint menu.

I believe that my publication will speak to everyone – starting with sommeliers through distributors, restaurant owners up to visitors of wine trails and all fans of Slovak wine. I hope to meet you again in regularly updated editions of this book.

V. H.

VITICULTURE AND WINEMAKING IN SLOVAKIA

The quality of Slovak wine has distinctively improved in the fifteen years since the publication of my first book on Slovak wines. The viticulture and winemaking structure in Slovakia has also undergone a complex change. Many new wine producers have emerged, while others no longer exist. However, the majority of traditional entities overcame the entry to the common European market with high quality wine with attractive bottling and labeling. The young generation of winegrowers and winemakers operate on a smaller area of vineyards, but they stride with greater professional enthusiasm on the path towards world quality Slovak wine. This has been proved by dozens of awards from prominent international competitions. And from year to year their numbers grow.

Viticultural Region of the Small Carpathians	13
Viticultural Region of Southern Slovakia	14
Viticultural Region of Nitra	15
Viticultural Region of Central Slovakia	17
Viticultural Region of Eastern Slovakia	18
Viticultural Region of Tokaj	19
Vintage Quality Overview	21

Grapevines (Vitis vinifera) are cultivated in the Slovak Republic in viticultural areas (vineyards) registered in the viticultural land register. Pursuant to Act No. 313 on Viticulture and Winemaking of July 30, 2009, which entered into validity on December 1, 2012, the **Slovak Viticultural Country** is the largest geographical unit. It is segmented into six viticultural regions, 40 viticultural areas and 603 viticultural villages. In 2012, there was a total of 18,705 hectares of registered vineyards in Slovakia. Each **viticultural region** has distinctive natural conditions that affect the character and quality of the wine. **A viticultural area** is a smaller section of a viticultural region that is characterized by a higher degree of homogeneity of climatic, soil and orographic conditions which have an impact on the character and quality of the wine. **Viticultural villages** are another important geographical unit. Viticultural areas are situated within their cadastral territories. Basic geographical units (vineyards) with a high degree of homogeneity of natural conditions are called **vineyard sites** (vineyards). They represent a compact part of viticultural areas. They may also be a part of the cadaster of one or several neighboring viticultural villages.

The **climatic conditions** crucial for grapevine cultivation include the temperatures in individual growing seasons (winter, spring, etc.), the sum of active air temperature, the absorbed thermal energy of the sun on a unit of grapevine leaf area, the length of exposure to the sun, annual precipitation totals in individual growing seasons, cloud cover, wind direction, and the frequency and intensity of storms and hailstorms. The following **soil conditions** are important: geological subtype of soil, kind of soil, soil skeleton, carbonate and salt content, as well as drainage. **Orographic conditions** are related to the orientation of vineyards to cardinal points, elevation, incline, super-elevation and shade cast on the horizon. You can read more about the classification of Slovak grape wine according to geographical origin in the chapter What Do the Labels of Slovak Wines Reveal.

All but one of the viticultural regions of Slovakia are situated in zone B pursuant to European **zoning guidelines;** the Tokaj viticultural region is in zone C. The viticultural villages with the warmest soil and microclimatic conditions are in the B1 sub-category. They are situated in the areas of Bratislava, Hurbanovo, Modra, Pezinok, Strekov, Želiezovce and Žitava.

This sub-category also includes all of the villages of the Tokaj viticultural region, which are evaluated even better than the B1 wine viticultural areas in terms of soil and orographic conditions. The soil and orographic conditions of B2 sub-category viticultural areas meet the requirements for the B1 subcategory in the grapevine growing season; however the sum of active temperature is lower. B3 sub-category viticultural areas are on the break-even point of winegrowing, and situated in areas with an unsuitable orientation, more shade cast on the horizon, and a colder microclimate.

The Tokaj viticultural region is Slovakia's only closed viticultural region, i.e., a territory with specific soil and climatic conditions, with a designated exposition of vineyards, a permanent variety composition, and a special winegrowing and winemaking regime. Slovak Tokaj is not broken down into areas but directly into viticultural villages based on the heritage of the unique Tokaj zoning which was formed, developed and renovated by generations of our predecessors.

Viticultural Regions of the Slovak Republic in Numbers

Area of registered vineyards	18,705 ha
Bearing vineyards	15,038 ha
Non-bearing vineyards up to 3 years from planting	440 ha
Share of must varieties designated for wine production	98.57 %
Rootstock vineyards and grapevine nurseries	1.43 %
Average yield in registered vineyards	5.14 t/ha
Total wine production in 2012	360,000 hl
Import to EU countries in 2012	166,000 hl

VITICULTURAL REGION OF THE SMALL CARPATHIANS

The oldest winegrowing region is situated in southwestern Slovakia, where the vineyards are bathed in the sunshine of the southern, southeastern and southwestern slopes of the Small Carpathians. The southern and western viticultural routes of this region are situated on the elevated plains and rolling hills at the foot of the Small Carpathians.

The 5,488 hectares of registered vineyards in this region are divided into 12 viticultural areas with cadasters of 120 viticultural villages. The soil in the vineyards is medium skeleton, loamy sandy and rocky on the slopes, with loess or drift sand on the edges. It features low water retention and high sun energy absorption. The geological bed is composed of paragneiss, granite and granodiorite. The vineyards are situated from 100 to 260 meters above sea level. The Viticultural Region of the Small Carpathians (hereinafter referred to as the "VRoSC") lies in a continental climate zone. Atmospheric precipitation is evenly spread throughout the entire year with 670 mm on average. This is a windy region with a predominant northwest air circulation. The average temperature in the growing cycle is 17.5 °C, the average annual length of exposure to the sun is 2,100 hours and the sum of the active temperature during the growing cycle is more than 3,000 °C. The temperature difference between day and night in the grape ripening period is approximately 15 °C, which ensures a higher acid content in the must.

The most important cultivated varieties are Grüner Veltliner, Italian Riesling and Lemberger (Blaufränkish). The wineries associated with the Small Carpathian Wine Route feature local varieties in every viticultural village in which the local microclimate along with the soil and efforts of winegrowers result in outstanding sensorial qualities. Grüner Silvaner from Limbach, Kerner from Grinava, Feteasca Regala from Svätý Jur, Italian Riesling from Modra, Feteasca Alba from Kráľová, Blauer Portugieser from Orešany, Pinot Blanc from Šenkvice, as well as Chardonnay from Skalica are worth mentioning. In addition, we would be remiss if we failed to acknowledge traditional branded wines such as **Račianska frankovka** (Rača Lemberger), **Skalický rubín** (Skalica Ruby) and **Skalická frankovka** (Skalica Lemberger). We can also discover wine from complementary varieties and varieties that are no longer part of the current assortment (Red Silvaner, Chasselas, Muscat Ottonel, Veltliner Frühroter Malvasia, Dornfelder) and wines from new clones of varieties (Devín, Aurelius, Pálava, Dunaj, Hron). Cultivating international varieties, such as Viognier, Syrah and Merlot, in new vineyard planting which has not yet been registered in Slovakia is a regional rarity.

VITICULTURAL REGION OF SOUTHERN SLOVAKIA

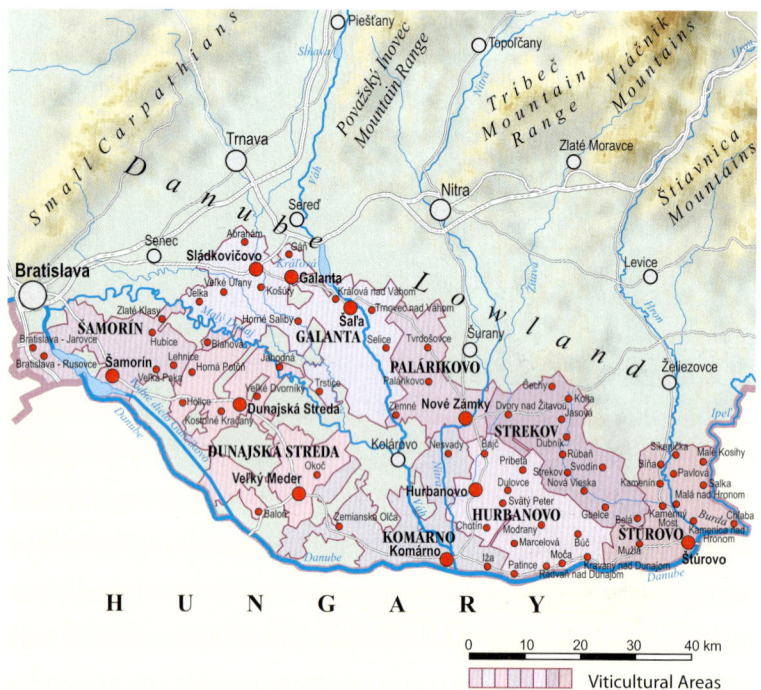

The vineyard sites of Southern Slovakia are situated on lowland plains, loess hills and clayloam soil terraces north of the Danube River basin. This region incorporates 8 viticultural areas with cadasters of 114 viticultural villages. The plains on the boundaries of the Danube lowlands change into slightly rolling hills with fertile river terraces due to Neogene river sediments. Terraces are brilliant sites for all varieties requiring high sun energy concentration. The average air temperature in the growing season is 18.5 °C; the sum of active temperature during the growing season exceeds 3,400 °C, while the average annual length of exposure to the sun is 2,200 hours. The Viticultural Region of Southern Slovakia

VITICULTURE AND WINEMAKING IN SLOVAKIA

(hereinafter referred to as the "VRoSS") is the hottest viticultural region in Slovakia with a dry climate and moderate winters. The conditions are excellent for growing varieties with later ripening grapes designated for the production of wines with attribute of supreme quality.

The total annual precipitation - 550 mm - is evenly distributed. Sufficient warmth, a deep soil profile and an optimum water regimen are the preconditions for a rich yield of must with high sugar content. In the case of new planting and renovation, grapevines are no longer cultivated on unprotected lowland plains where there is a danger of freezing temperatures. Most of the planting is concentrated on the uplands and alluvial terraces around the river basins of the Danube, Váh, Hron, and smaller rivers such as the Small Danube, Nitra, Žitava, and at the confluence of the Ipeľ and the Danube in the easternmost corner. The region's 4,558 hectares are not fully utilized. However, ideal conditions for winegrowing enable its full use and further extension. The most common varieties in this region are the white wine grape varieties of Italian Riesling, Grüner Veltliner, Rhein Riesling, Pinot Blanc and Chardonnay. Red wine grape varieties include Lemberger (Blaufränkish), Cabernet Sauvignon, Pinot Noir and Saint Laurent. The cultivating of new clones of varieties was successfully developed in this region during the Socialist era. The cooperation of the former viticultural cooperatives of Mužla, Rúbaň, Dvory nad Žitavou, Strekov, Svodín, Dulovce, Modrany, Pribeta, Okoč and Moča with domestic breeders resulted in dozens of new wine grape and table grape clones of varieties which found their home in the viticultural areas of Strekov and Štúrovo. In addition to these new varieties, local winegrowers and winemakers discovered forgotten varieties such as Bouvier, Honigler, Pamid and Lipovina (Harslevelü), which were the most widespread here before the Phylloxera louse. Tasting these varieties is a treat and spiritual experience for every wine connoisseur.

VITICULTURAL REGION OF NITRA

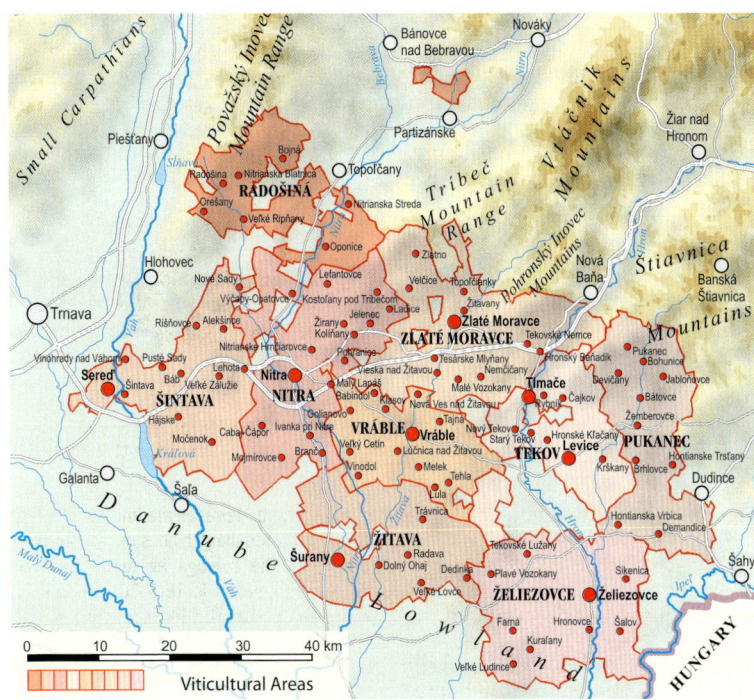

Vineyards in the Viticultural Region of Nitra (hereinafter referred to as the "VRoN") are among the most picturesque and diverse in Slovakia in terms of exposition, soil and microclimatic conditions. They are situated on the southern, southwestern and southeastern slopes of the Tríbeč mountain range and stretch along the borderline of the Danube lowlands to the hillsides of the Považský Inovec mountain range. The south of this region has a warm and dry climate with moderate winters; the north has a colder climate and higher precipitation. Vineyard sites begin in the west along the right bank of the Váh River towards the towns of Veľké Zálužie and Nitra, and southbound towards the town of Mojmírovce. The northern vineyard sites in the vicinity of the town of Radošina are protected by the Považský Inovec hills, while the vineyards in the towns of Jelenec and Topoľčianky are protected by the Vtáčnik mountain range. The charming uplands of the towns of Vráble, Čajkov and Tekov hide scattered vineyard sites which descend to the Hron River and continue through the southern gate to the towns of Levice and Želiezovce. The foothills of Štiavnické vrchy (Pukanec) and Krupinská pahorkatina (Žemberovce) create the borderline of VRoN in the east.

The region has 9 viticultural areas and 159 viticultural villages. Thanks to the chain of mountains, the total precipitation average – 550 mm - is more inclined to the growing season when there is 30% more precipitation than in the winter. Average air temperatures between the northern and southern latitudes vary from 16.8 °C to 17.6 °C. The sum of active temperature also varies: 3,100 °C in the south and 3,000 °C in the north. The average annual length of exposure to the sun is 2,200 hours. Vineyards occupy a total area of 3,823 hectares. Vineyard sites on the north and east take advantage of the skeleton formed by Mesozoic limestone, dolomite, quartzite and sandstone. The central, southern and southwestern vineyard sites are planted in Neogene sediments which extend here from the VRoSS. The diversity of climate conditions is also significantly affected by altitude. Lowland vineyards are situated in altitudes of 100 to 150 meters, mountain vineyards extend along the south slopes of the Tríbeč mountain range on medium heavy, heat absorbant and nutritious soils with skeleton in altitudes ranging from 240 to 350 meters.

The diversity of natural conditions in the Nitra region is confirmed by the variety of grapevines with different environmental requirements. Pinot Blanc, Pinot Gris, Sauvignon Blanc, Müller-Thurgau, Feteasca Regala, Traminer and Lemberger (Blaufränkish) are the basis of the best quality wines from the mountainous north of this region. They are characterized by a higher acid content, a piquant bouquet and expressive fresh taste.

In years with long, dry autumns, local winegrowers impatiently wait for the first frost when the air temperature drops under the magical minus seven degree mark for at least for 24 hours. Berries of medium late varieties with firm skin freeze in the vineyards and after harvesting winemakers use them to make precious ice wine. If the vintage fails to bring an early frost, the healthy grapes are harvested and stored in small containers. After sorting, winemakers hang the clusters of grapes in a well-aired room on strings or place them on straw-covered racks. By law, overripe berries must be dried for at least three months. The precious concentrate of sweet must is pressed from straw grapes, which after fermentation is valued by aficionados of naturally sweet straw wines.

The heart of this region is situated in a milder and dryer climate with excellent variety wines: Italian Riesling, Müller-Thurgau, Grüner Veltliner and Saint Laurent. Pálava, Devín and Dunaj plantings (in the viticultural villages of Čajkov, Tajná, Šintava, Lúčnica, Dolný Ohaj) are attractive from among the new clones of varieties. The bearing intensive plantings of red Cabernet Sauvignon and Lemberger (Blaufränkish) varieties raised interest in the production of quality rosé wines in the south of this region. Rhein Riesling and Pinot Noir, as well as Semillon from forgotten minorities, have reappeared among classical varieties. However, the largest share of grapes does not end up in wines with high attribute but in harmonious wines with fine bouquets; many are used for the production of quality sparkling wine (J. E. Hubert, Pálffy, Sekt 1933).

VITICULTURAL REGION OF CENTRAL SLOVAKIA

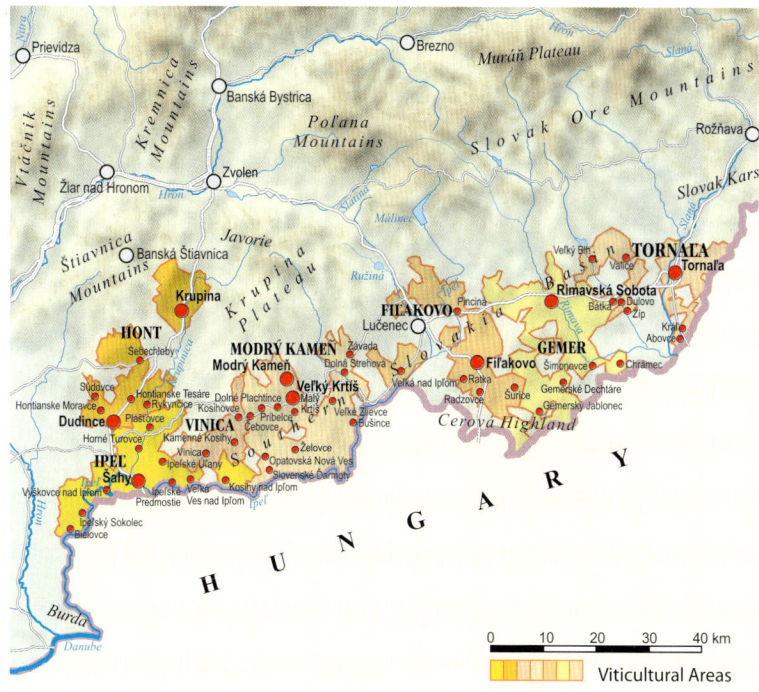

This is an interesting region in terms of its geology and rich winegrowing and winemaking tradition. It has no compact vineyard sites; however it offers many diverse **terrorirs** from the highest situated slopes of the hills of Krupinská pahorkatina through the volcanic mountains of Sitno and Štiavnické vrchy up to the elevated plains of Ipeľská nížina. The Viticultural Region of Central Slovakia (hereinafter referred to as the "VRoCS") is comprised of 7 viticultural areas and 107 viticultural villages with a total registered area of vineyards of 2,289 hectares. The climate is dry with an average precipitation of 450 mm. Average air temperature during the growing season reaches 16.2 °C. The length of exposure to the sun is 2,100 hours per year. The northern microclimate is harsher and colder and slightly humid. A more moderate climate with milder winters can be found in the south. The region's geological bed is diverse. It is created by Neogene sediments, argillaceous sandstone with no skeleton, with nutritious, heavy clay-loam soils and medium heavy loam soil on top. In the mountainous northwest part of this region grapevines grow on andesite substrates with higher mineral content. Volcanic activity left its traces here. Even today, wine is stored in tuff cellars from the 16th century that were originally used by the locals as hiding places from the Turks (Sebechleby). Italian Riesling, Rhein Riesling, Müller-Thurgau, Grüner Veltliner, Pinot Blanc and Chardonnay are the most frequently cultivated white varieties. The aromatic Traminer and Devín make excellent wines. Sauvignon Blanc and Pinot Gris are popular from local variety wines, as well as the relatively rare, self-grown hybrids which are called **samorodne** (Izabela, Jeruzalem, Otthelo, Delaware). They were left after the period of the Phylloxera louse which destroyed a large part of vineyards with high-bred grapevine varieties in Europe. Wines from **samorodne** varieties have been and still are the subject of small-scale, home production and are not introduced to the wine market. However, you can taste them on a visit to the ancient cellar directly under Stará hora. This region's red wines are made of Lemberger (Blaufränkish) and Saint Laurent. The selection of international varieties has been supplemented by Cabernet Sauvignon and Pinot Noir with noteworthy results.

The ecological production of grapes and wine is successfully developing in this region due to its extremely clean natural ecosystem. The first registered bio-vineyard was planted in the viticultural site of Katovka in the vicinity of Modrý Kameň in 1998. Today, the certified production of bio-wines is centralized in the viticultural areas of Modrý Kameň and Vinica in the viticultural villages of Veľký Krtíš, Modrý Kameň, Dolné Plachtince and Vinica.

VITICULTURAL REGION OF EASTERN SLOVAKIA

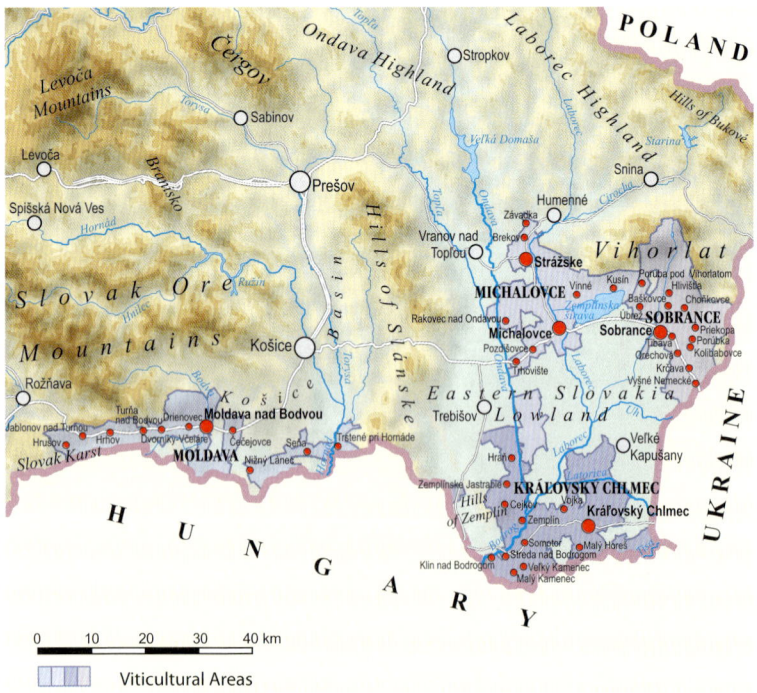

This region is composed of four viticultural areas with 89 viticultural villages in the southwest near Moldava nad Bodvou, in the northeast near Vinné, Sobrance, Orechová, Priekopa, Poruba pod Vihorlatom and Vyšné Nemecké, and in the southeast in the vicinity of the Topľa, Ondava and Bodrog river basin near the town of Streda nad Bodrogom and Kráľovský Chlmec. The soil composition and geographical diversity of the Viticultural Region of Eastern Slovakia (hereinafter referred to as the "VRoES") provides sunny and airy locations on volcanic igneous rock with a heavy clay loam bed. Vineyards situated in the karst area have an andesite skeleton which, south of the Zemplín region, turns into light sandy

VITICULTURE AND WINEMAKING IN SLOVAKIA

soil with a distinctively dry profile. The average altitude of viticultural sites begins at 100 meters and rises as high as 250 meters. The rewarding warm, slightly dry continental climate enables a regular harvest of highly ripened grapes in the fall. The average air temperature in the growing season is 16.6 °C and accumulated precipitation is 373 mm. The production of extractive wines with velvety bouquets and full taste from Pinot Blanc, Pinot Gris and Pinot Noir varieties is successful in this region thanks to an average length of exposure to the sun of 2,200 hours and a sum of active temperatures of more than 3,300 °C during the growing season. The almost forgotten variety of Grüner Silvaner and the almondy Grüner Veltliner are also enjoying a renaissance.

The more southern locations are suitable for Müller-Thurgau, Italian Riesling, Chardonnay and Traminer, while Lemberger and the new Dunaj clone are extremely interesting red varieties. Rhein Riesling and Sauvignon Blanc from old plantings at the foot of Vihorlat mountain have a piquantly fresh and long mineral body with a rich herbal and honey-fruity aroma. In comparison to more southern regions of Slovakia, the wines from the VRoES are more extractive, full and more mineral at first taste. The stable microclimate combined with integrated ecological winegrowing enable more progressive wineries (Tibava, Orechová, Malý Horeš) to produce wines that respect the local terroir.

VITICULTURAL REGION OF TOKAJ

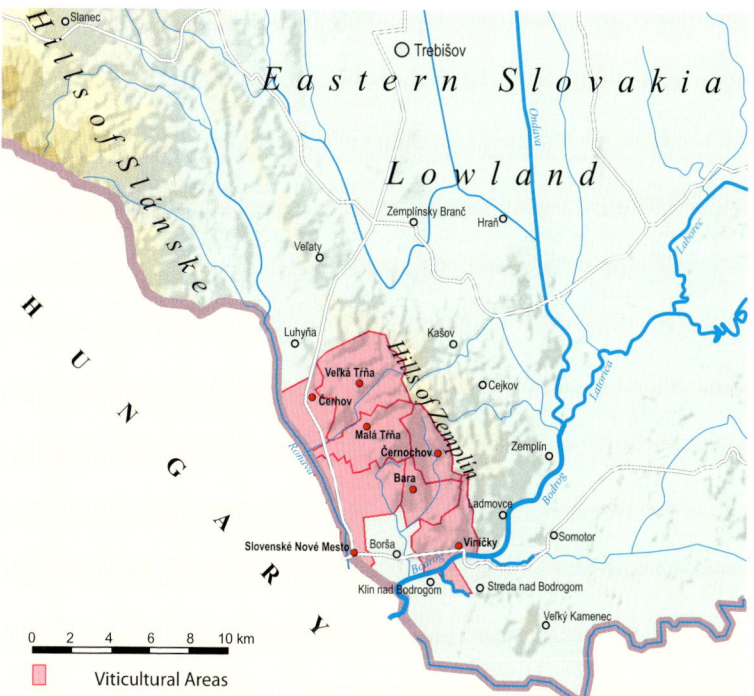

This region is small in area, but one of the most precious pearls among the viticultural regions of the world in terms of its significance and history. The first information regarding winegrowing here dates back to the Roman Empire in the 2nd century. Later, the first wine settlement named Stokaj (from the Slovak for conduit, confluence) was founded beyond the

Slav settlement in the foothills above the confluence of the Bodrog and Tisa rivers. The area of the Viticultural Region of Tokaj (hereinafter referred to as the "VRoT") in the Slovak Republic is 908.2 hectares. After years of transformation and complicated property settlements, it has been gradually filled with new plantings and boasts of well-reconstructed, bearing vineyards. Tokaj vineyards, located in the Slánske vrchy mountains in the south, southwest and southeast parts of the Zemplín region, are situated in the historical cadastral territory as declared by church and royal legislation in the Middle Ages, imperial legislation in the times of the Revival and the legislation of the first Czechoslovak Republic.

In the 13th century, Hungarian King Béla IV invited Italians from near Bari to settle in the territory of the south Zemplín region that had been plundered by Tatars, and they brought a variety of Furmint with them. The 170 year rule of Turks, which caused the local inhabitants to build underground hiding places for their families and crops, had a significant influence. Tuff cellars with their uniquely stable microclimate later became a significant place for aging and storing Tokaj wine. According to historical documents, the first quality wine with attribute was made in 1650 by Ladislav Sepši Máté, a local priest, in the cellars under Šiator Hill not far from the present day town of Slovenské Nové Mesto. The rules for the production of Tokaj assorted wines were established five years later under the reign of Francis II Rákóczi. This outstanding native of Trebišov was also responsible for the fact that French King Louis XIV was introduced to Tokaj wine. It became a favorite of his Court and won the title **Vinum Regnum – Rex Vinorum** – Wine of Kings – King of Wines. Tokaj wine has won the hearts of many eminent personalities in history. It was served at the table of Czar Peter the Great, Empresses Elizabeth I and II and Catherine I and II. Maria Theresa sent Tokaj as a gift to Pope Benedict V, who upon drinking it for the first time said, "Blessed be the land that gives birth to you, blessed be the woman who sends you and blessed be me because I am drinking you."

The Tokaj region is noted for its warm, moderately dry summers and warm and dry autumns. The average air temperature in growing seasons is 16.8 °C with 336 mm of precipitation. Average annual accumulated precipitation amounts to 608 mm and the sum of active temperatures in the growing season is 3,100 °C. Dry autumns are followed by cold and humid winters. The Slovak Tokaj region is a closed viticultural region with a specific compositional variety of plants and a special winemaking method. Seven viticultural villages are included in this region – Bara, Čerhov, Černochov, Veľká Tŕňa, Malá Tŕňa, Viničky and Slovenské Nové Mesto. The vineyards with highest altitude are situated in Malá Tŕňa with an altitude of 360 m, while the vineyards with the lowest altitude are outside Viničky at an altitude of 105 m. The secret behind the success of Tokaj wines, which globally have no competitor in their category, are the exceptional natural conditions.

Slovak Tokaj wine may only be produced from grapes from the VRoT, and the wine must be produced and bottled here. Traditional wine grape varieties for the production of Tokaj wine include Furmint, Lipovina (Hárslevelű) and Yellow Muscat. In addition, the autochthonous Kövérszőlő variety appears in old plantings, while the new Zéta and Kabár clones can only be found marginally in new plantings. The last three varieties are not registered in the **List of Registered Varieties**.

The Tokaj region is characterized by its stony, sandy loam soil. It was formed on the geological bed of volcanic rhyolite, andesite and tuff. The distinctive portion of fault rock in Tokaj vineyards on the slopes with a southern orientation enable the absorption of the sunlight throughout the long, sunny autumn. The accumulated energy gradually evaporates on the surface after sunset and thus warms the colder air around the ripening grapes. The abundant early fog, which aids in the creation and development of the "noble rot" **Botrytis cinerea** on the grape, is another significant phenomenon with an impact on the ripening and quality of Tokaj grapes.

Nobly rotten raisins occur in favorable years due to evaporation which concentrates the organic acids in the must, while the noble rot concentrates the glucose and fructose content. The creation of moisture on the surface of the grape enables the growth of the fungus's hyphae. When the moisture of the grape evaporates in the Tokaj sun, the fungus's activity shifts from growth to breathing and the secretion of its hyphae softens the grape's skin. The sweet Tokaj essence is the result of the slow process of ripening of the grapes aided by the botrytis rot, and it is added in a precise amount to the **Tokaj samorodne wine**. However, the final stage in the creation of the wine features the slow oxygen-aided maturing process in traditional 136-liter **Gönc** oak or acacia-oak casks which are stored for several years in tuff cellars.

VINTAGE QUALITY OVERVIEW

Comparing the quality of individual vintages means that hundreds of wines produced in all corners of Slovakia must be tasted in various stages of production and development, and voluminous sensory notes and personal evaluations must be taken and independently compared with the personal evaluations of other enologist colleagues. The subjective evaluation of each viticulture region, area or vineyard is affected not only by one's own abilities, but also by nature which prepares many surprises for winegrowers and winemakers. Producing the ideal wine is the most precious goal for each viticulturer, and an unpredictable, lifelong experience. This is also why my humble overview is subjective and does not fully mirror the rating and observations of other specialists. As an enologist, I recognize that my chart is statistically imperfect, because great wines worthy of high marks can appear in the poorest vintages and vice versa.

Vintage	Rating
2000	★★★★
2001	★★★
2002	★★★★
2003	★★
2004	★★★★
2005	★★★
2006	★★★★★
2007	★★★
2008	★★★
2009	★★★★★
2010	★
2011	★★★
2012	★★★★
2013	★★★
2014	★★

Scale of Quality of Vintages and Its Interpretation

Rating	Vintage Quality	Interpretation of Vintage
★★★★★	outstanding	Prestigious vintage of outstanding quality where the intensity, purity and harmony of individual wine qualities fully shows as a fascinatingly rich and well balanced whole with high extract, length, personality, comprehensive style and attractive maturing potential.
★★★★	very good	Pure, elegant appearance, intensive aroma and taste, harmoniously reflects the very good quality of grapes and precise conditions of vintage processing in interesting wines with pleasant length and a comprehensive overall impression.
★★★	good	Represents good quality wines which also include outstanding wines of excellent varietal quality, sensory delicacy and characteristic features with a pleasant harmony and pleasing overall impression. It offers good quality wines for a reasonable price.
★★	average	Provides wines of average quality with less distinctive intensity, purity and fullness in aroma and taste. However, the wines of this vintage are acceptable and suitable for daily consumption without distinctive sensory experiences.
★	poor	Vintage of a substandard quality with distinctive deficit of technological maturity of grapes with low purity of sensory qualities affected by the poor health of grapes. Due to poor climatic conditions and many processing deficits, it is unsuitable for production or sale of wine.

GRAPEVINE VARIETIES IN SLOVAKIA

Slovakia is a small country with a rich history of viticulture and a broad selection of original and international grapevine varieties and new clones. You will appreciate becoming acquainted with them not only at wine tasting events, but also when travelling our wine routes and deciding on the next purchase for your wine cabinet.

Traditional White Varieties	25
Traditional Red Varieties	33
Tokaj Varieties	37
New White Clones	39
New Red Clones	43

GRAPEVINE VARIETIES IN SLOVAKIA

Nowadays, 39 wine grape and 16 table grape varieties of common grapevine (vitis vinifera) are registered in Slovakia. Considering the total area of registered vineyards (18,705 hectares), the varietal grapevine composition is extremely diverse.

Grapevine varieties can be divided into traditional groups of **table grapes and wine grapes** according to the purpose of cultivation. While table grape varieties are designated for fresh consumption, the wine grape varieties provide plenty of grape juice (must) for the production of white, rosé and red wine. We divide wine grape varieties into **white and red** according to the color of their skin. White wines are made of the juice of white varieties, while red varieties are used to make red, rosé as well as white wines.

According to the character and intensity of smell, the white wine grape varieties provide **non-aromatic or aromatic** white wines. Slovak wines are crystal clear; in color they correspond with the variety, labeling and vintage. Their freshness, harmony, typical aroma and pure, distinctive and persistent taste stand out.

Based on a wine's growing importance, dissemination and wine history, traditional white varieties in Slovakia include Grüner Veltliner, Italian Riesling, Pinot Blanc, Rhein Riesling, Feteasca Alba, Traminer, Feteasca Regala, Frührer Roter Malvasier (Veltliner Frührot) Chardonnay, Pinot Gris, Grüner Silvaner and Sauvignon Blanc. Red varieties include Lemberger Blaufränkisch, Saint Laurent, Cabernet Sauvignon, Pinot Noir and Blauer Portugieser. Traditional white varieties also include Müller-Thurgau and Irsai Oliver (Muscat Oliver) while red varieties include Zweigeltrebe and André, despite the fact that they belong to the group of "older" new clones. However, since these varieties were bred and entered in the List of Registered Varieties in the first half of the last century, we present them among traditional varieties. Traditional varieties in the Tokaj viticultural region are Furmint, Lipovina (Hárslevelű) and Yellow Muscat.

All varieties indicated in the List of Registered Varieties is may be grown in the Slovak wine country. The varieties are listed according to how widespread they are from those with the largest areas to those with the smallest growing representation. The below table provides an overview of registered new clones of Slovak origin.

New Clones of Slovak Origin

Name	Parental varieties (Clone No.)	Registration year
Devín	Traminer x Veltliner Frührot 15/4	1997
Noria	Rhein Riesling x Semillon 23/33	2002
Milia	Müller-Thurgau x Traminer 65/4	2002
Hetera	Traminer x Veltliner Frührot 4/13	2011
Breslava	(pink Chasselas x Traminer) x St. Maria d´Alcantara 10/28	2011
Dunaj	(Muscat Bouchet x Oporto) x Saint Laurent 6/10	1997
Hron	Castets x Abouriou Noir 3/22	2011
Váh	Castets x Abouriou Noir 3/13	2011
Nitria	Castets x Abouriou Noir 3/8	2011
Rimava	Castets x Abouriou Noir 3/12	2011
Rosa	(Picpoul x Blaufränkisch) x Traminer 15/3	2011
Rudava	Castets x I-35-9 (Teinturier x Aleatico x Puchljakovskij) 6/28	2011
Torysa	Castets x I-35-9 (Teinturier x Aleatico x Puchljakovskij) 9/17	2011

TRADITIONAL WHITE VARIETIES

Grüner Veltliner
(Veltlínske zelené)

This is the most universal variety in the wine regions of the Small Carpathians and Southern Slovakia with a 16 % representation in vineyards. Grapes of this variety ripen in the second half of October. It gives quality wines a well-balanced, floral-fruity smell and a fresh spicy taste fortified by a green almond bouquet finish. A higher extract of the wine and fullness of taste is achieved by reducing the yield, by means of which Grüner Veltliner acquires its intensity. This is particularly manifested on loess and clay soils where piquantly spicy tones moderated by a honey note are part of the varietal bouquet in higher attributes. In recent decades, Grüner Veltliner has become attractive as a young wine without a longer aging process. Although in young wines it surprises by its freshness and spicy bouquet, most Slovak wineries make more structured and longer aging wines of this variety with aromatic nuances of celery tops, white pepper with an admixture of a honey-citrus drop and frequently also with higher alcohol content. Matured late harvests do not have a distinctive aroma; however, the elegance is multiplied in their full taste due to its honey-spicy smell and tender residual sugar content.

Synonyms: Zelený muškátel, Bielošpičák, Veltlín zelený, Ryvola bílá

Italian Riesling /
Wälschriesling
(Rizling vlašský)

This later ripening variety has roots which, according to certain sources, reach back to the south of Eastern Europe. Theories claiming that Italian Riesling came from France have not been confirmed. The name Wälschriesling was most probably derived from Walachia, a mountainous inland region in present day Romania. The alternative to this name is connected to northeast Italy where it is cultivated with the name Riesling Italico. The cultivation of this variety is widespread in several regions from the Small Carpathians to Transylvania. It occupies almost 13 % of the total bearing vineyard area. In our country, it does well on the sunny alluvial hills of the Danube Lowland in the wine region of Southern Slovakia. In good years, its grapes reach a satisfactory sugar content with a higher acid content; on the contrary, in colder and humid periods, the varietal wines are green and hard. Noble rot Botrytis cinerea grows on the grape berries in the best locations with a long and sunny autumn and with adequate humidity in the vicinity of rivers (Dunaj, Hron, Bodrog). The skin of Italian Riesling is thin and elastic. It accumulates a relatively rich varietal bouquet supported by a piquant content

GRAPEVINE VARIETIES IN SLOVAKIA

of fruit acids in a short ripening period. Young quality wines with a Kabinett attribute up to late harvest show themselves by tones of currants, later by their kernel-nutty character and opulent taste by pleasant acidity after maturing. The aftertaste is characterized by a more distinctive tone of fresh gooseberries. The longer growing season enables winemakers to make naturally sweet wines, including ice wines from Italian Riesling, which have a delicate smell of honey and meadow flowers.

Synonyms: Vlašák, Welschriesling, Olaszrizling, Taliansky rizling

Müller-Thurgau

This intraspecific variety, which has modest soil requirements, did not make its way to former Czechoslovakia until after World War I. Older German sources state that it was created by the cross breeding of Rhein Riesling and Grüner Silvaner. However, there are scientific disputes regarding the paternal variety, because the molecular analyses of genomes confirmed the existence of genes identical to Chasselas and not Grüner Silvaner. This variety occupies 8 % of the area of bearing vineyards and its fruit-bearing coefficient is high. Grapes ripen by the end of August. Quality wines in new vintages are pleasantly drinkable, with a lower acid content and a decent Muscat character in their smell. In wet years, Müller-Thurgau suffers from fungal diseases which decreases the quality. Progressive winemakers use it to produce excellent fresh young wines full of a primary peachy aroma. Thanks to modern grape processing and must fermentation technology, it became the hit of the season of Saint Catherine wines. However, their beauty fades with the time of

maturing in bottles. This is also why young wines of this variety should be consumed within three months after bottling and qualitatively more mature vintages should be gradually blended with wine with a higher acid content.

Synonyms: Müller, Müllerka, Rivaner, Riesling Sylvaner

Rhein Riesling / Riesling (Rizling rýnsky)

Rhein Riesling suffered many losses in the past century in Slovakia due to political dogma and later in competition with the ridiculously fashionable Chardonnay. One hundred years ago, the value of German Rieslings from the best vineyards of the Rhineland easily exceeded the value of the best red wines of Bordeaux. The global practices of Riesling makers changed in the past century since they allowed the wines of this variety to become popular so to speak. The same situation occurred in our country but to a lesser extent. Rhein Riesling, the best German variety, was not desirable during the

Socialist era. Even its rare viticultural potential, which was respected by winemakers, did not allow it to fully develop its possibilities in the era of quantitative winegrowing. At first, the variety was blended with dull wines in order to enhance the intensity of their taste; later, it was avoided because of the difficulties with selling it. On one hand, this was related to fashionable tastes that consumers were used to, and on the other hand with a longer period of aging in comparison to quickly sellable universal wines. The Riesling revolution began only in the last decade of the 20th century and was triggered by Egon Müller, the famous winegrower and winemaker from the Mosel region. In cooperation with Ing. Miroslav Petrech, an experienced winegrower and winemaker from the village of Mužla, they brought the excellent terroir of Riesling back to life on the basic soils of sunny Southern Slovakia. This variety has returned to the pedestal in several vineyards of Slovakia and occupies 4.9 % of the total planting area. Tasting the wide range of Slovak Rieslings from dry up to naturally sweet is a unique experience. Its spicy freshness and piquantly honey smell of linden blossom, the concentrate of dried apricots, marmalade tangerines and the rich extractiveness of mature vintages can rarely be multiplied by kerosene tones. Rieslings of the regions of the Small Carpathians, Southern Slovakia, Nitra, Central and Eastern Slovakia have their undeniable identity. However, despite many significant awards and endless possibilities for use in gastronomy, they are still waiting to be discovered.

Synonyms: Ryňák, Rizling, Riesling, Roháč, Lipka

Pinot Blanc (Burgundské biele)

A variety of the Small Carpathians with an original Burgundy genealogy, it served as a synonym for quality wine in the past. It does well in nutritious soils with sufficient airiness, high sun exposure, an abundance of humidity and without the threat of spring frosts. Soils with an elevated calcium content produce a fuller fruity bouquet. In the post-World War II period, it was widespread in the Nitra wine region and produced very good results in grapes and wine quality. It is also cultivated in Eastern Slovakia. In heavy nutritious soils it gives high extracts in musts, the wine after fermentation acquires a distinctive aroma ranging from cream to almonds to exotic fruits. In this way it differs from wine from the original regions. Pinot Blanc has more modest yields; its grapes ripen from the end of September and with sensitive reduction make excellent wines with a well-balanced acid content, and an elegant olfactory and taste structure. Overall, the style of the wine and its

intensity are emphasized by aging in oak casks or after resting on yeast lees and later in bottles. Its current share of bearing plantings in Slovakia is 4.3 %.

Synonyms: Rulandské biele, Ruland, Burgunda, Roučí bílé

Traminer (Tramín červený)

This very old wine grape variety is represented in Slovakia by various styles of full wines with attractive bouquets and adequate acid content. Depending on the cultivated sub-variety and its exposition in vineyards with various soil profiles, the bouquet of Traminer has a spectrum of white pepper, tea rose, honey grapes or violets and even tropic oranges and cinnamon in bottle

GRAPEVINE VARIETIES IN SLOVAKIA

maturity. Traminer is more widespread in Slovakia than Gewürztraminer (Tramín korenistý). Breeders presented several clones from sub-varieties, of which those of the best quality made their way in new plantings in the wine regions of the Small Carpathians, Nitra, Central and Eastern Slovakia. In comparison to Traminer, Gewürztraminer provides wines of more intense aroma with a more distinctive spicy bouquet in which creamy tones of rose oil and lychee appear. Both sub-varieties ripen in mid-October and comprise 2.1 % of planting in Slovakia. They have the ability to accumulate a high sugar concentrations and their grapes can be left on the vines for a long time. The skin of Gewürztraminer is thinner than that of Traminer and the bunches of grapes ripen unevenly. In the event of a long sunny autumn, the Traminer grapes ripen to grape selection and the Gewürztraminer bunches to raising selection. Traminer suffers from Chlorosis in poor calcareous soils; it requires deep heat absorbent soils with sufficient nutrients. On the contrary, Gewürztraminer obtains a distinctive spicy smell on calcareous soil, but like Traminer, it needs sufficient nutrients and warmth for the ripening of its grapes. When making wine from all sub-varieties of Traminer, care must be taken in preserving a sufficient concentration of acids, especially when processing grapes with a higher attribute. Many Traminer winegrowers confirm that the character of color of the grape skin and subsequently the wine is related to the type of soil on which the varieties are cultivated. For example,

the color of the skins of Gewürztraminer cultivated in soils with a higher calcareous content is orange, and more scarlet in acid or gravel soils. It is obvious that the processing and producing of wine from all sub-varieties of Traminer is demanding for each producer and requires greater attention. Similarly, as in the case of Rhein Riesling, the character of each Traminer is closely related to the soil. Traminers from Southern and Central Slovakia are elegant and give off a honey-fruity overall impression, while those from the Small Carpathians and Nitra are surprisingly spicy, and Traminers from eastern Slovakia are more massive and parfume.

Synonyms: Tramín, Ryvola, Livora, Traminer, Gewürztraminer

Feteasca Alba (Dievčie hrozno)

This old eastern European variety with rather early fruit-bearing comes from the territory between Transylvania (Romania) and Bessarabia (Moldova). It has a long tradition in the wine region of Central Slovakia, and later spread to the Small Carpathians and Southern Slovakia. Winegrowers from the town of Modra made passionate wines of this variety in the past. Currently it is not very widespread in our country; it occupies only 2 % of the planting area. Consumers frequently confuse it with Feteasca Regala, which originated in Romania at the beginning of the 1920s by cross breeding Feteasca Alba and Grasa de Cotnari. Because

GRAPEVINE VARIETIES IN SLOVAKIA

of its modest demands on soil, its sensitivity to spring frosts and its finer skins, it does well in higher hilly slopes with moderate precipitation and poorer stony or gravel soils. Wine made from Feteasca Alba has a golden-yellow color, is pleasantly drinkable, with a medium full, harmonious, with well-balanced acid content and a juicy, fruity-floral aroma and taste. More mature quality wines leave a persistent citrus-grapefruit aftertaste.

Synonyms: Leánka, Dívčí hrozen

Irsai Oliver

This very early ripening variety was bred between the two world wars in Hungary from Bratislavské biele (Pozsoni, White of Bratislava) and Čabianska perla (Csaba Gyöngye, Pearl of Czaba). Its golden-yellow berries ripen for consumption at the beginning of August. Its young wines are full of a delicious Muscat fruity, slightly spicy bouquet and a light taste of grapes. However, as time passes, they lose their piquant freshness in aroma and taste intensity. This variety is mostly used for making young wines or wine musts for non-alcoholic beverages and juices. After 2000, its planting area slightly grew to 365 ha and comprises 2 % of the total vineyard area. Since it does not do well in frosty locations, it is cultivated on hills. It does not require nutritious soils; however it is sensitive to downy mildew.

Synonyms: Iršaj, Irsay Olivér

Feteasca Regala

This is an interesting variety in terms of cultivation with a high fruit-bearing coefficient. Wines of this variety have a decent Muscat aroma which in the best vintages shows tones of apricot blossom with a note of white pepper. Wines with a fresh taste keep a higher acid content. This variety allows the production of wines with a longer aging potential with the use of various methods or sparkling wines with the use of the classical method of fermentation of wine in bottles. Deeper fertile soil with good precipitation and draining on slopes facing south or south-west, where the grapevines cannot be damaged by frost, is the ideal environment for this variety. It was first planted in Slovakia in the 1930s in the village of Pesek, before spreading out, but not extensively, to the wine regions of Southern Slovakia (Mužla), Central Slovakia (Sebechleby) and the Small Carpathians (Modra). The total area of plantings of this variety comprises 313 ha, which is 0.1 % less in comparison to the area of Feteasca alba.

Synonyms: Pesecká leaňka, Pesecká leánka, Feťaska, Kráľovská leánka

GRAPEVINE VARIETIES IN SLOVAKIA

Früher Roter Malvasier / Frühroter Veltliner (Veltlínske červené skoré)

In the past, this probably accidental cross breeding clone of Grüner Veltliner and Grüner Silvaner was planted in the northernmost locations in Slovakia due its early ripening (second half of September) and its ability to bear higher grape yields. In addition to traditional processing into must and wine, it is harvested for direct consumption. It favors sufficiently aired sites where it is not endangered by fungal diseases in periods with higher relative humidity. Reductive wines made of this variety are pleasantly drinkable. Their aroma creates a rather neutral, fruity-floral (elderberry) impression. The best dry hilly locations in the wine regions of the Small Carpathians and Nitra support the character of its fine almond up to banana aroma in young wines.

Synonyms: Skorý červený muškátel, Véčéeska, Veltlínske červené rané, Malvazinka, Babovina

Chardonnay

Until the middle of the 1980s, this variety was cultivated in our country in a mixture with Pinot Blanc. Increased demand for sensually well-balanced and full wines with a pleasant fruity aroma and a fresh taste of apricots and tropical fruits in the 1990s, and later for structured vanilla-cream up to nutty-butter wines of the barrique type caused the extension of plantings of Chardonnay clones in Slovakia. The area of this Burgundy variety grew after 2000 from 213 ha to 341 ha. Chardonnay is an accidental clone of Pinot Blanc and Heunisch varieties. It does fairly well in several winegrowing regions of Slovakia with loam and marl soils with a higher calcium content and adequate water drainage and which are well heated by the sun. In the best, slightly hilly protected south-oriented locations, it gives average grape yields which begin to ripen in the last decade of September and the beginning of October. Medium large bunches have a short stem and less weight. Because of its thin skin, it is vulnerable to by grey mold (Botrytis cinea). Wines made of Chardonnay are harmonious, fruity, and in colder locations with an aroma of green apples and an admixture of wild acacia. More mature wines offer a bouquet of honey with a note of hazelnuts. In warmer locations, the wines provide an exotic bouquet

of bananas, mango with a hint of cream and cantaloupe. After a short pre-soak of the grape mash, Chardonnnay releases a higher content of phenols (esters of cinnamic acid) in the must, which is undesirable for the production of sparkling wines, for example Blanc de Blancs. However, this quality is successfully used in the production of barrique wines.

Synonyms: Chardonnay Pinot blanc, Chardonnay blanc, Pinot

GRAPEVINE VARIETIES IN SLOVAKIA

Pinot Gris
(Burgundské sivé)

This is the first of the Burgundy varieties to ripen, and in good locations with climatically favorable years, its grapes have a high sugar content. The cultivation of this old French variety spread to Slovakia at the beginning of the 20th century. It produces full wines with a honey-fruity and frequently sweetish smell. In taste, it has tones of pears, oranges and spice, while the note of bread crust is impressive in drier vintages after maturing. Because of the higher concentration of colors in its skins, the wine, after a short fermentation of mash, has a golden-yellow up to light rose color. This variety does well in first-class locations and soils with sufficient nutrients. In our vineyards, it comprises 1.9 % of planted areas. An interesting terroir for this variety is the wine region of Eastern Slovakia, where thanks to its deep and heavy soils it develops the potential of extractiveness, richness, and spicy-honey fruitiness with a distinctive bread character. In selections of grapes with attribute, the Pinot Gris has a more distinctive fruity and honey bouquet in the wine region of Central Slovakia, while in the northern vineyards of Nitra and the Small Carpathian regions it shows a decent fruity-spicy up to exotic citrus tone in the nose and mouth. The diversity in labeling quality single-varietal wines may confuse beginning wine lovers. Pinot Gris is the most frequently used name for this variety in France, and it was registered in Slovakia in 1941 as Burgundské sivé; however, it is better known under its commercial name – Rulandské šedé. Two facts triggered its naming. In 1711, Johann

Segner Ruland noticed this variety and disseminated it successfully. Thanks to his commercial activities, the name Ruländer was used in German-speaking territories, and Rulandské later in Slovakia. Since the wines from the family of Burgundy varieties cannot be labelled by appellation, the name of a historically recognized geographical area with protected designation of origin, the official name Rulandské šedé was introduced in Czechoslovakia for Burgundské sivé. After changes in legislation and Slovakia's entry to the European Union, the original name Pinot Gris is used more frequently.

Synonyms: Klevner, Rulandské šedé, Špinavý hrozen

Grüner Silvaner
(Silvánske zelené)

This Central European variety became rooted in the hills of the Small Carpathians, particularly in the towns of Limbach, Grinava, Pezinok and Modra thanks to Roman legionaries. The fame of Grüner Silvaner and its sub-variety Roter Silvaner (Silvánske červené) culminated at the end of the 18th century and the beginning of the 19th century when these two varieties comprised 10 % of the area of plantings. After World War II, this variety was pushed out of the vineyards by Müller-Thurgau, Rhein Riesling, in the best locations, as well as other varieties attractive for consumers. In spite of this, Grüner

Silvaner has marginally held on to its position in traditional locations; in fact a new planting recently appeared in eastern Slovakia. In total, it occupies 1.1 % of bearing vineyards. This variety with medium requirements for location, needs deeper nutritious soils with a sufficient supply of water. It does not stand up well to winter frosts. In the case of drought and the high training of high bud load plants, the grapes on one-year old plants do not ripen well. Wines from plants with smaller spacing and reduced yields are surprising by their attractive freshness and harmonious fruitiness of taste. Their captivatingly spicy bouquet suggests a mixture of green tomatoes with tones of acacia and pome fruits. In the eastern Slovak villages of Tibava and Orechová this variety produces extractive wines with delicate acid and residual sugar content.

Synonyms: Cyrifandel, Cynifádl, Sylván, Sylvaner

Sauvignon Blanc (Sauvignon)

The first Sauvignon Blanc plants mixed with Semillon were planted by winegrowers in the vicinity of Nitra and Vráble before World War II. Because of its high sensitivity to winter frosts, it is cultivated in warmer locations, but it is not very demanding in terms of nutrients and depth of soil. Its plantings comprise 1.4 % of the total vineyard area. It does well in dry, light and shallow soils in open, airy vineyards where it does not show its growth vitality more distinctively. Grapes ripen in mid-September and for winemakers it is a great challenge, not only in terms of the higher concentration of volatile substances such as methoxypyrazine and thiols, which are released enzymatically in the wine during the fermentation of wine must. Higher levels of methoxypyrazine in the skins of unripe grapes from marginal vineyards have the smell of green grass and nettle, its content is reduced in riper grapes and its must has the smell of fruit, peaches in particular. Our winegrowers and winemakers offer several profiles of this variety, according to the planted clone, vintage and location of the vineyard. The basic profile is traditionally linked to grass, whose bouquet in selections of unripe grapes features floral tones with an herbal, sometimes distinctively peppery up to asparagus taste and with adequate acid content. The second

profile, which is sweeter and more mature, is typical for the processing of ripe grapes when the aromas of black currant, gooseberries, frequently peach or kiwi appear. The third, a mineral profile, is affected by the sur lie, where the young Sauvignon with higher acid content matures for a longer period of time in yeast deposits in newer oak casks. Such wine provides vanilla-Muscat tones of aroma and a full spicy-honey taste with a hint of hazelnuts and mowed meadows.

Synonyms: Sauvignon Blanc, Sauvignon biely

TRADITIONAL RED VARIETIES

Lemberger / Blaufränkisch (Frankovka modrá)

This reliable fruit-bearing Central European variety is from Lower Austria (Niederösterreich) from where it gradually made its way to our region. It is one of the most widespread red varieties in Slovakia and currently it occupies 1,560 ha, which is 8.4 % of the area and 35.7 % of all cultivated red varieties. Wines made of Lemberger are noted for their darker, ruby-red color and pleasant, fruity-spicy bouquet of cranberries, dried plums, sour cherries and cinnamon. Its harmonious taste with a piquant content of tannins contains fruit acids. The grapes ripen in late harvest quality in most regions according to soil type and location. In warmer loamy-sand soils, it provides regular grape selections and raising selections and selections of berries with a rich extract and a firm structure suitable for longer aging in oak barrels or bottles. After ripening in favorable years, grapes do not rot or drop; therefore, some winemakers use them for the production of a smaller volume of naturally sweet, straw or ice wines. Slovak Lembergers do well with fine micro oxidation in wooden barrels and slow aging in new barrique casks; they can also be used to make fresh rosé wine. Rosé made of Lemberger is characterized by its spectrum of colors ranging from rose-violet up to salmon-pink and orange, as well as its graceful, fruity smell of raspberries, cherries or garden strawberries. It preserves its higher acid content in its taste which predetermines it for many gastronomical combinations with traditional regional and international cuisine. Some of the most famous locations for the production of quality and full red wines made of Lemberger are Skalica, Rača, Vajnory, Hlohovec in the west, Levice, Strekov, Mužla in the south, Bušince in the center and Slovenská Moldava and Sobrance in the east. The Lemberger (Blaufränkisch) variety is the queen of original vineyards and sites and its wines deserve a regular place in every wine cabinet.

Synonyms: Limburské, Skalické černé, Neskorák, Karmazín

Saint Laurent (Svätovavrinecké)

A seedling with similar qualities to Burgundy varieties was planted in several northern vineyards of Slovakia by the generation of winegrowers at the beginning of the 19th century. Saint Laurent is a less demanding variety in terms of location and soil. It does well on mild slopes facing southeast or southwest with lighter quartzite and sandy and limestone soils with good drainage. Grapes ripen at the beginning of September; however, in years with a wet autumn they are prone to rotting. The young wine is of a dark, garnet-red color with violet hues. In average vintages, it is characterized by a fruity bouquet of black currant and forest fruits with a medium full taste and higher acid content. In warm locations with high training, it brings quality harvests. Bunches on older plantings may drop after blooming. This is also why winegrowers begin to prefer reliable clones in newer plantings. It occupies 6.1 % of our registered areas. Saint Laurent is also suitable for the production of blends with related varieties and rosé wines and sparkling wines. Red wines are pleasant and harmonious after maturing in wooden barrels. The original harsh tannins make a velvety smooth impression, and thus Saint Laurent acquires a full aroma and an elegant taste.

Synonyms: Vavrinecké, Svätý Vavrinec

Cabernet Sauvignon

This popular international variety found its place in our assortment at the end of the past century. It was registered in former Czechoslovakia in 1980 as a late fruit-bearing variety which does well in especially warm and sunny locations, schist soils and soils with higher gravel-sand content. In soils with a higher nutrient content it gives higher grape yields, which however is reflected in the decreased quality of wine. Therefore, in our country it is planted on southern slopes with sufficient sun exposure and higher aggregate temperatures, especially during the growing season. The slow warming of the climate is beneficial for new and older plantings. Cabernet Sauvignon buds late in the spring and also blooms later. Grapes begin to ripen only in the second half of October. Thanks to its medium firm skin, smaller diameter of berries and straight growth, mechanization can be used for pruning and harvesting. Consumers look for bottle-matured, claret-red wines with a characteristic aroma of violets and a harmonious taste. After slowly aging in barrels, it acquires a bouquet of black currants, licorice and occasionally white pepper and sweet almonds. It achieves excellent qualities by maturing in barrique barrels, when specific tones of vanilla, cedar wood, sweet pepper and resin develop. In the past thirty years, the experiences of Slovak

winemakers and winegrowers with Cabernet has advanced to such a degree that thanks to their late harvests and grape selections and resting in barrels, they are successful at prestigious international competitions and exhibitions. However, we must wait at least for the next generation of winegrowers and winemakers for a more specific description of wines made of Slovak Cabernet. The current area of Cabernet in Slovakia amounts to 600 ha, which represents almost 3.2 % of the total planting area.

Synonym: Kabernet

André

Several new domestic clones appeared in our vineyards during the socialist era. André came from Veľké Pavlovice, Moravia and got its name from Christian Karl André, who founded the first breeding society in the world in Brno in 1806. The Lemberger and Saint Laurent cross breed is a massive plant which forces growers to reduce the number of canes. It is recommended that the canes be shortened to six buds. With high training, it gives regular and rich grape yields. It does well in deeper loam soils with good drainage and sufficient nutrients, and on sunny and warm slopes it reaches a medium long phase of ripening. The best reduced yields produce grapes in late harvest quality in the second half of October and in warmer years even sooner. The taste of these intensive red up to garnet-red wines resemble a mixture of blackberries and plums and feature a high concentration of tannins with a note of green pepper. At least half a year of aging in wooden barrels is needed to soften their temperament. The overall extract is gradually harmonized and the fullness of taste is emphasized. This complementary red variety occupies approximately 1.2 % of the registered vineyard area.

Synonym: Andrea

Pinot Noir (Burgundské modré)

This is one of the oldest, noble red wine grape varieties cultivated in Slovakia. Ancient Romans knew of it, but it did not appear in our geographical latitude until the second half of the 14th century. However, it experienced a true Renaissance at the end of the 20th century (1.2 % of total plantings) because during the socialist era, despite its excellent qualities it did not achieve the required yields without clone selection. Moreover, young, prematurely consumed single varietal wines lacked the esprit of bottle maturity. Like most top red varieties, it requires warm and mild southern slopes and relatively nutritious chalkstone and limestone soils or loamy sandy soils with good drainage. Its berries have a relatively thin skin; therefore they are easily infected by Botrytis. In humid years, they are vulnerable to rotting. New intensive plantings have inspired Slovak winemakers to make high quality, single varietal and blend wines (cuvée). When processing the grapes, they use both traditional and progressive methods of maceration (e.g., carbonic maceration) and a longer contact of the wine with wood in the maturing process (if conditions allow). Contemporary Pinot Noir from Slovakia has a light, brick-red color which acquires mahogany-brown shades by maturing. Its aroma resembles plum and blackberry marmalade, while bitter almonds with an attractive touch and licorice appear in the bouquet in southern locations. The taste is usually harmonious, with a velvety tannin and a pleasant bitter aftertaste.

Synonyms: Burgunda, Rulandské modré, Červený Klevner, Roučí modré

GRAPEVINE VARIETIES IN SLOVAKIA

Zweigeltrebe

This crossbreed of Saint Laurent and Lemberger was born in Klosterneuburg, Austria, near the Slovak border, in 1922. However, it went unnoticed by Slovak winegrowers and didn't make an appearance here until the second half of the 1990s. It produces regular and abundant yields. It is a resistant variety with a shorter growing season and less demanding requirements regarding soils and location. In northern areas it requires more nutritious potassium soils. The grapes ripen in the last decade of September. With regulated harvests it gives pleasant spicy wines with sufficient extract and smooth tannins. Its aroma resembles black sour cherries and berry fruits. The young and more mature vintages of Zweigeltrebe keep their intensive ruby-red color. In young wines, the expression of the tannins on the tongue is more distinctive at the beginning; in colder vintages it is rougher, but the hardness drops down upon maturing. The greatest expansion has been recorded in the Small Carpathians (Vištuk). It is also cultivated in the regions of Nitra (Topoľčianky, Moravany), Southern Slovakia (Mužla, Dunajská Moča) and Eastern Slovakia (Tibava). The fruit-bearing plants of Zweigeltrebe covered an area of 134 ha in 2012.

Synonym: Zweigelt

Blauer Portugieser (Modrý Portugal)

This legendary variety is definitively connected with František Hečko's novel Červené víno (Red Wine), which takes place in Horné and Dolné Orešany. However, the Portuguese origin of this variety has not been conclusively verified. Older sources claim that it was brought here by Count Johann von Fries from Oporto in 1772. In favorable years, the grapes ripen in mid-September and are used for direct consumption. Our predecessors named it štrudlák (strudel grapes), because it was used as a significant ingredient in the pulled strudel of our grandmothers. Blauer Portugieser wines are of ruby-red color. In aroma they resemble tones of stone fruits with a hint of violet in warm years. May cherries supported by a lighter tannin content and a fine hazelnut aftertaste dominate the taste on the tongue. Blauer Portugieser is sensitive to frost and in the growing season it is prone to fungal diseases; therefore it does well in airy, drier locations and poorer soils with various profiles. Grapes ripen at the end of September and on southern slopes they produce quality yields. In addition to the villages of Orešany, it is traditionally cultivated in Hlohovec and Skalica, and in newer plantings on terraces in the vicinity of Dunajská Moča, Strekov and in Tibava in Eastern Slovakia. Blauer Portugieser is planted on 0.7 % of the total area in Slovakia.

TOKAJ VARIETIES

Pursuant to the Act on Viticulture and Winemaking, only three basic Tokaj varieties may be planted in the Tokaj viticultural region: Furmint (61.3 % of the area), Lipovina (Hárslevelű) (29.5 % of the area) and Yellow Muscat (Muškát žltý) (9.2 % of the area). The combination of unique qualities of the warm continental climate on the dry, southern slopes of the Slánske vrchy mountain range, the great diversity of volcanic soils rich in minerals with an accumulation of sun energy and production perfected by generations of winegrowers have turned this area into a unique terroir, which has no competitor among other wine regions of Slovakia or the world. In addition to the aforementioned varieties, the original seedling, Tučné hrozno (Kövérszőlő – Fat Grapes), which got its name from the viscous or even buttery texture of its pulp, as well as Zéta, which is crossbred from Bouvier and Furmint, are marginally cultivated here. However, they are and Kabár, crossbred from Bouvier and Lipovina are not on the List of Registered Varieties.

Furmint

Furmint is our main Tokaj variety, although its origin is unknown. Some sources claim that it comes from the province of Formia in southern Italy and that it was brought here by Italian settlers who came to the Zemplín territory in the 13th century at the invitation of Hungarian King Béla IV. Other sources believe that it originated in the Serbo-Croatian province of Sriem, which is part of Vojvodina, and in Tirnava, Romania. The first reference to the cultivation of Furmint in the Tokaj region is from 1623. Nowadays, this variety is cultivated on almost 480 ha in Slovakia. It does extremely well in deep soils rich in minerals, especially on stony soils of volcanic origin and loess loams. However, it does not like dry sands and alluvial gravel and sands. It features leaves with thicker veins with three lobes and smaller cuts and thin cylindrical bunches with or without wings. The berries have thin, waxy, light green skins with brown dots. Their pulp contains a higher must content. Furmint is not resistant to frost or mold. However, drier locations with frequent morning fog are ideal for the harvest of nobly rotten raisin selections. Old Furmint vines planted 60 to 80 years ago produce small and dense bunches. Furmint biely (White Furmint), Furmint kučeravý (Curly Furmint) and Furmint zlatý (Golden Furmint) are precious, original clones in terms of their cultivation and technology. Their wines are concentrated with a rich aroma and full mineral taste.

Synonyms: Mosler, Zapfner, Šipon, Moslavac

GRAPEVINE VARIETIES IN SLOVAKIA

Lipovina (Hárslevelű)

This old Hungarian variety probably originated in the region of Zemplín as an accidental seedling. It is cultivated in Slovakia on an area of 179 ha in the Tokaj region, where it is the second largest variety after Furmint. Before the phylloxera plague, this variety was part of smaller plantings in the vicinity of Štúrovo and Strekov. It prefers warm volcanic soils and loess loam mixtures. It has long cylindrical bunches (frequently over 40 cm long) with occasional wings. Its green-yellow berries have brown freckles when ripe. A wax film is visible on the surface. A sufficient amount of must with a neural fruity taste that is pleasantly sweet when fully ripe is released from the pulp during pressing. Lipovina (Hárslevelű) berries are prone to the creation of raisins similar to Furmint berries. Its leaves are medium large and tooth-shaped like linden leaves. This is also why this variety has its traditional Slovak name Lipovina (Linden Tree).

Synonyms: Lindenblätrige, Kerekes

Yellow Muscat (Muškát žltý)

This is one of the oldest original varieties in the Tokaj viticultural region, where it currently occupies an area of 65 ha. According to several sources, Yellow Muscat was known and cultivated by the original inhabitants of the Zemplín region at the height of the Roman Empire in Europe. In general, this variety, which is less demanding regarding soil, produces quality aromatic wines even on dry stony soils. Its leaf has three to five lobes. It does well even on poorer sandy loams especially in locations with sufficient sun exposure. The fruit-bearing coefficient is also affected by the training and yield reduction methods. A burden of up to 6,000 kilograms of grapes per hectare is suitable for high quality wine because the average sugar content of the must is over 30 kg/hl. It does not like frosty locations, and therefore it is cultivated on high, airy slopes. Its bunches are medium large; they have a cylindrical-conical shape with a high density of berries. They begin to ripen at the end of September. In addition to a higher extract of acids and sugars, grapes infected by noble rot Botrytis cinerea also have relatively concentrated primary aromas in pulp resembling Muscat and spicy tones with honey, and a hint of exotic fruits.

Synonyms: Muškát Lunel, Muscat Blanc, Yellow Muscat

NEW WHITE CLONES

Moravian Muscat (Muškát moravský)

This medium aromatic wine grape variety was bred at Polešovice (V. Křivánek) from Muscat Ottonel and Prachttraube. In 1987, it was registered in the state varietal book under the official name *Mopr*, and then as *Moravský muškát*. Since 1993, it has been known as *Muškát moravský*. The taste of this lovely aromatic wine with a Muscat bouquet is more delicate and the acid content is lower. This is also why this variety is used for the production of young wines, which are sought after by consumers in cellars and wine shops from the first Monday in November until the end of the year. This variety is modest in terms of its location and occupies smaller areas of planting in marginal vineyards (178 ha) where it is a reliable bearer. This enables growers to produce delightful, spicy-muscat fruity wines with a lower extract. It suffers from a lack of water in dry locations, nor does it prosper in light sandy and gravelly soils. The results of new plantings by winegrowers in the town of Šenkvice are interesting. The cryomaceration of freshly harvested grapes combines herbal and honey aromas with the pleasant juicy taste of citrus fruits and a light spicy aftertaste.

Synonym: Mopr

Devín

This variety was bred at the Research Institute of Viticulture and Enology in Bratislava from the Traminer and Rotweiss Veltliner varieties in 1958 (D. Pospíšilová, O. Korpás). Its clone 15/4 with the best qualities was eventually registered in the *List of Registered Varieties* in 1997. It is cultivated in all wine regions except the Tokaj region. Its current planting area of 157 ha is slightly growing each year. Devín's budbreak is late, while the blooming and ripening is medium late; it is not too demanding in terms of location or soil. Its ability to create high sugar content is one of its most valuable qualities. In warm years with a long, dry autumn, the grape must reaches a sugar content of 28 up to 30 g/l and average yields of grapes exceed 9 tons per hectare. Noble rot is frequently created on berries. Wines are noted for their charming yellow-green hues, and piquant fruity and spicy bouquet of exotic fruits, wild roses and nutmeg mace. In higher attributes, the taste of the wine is affected by tones of butter pear and pineapple; in naturally sweet raisin selections it is the mixture of dried summer fruits, honey and rhubarb. In heavier clayey and argillaceous soils (the village of Orechová), its elegant bready character stands out; on sands with optimum irrigation (the village of Malý Horeš) it provides charming spicy and herbal notes.

Pálava

This cross of Traminer and Müller-Thurgau was bred in Perná na Morave in 1953 (J. Veverka). It occupies an area of 55 ha in Slovakia. Grapes ripen in mid-October; in good vintages it is suitable for making high quality, single varietal wines. The average sugar content of its must is 20 – 23 g/l with an acid content of 6 – 10 g/l. It does not agree with dry locations and is susceptible to spring and winter frost. It also has a low resistance to fungal diseases, which is why this variety is not intensively extended. In quality, frost-free locations with vineyards with a southern exposure and warm soils with a sufficient soil profile depth it gives more stable yields of grapes suitable for the production of quality wines with attribute. These wines resemble Traminer varieties; they refresh with piquant acidity and a distinct muscat-spicy bouquet. In higher attributes acquired from the grapes of reduced harvests from poorer locations the wines are well balanced in residual sugar content and acids and their smell hints of tea rose and false acacia. In terms of taste, Pálava preserves a fruity freshness, with a fine hint of vanilla in the best vintages even after several years of maturing in bottles.

Aurelius

This is a new clone from the cross breeding of the Neuburger and Rhein Riesling varieties in 1953 in Veľké Pavlovice, and later in Perná pri Mikulove (J. Veverka, F. Zatloukal). It was registered in Slovakia in 1983. Grapes ripen medium late, at the end of September and the beginning of October. Its ability to accumulate high sugar content until full ripeness is a typical quality in warm and dry vintages. Aurelius has no specific soil or location requirements. It enjoys the best results on airy slopes with limited pressure of fungal diseases and in heated soil with good water drainage. Soils with good nutrition ensure high yields; it has a spicier bouquet in poorer vintages. The sensory qualities of wines made of this variety resemble Rhein Riesling wines; however their smell incorporates a wider variety of aromatic substances. Noble botrytis rot appears on the thin-skinned berries in warm years. The maceration of skins can distinctively support a lovely bouquet of single varietal wine. Late harvest up to the selection of the berries of these single varietal wines are characterized by a green-yellow to golden hue, and a floral-fruity aroma with tones of peaches, dandelion and elm tree. The taste is full, fresh and harmonious, spicy with hint of lemon zest and honey on the palate. Medium-sweet and sweet selections of grapes are noted for their fruity-spicy aroma and fresh elegance. Despite all of this, Aurelius is not widespread across Slovakia. Its total of planting area amounts to less than 17 ha the largest areas are in the Small Carpathian wine region (Šenkvice, Dubová pri Modre).

GRAPEVINE VARIETIES IN SLOVAKIA

Noria

This young Slovak variety was created in 1974 by the cross breeding of Rhein Riesling and Semillon in a former branch breeding station in Opatovská Nová Ves near Veľký Krtíš (A. Foltánová), but it was entered in the *List of Registered Varieties* in 2002. To date, its cultivation has confirmed the hereditary qualities of Rhein Riesling, which is extremely positive for its further expansion in our northern regions. Noria's budbreak and blossom are medium early, and bring higher average yields than Rhein Riesling; the grapes ripen in mid-October. It is not too demanding in terms of location and soil. Furthermore, it is very resistant to winter frosts. It is susceptible to grey mold and has medium resistance to other fungal diseases. Currently, it is only locally cultivated on an area of 3 ha in Dolné Plachtince and Strekov. In warm fertile soils with good drainage on hills facing the south it gives excellent yields of grapes with a pleasant bouquet. The young wines resemble Semillon in smell with tones of apricot, nectarines and mango after its fermentation and medium long maturing and slight micro-oxidation in oak casks; they feature a charming hint of hazelnut and butter toast. They can mature to full elegance in several years. The taste is fresh, complex, supported by a higher acid content and extract. You can also find tones of gooseberries, elderberry and citrus fruits. Wines from better quality locations have a potential for longer maturing in bottles. The verification of the qualities of naturally sweet single varietal wines made of noble rot raisin harvest which have a potential for interesting enrichment of assortment is only a technological question.

Milia

This variety was bred from the Müller-Thurgau and Traminer varieties in Šenkvice in 1973 (I. Novák, V. Bobeková, M. Matochová) and was registered in the *List of Registered Varieties* in 2002. It is one of the early varieties. Its grapes begin to ripen by the end of August and reach optimum technological ripeness in mid-September. Similar to Noria, it is only found in the wine regions of Southern Slovakia and the Small Carpathians (3 ha). It does well in loess and even poorer gravel-sandy soils in vineyards with a southern orientation. The grapes must be processed according to sugar content and acid concentration. The must sugar content reaches 23 g/l, however the acid content quickly drops in over-ripened berries. Young wines are deliciously aromatic with pleasant fruity acids. Shorter grape maceration, the fast processing of grape mash in low temperatures with reduced oxygen and in the case of low acid content in musts with an early racking of young wine from wine sediments are required because of the similarity of taste qualities with the Müller-Thurgau mother variety. Single varietal wines made of Milia are attractive thanks to their residual sugars in higher attributes, which is appreciated by lovers of sweeter wines.

Hetera

The rare Inzucht-hybrid variety was bred by crossing Traminer and Veltliner Rot Weiss in 1965 in Bratislava (D. Pospíšilová). The difficult crossing technique emphasized certain cultivation signs in the offspring variety such as the growing strength of grapevines, the ripening of grapes with high sugar accumulation (25 – 29 g/l) and regular high yields (16 – 19 tons per hectare). Hetera was registered in the *List of Registered Varieties* in 2011. It does well on warm slopes with good water deposits. It has low resistance to mildew and a slightly higher resistance to powdery mildew. However, the medium thick skin resists the grey mold well. Wines made of the yield in earlier harvests are rougher and contain more green acids. Late harvests and grape selections from nutritious deep soils provide harmonious and bouquet wines with tones of tropical fruits and honey, in naturally sweet attributes they differ in typical bready character. The perspective growing potential of this variety needs to be fully tested in several winegrowing regions of Slovakia. Its extraordinary ripening potential, which exceeds that of Traminer in all compared attributes, can be a great advantage for winemakers.

Breslava

This variety was named after the ancient name of the city of Bratislava. It was bred by triple crossing on a maternal plant which grew from Pink Chasselas and Traminer in 1951 (D. Pospíšilová, O. Korpás). Santa Maria de Alcantara is its paternal variety. In 1960, the cultivators picked the two best vine seedlings from triple crossing which advanced to next testing. Type 10/28 eventually passed the state varietal testing. Breslava has a shorter vegetation cycle. It buds and blooms early in the spring and the grapes ripen at the end of September. Because of its firm and flexible skin, which can withstand pressure of 930 g on the berry, it is also suitable for direct consumption as a table grape variety. The pulp of Breslava disintegrates easily and is juicy with a pleasant Muscat aroma. The young wines are noted for their smell and taste of ripe grapefruits with fresh herbal tones of mint leaves and a pleasant citrus fruit aftertaste.

NEW RED CLONES

Odessa red (Alibernet)

A Ukrainian cross of the Alicante Bouchet and Cabernet Sauvignon varieties was bred in 1950 in Odessa. It was used as teinturier grape in blends with traditional varietal wines. Because of the interest of consumers they began to plant it as complementary red variety suitable for longer aging in wooden casks. Its berries are characterized by the high color intensity of the must. The hard skin has a purple-red color and its surface is covered with a wax layer. Grapes ripen in the second decade up to the end of October. This variety brings the best quality yield in warm sub-regions with a sufficient number of sunny days. In nutritious soils it has better gains while bunches in bloom are prone to blossom drop. In terms of the quality of grapes, this variety does well in medium fertile, deeper and warm soils. Alibernet's bearing area in Slovakia exceeds 253 ha. It has a strong resistance to frost as well as grey mold and a satisfactory resistance to other fungal diseases. Grapes for the production of more extractive wines must be harvested in the phase of technological ripeness, when the colored anthocyanes and other tannins are mature in addition to a sufficient amount of sugars in the skins and pulp. Wines made of Alibernet agree with long-term storage in new as well as frequently used oak casks with a small process of micro-oxidation. The young wines are relatively rough and difficult to drink, with a higher content of fruit acids and tinted color substances. Mature vintages will surprise you with their rich blackberry bouquet and neutral taste with tones of black currant and green poppy head. Thanks to oxidation, the bouquet extends by a spectrum of gingerbread spices with note of chocolate and elderberry wood in the background.

Dunaj

This later ripening plastic variety was bred by crossing the Muscat Bouchet and Oporto varieties in 1951 (D. Pospíšilová, O. Korpás). Because of its high blossom drop, it was crossed with the Saint Laurent variety seven years later. Based on the proposal of the state varietal commission, it was included in the assortment of permitted varieties in 1997. Its frost resistance and ability to produce high sugar content in must (21 – 26 g/l) and regular high yields of grapes (10 tons per hectare) are great advantages. It has no specific requirements for soil. However, it is sensitive to powdery mildew. In deeper fertile soils, the grape must contains more acids than in warm soils with fewer nutrients. Young wines keep their dark carmine-red color with high tannin content and a surprisingly round, harmonious, fruity taste. After maturing in wooden casks, the structure of the wine becomes even finer and notes of plums, black berry fruits and chocolate come to the fore. Dunaj from drier and warm sites surprises by its fine "Bourgundy/Pinot" animal tones. The grapes must be harvested on time, because the bunches dry out in later phases. This variety is also suitable for the production of naturally sweet wines in a quality selection of berries or raisins. New plantings are doing well in the west of Slovakia in the vicinity of the towns of Pezinok and Vištuk, in the south in Strekov, in the surroundings of Nitra, near Čajkov, Rybník and Tajná, as well as in the east of Slovakia in Orechová. The total area of newly planted Dunaj vineyards exceeds 78 hectares.

Hron

This variety was cross bred from the southern French varieties of Castets and Abouriou Noir in 1976 (D. Pospíšilová et all.). From the original 85 vine seedlings, type Nos. 3/8 (Nitra, later Nitranka), 3/12 (Rimava), 3/13 (Váh) and 3/22 (Hron) were interesting in terms of cultivation and physiology. Hron is one of the late budding and blossoming varieties and ripens in mid-October. It does well in deeper loamy sand soils on mild southern slopes. As opposed to Dunaj and Alibernet, this variety is sensitive to winter frosts. However, in comparison to Dunaj, its berry set of the yield is lower; according to the type of vine training and selection of bud load, it produces 7 up to 14 tons per hectare on average. The wines are of dark-red color with well-balanced content of varietal tannins, fruit acids and residual sugar. They can also be consumed as young wines. Patient consumers appreciate more mature vintages made from the grapes in later harvest or grape selections that were stored in oak casks for a longer period of time. In their aroma their slightly resemble Cabernet Sauvignon, but they are much more harmonious. They show a full fruity extract in their taste.

Neronet

This variety was bred from triple crossing (Saint Laurent x Blauer Portugieser) x Alibernet in 1965 in Lednice na Morave (V. Kraus). The aim of the selection and hybridization was to achieve a variety similar to Alibernet with an intensive content of color substances and an earlier grape ripening period. Neronet is demanding in nutrients, and in the course of its growing season it requires a sufficient amount of water in the soil. Since it can be damaged by late spring frosts, it must be planted in airy, non-frosty locations. Its bunches are thin which increases the natural resistance of the berries to grey mold. However, it is sensitive to powdery mildew and downy mildew. From the technological aspect, even in average vintages it preserves a satisfactory production of sugars in must, which with regular rich yields (8 – 12 tons per hectare) enables the production of wines of neutral smell and a medium long taste of forest fruits. Mature vintages have an intensive red-purple color and a harmonious taste of black sour cherries fortified by a rich tannin content. It pays off to store them in wooden casks for several months where they acquire an elegant structure. Young Neronet wines designated for earlier consumption are made by the partial storing of grape mash without fermentation and simple fermentation after

the gravitation straining of the must in a press or straining vessel. The fruity aroma supported by primary tones in young Neronet resembles mulberry and ripe blackberries. Neronet is very rare in Slovakia. It is marginally cultivated on small areas in the Small Carpathians (Pezinok), Nitra (Tekov) and Southern Slovakia (Rúbaň).

Váh

Bred as vine seedling No. 3/13 from the same breeding as Hron, it is one of the late budding and late bearing varieties whose berries begin to soften only in the second half of October. Váh is medium resistant to winter frosts, which however must occur gradually without swift changes in temperature. Spring frosts do not damage it. It blooms early and in the growing season it displays a strong growth of foliage; therefore, winegrowers thin the shade-casting leaves from the zone of bunches and break off sterile shoots. Despite its medium large bunches with small berries, this variety's yield is above average (10 – 13 tons per hectare) with a higher sugar content of must (19 – 25 g/l) on warm southern slopes. Young single varietal wines have a dark-red up to ruby-red color and distinctive cabernet smell of black currents and false acacia. Its higher green tannin content creates a rough impression in taste, even paprika-like in average vintages. In order to achieve optimum harmony and elegance, Váh needs to be stored for 2 to 3 years in wooden casks and then in bottles.

Nitria

Nitra, the original name of vine seedling No. 3/8 from the cross breeding of Castets and Abouriou Noir, was changed to Nitria when entered in the *List of Registered Varieties* (2011). In comparison with Váh and Hron, it features an early start of all phenostages. Grapes begin to ripen in mid-September and the harvest in technological ripeness is possible at the beginning of October. Because of late budding, spring frosts may damage this variety, but it also has low resistance to winter frosts. Successful cultivation requires protected frost-free locations. But it does not have any particular requirements for soil; it does well in deeper soils with good drainage, poorer gravel sandy soils and stony soils. In drier vineyard sites it produces smaller yields, but in deep warm soils the average yield per hectare varies between 11 and 19 tons of grapes. The sugar and acid content of the Nitria must corresponds with the Hron variety according to the cultivation conditions. In favorable years in terms of climate it gives high quality, dark-red wines with a smell of black currants, sour cherries and rhubarb. Colder vintages bring lighter wines with a light color of pomegranate and a piquant smell of ripening forest fruits. Like all related sibling offspring clones, Nitria will also reward you with its smooth, well-balanced aroma and taste after several months of aging in new oak casks.

Rimava

Of all the cross breeding new clones of Castets and Abouriou Noir, this variety provides red wines of cabernet type with a supreme intensity of cassis aromas and a rich extractive taste with long aging potential. It is damaged by winter and spring frosts, therefore it should be planted in protected airy locations. Rimava buds and blooms slightly late, and at the time of blossoming it does not handle cold and rainy or hot and dry weather. Then it shows it most serious defect – blossom drop. The regular high hectare yields with higher sugar content of must which manage to compensate for its blossom drop is an advantage. Because of its strong growth of foliage in the growing season, the shade-casting leaves must be thinned from the zone of bunches and sterile shoots must be broken off in order to ensure their better development. Young varietal wines made of Rimava will charm you by their relatively full fruity bouquet of blackberries and raspberries which will be elegantly developed in neutral varietal wines stored in wooden casks. The distinctive wine aroma creates the pre-condition for the creation of blends with less distinctive and single varietal wines. The use of barrique type casks gives Rimava a new sensory and value dimension in diversity, richness and complexity.

Rosa

This unusual teinturier grape with its charming smell of roses was bred in 1961 by triple cross breeding (Picpoul x Blaufränkisch) x Traminer (D. Pospíšilová et all.). Despite its massive growth, one-year-old plants ripen well. Winter and spring frosts are not particularly problematic for this variety; it buds as other later varieties and blooms at the same time as early varieties. High vine training suits it where abundantly growing shoots enjoy a larger assimilation area. Rosa requires regular green work. The zone of grape bunches must be thinned in order to preventatively lower the risk of powdery mildew, to which this variety is extremely sensitive. It does very well in soils with a sufficient water regime which retains precipitation. It suffers in dry locations where the bunches dry out. Rosa's yield is lower, it gives 5 – 8 tons of grapes per hectare on average. It is interesting by its ability to create raisins in long dry autumns. Therefore, Rosa is also suitable for the production of naturally sweet wines. Its dark-claret color and unique bouquet of tea roses with tones of overripe rose hips after the first frost and its sweet taste stand out in drier vintages accompanied by a piquant note of white pepper.

Rudava

This variety was bred in 1967 by cross breeding Castets with cross bred clone No. I-35-9 (Teinturier x Aleatico x Puchljakovskij) which came to us from the former Soviet Union (D. Pospíšilová, et al.). Rudava is a medium late to late variety which buds and blooms late. Thanks to the delayed beginning of its growing season, it resists spring frosts. Winter frosts do not present a problem either. It gives rich yields of grapes with a medium late harvest in the second decade of October. The grapevine is characterized by massive growth; one-year-old plants ripen very well in the fall. It is most sensitive to powdery mildew. Currently, its cultivation is rather scarce in the wine region of Southern Slovakia (Rúbaň), where it gives very good wines of dark ruby-red color with a smell resembling dark berry fruits. Rudava's taste is pleasant, medium full and neutral with tones of cabernet. Longer storage in casks or bottles contributes to its attractive harmony of tannins, fruity bouquet components and alcohol.

Torysa

Another registered variety from the series of precious vine seedlings of Castets x I-35-9 bred in 1967 (D. Pospíšilová et all.). Its growing season is longer thanks to which grapes ripen only at the beginning of October. It does best in high quality warm locations on mild slopes and deep nutritious soils with a good water regime. This variety is from the group of teinturier grapes because its pulp is of a dark violet and red color. Its bunches are medium large with medium thick berries with a firm skin which improves its resistance to fungal diseases except for powdery mildew. Wines made of late harvest selections keep their dark violet and red color and pleasant fruity taste of black currant. Its velvet taste is rich after several months of aging with pleasant fruit tannins; in high yields its loses its cabernet character.

Torysa is a suitable variety for blends. It distinctively affects the color intensity, harmonious fruity taste and comprehensive impression.

HOW WINE IS MADE IN OUR COUNTRY

Wine is an alcoholic beverage which is the result of the alcoholic fermentation of grape must. During fermentation, the natural sugars in the grapes (glucose and fructose) are converted into ethanol and carbon dioxide; this process is accompanied by released heat. Yeast (Saccharomyces cerevisiae) also plays a crucial role. Nowadays, many methods of production and technical equipment are used for preserving the quality and creating unique sensory features of wine. Being acquainted with the basic steps in wine making is essential for anyone who has a genuine interest in the life of wine and its tasting.

White, Rosé and Red Wines	50
Sparkling Wines	53
Tokaj Wines	56
Innovative Methods in Wine Production	59

WHITE, ROSÉ AND RED WINES

Collecting healthy and undamaged grapes is the first step in wine making. Since the grapes must be sufficiently ripe, the winegrower continually checks their acid and sugar content. The date for the harvest of each wine grape variety depends on the date on which it reaches its optimum **technological ripeness**, i.e., the ratio of natural sugar and acid content in the must. Because of changing climatic conditions, vintage winegrowers try to harmonize the harvesting of individual varieties with the winery's capabilities. All actions are adjusted to the earliest possible de-stemming and pressing of grapes after they are harvested. The fruit of white aromatic varieties are then left to rest on their skins. The pre-soak phase of fruits on their skins takes from 1 to 4 hours depending on the temperature of the environment. De-stemmed and finely chopped grapes (grape mash) of red varieties are left to ferment in fermentation tanks from several hours up to several days in various physical conditions. Winemakers use classical open fermentation tanks, closed roto-tanks or modern vinificators with carbon dioxide or nitrogen atmosphere for this purpose.

The result of this process with **white varieties** is the transfer of aromatic substances in the must prior to fermentation. Many Slovak winemakers use the most-up-to-date cryomaceration method (temperatures close to 0 °C) for the presoak of grape mash of white varieties. The application of enzymes in the grape mash speeds up the process of maceration and prevents the growth of undesirable microorganisms, acetic acid bacteria and oxidation enzymes in particular.

Rosé wines are made from the free-run must of red varieties or their instant pressing without fermentation. Because of the required intensity of the fruity aroma and the pleasant fresh taste with tones of garden fruits, their further processing is in fact identical to that of the production of white wines. White and rosé grape must is drawn off in a sedimentation tank. Soil particles, fragments of stems and skins and the residua of pesticides and original microflora settle and are separated from the pure must when the temperature is partially decreased and bentonite and sulfur dioxide are added. The purified must from insufficiently ripe or damaged grapes is usually further processed by the adding of beet sugar (chaptalization) and nutrients for yeast according to precisely established rules. Must with a sufficient content

HOW WINE IS MADE IN OUR COUNTRY

of fermentable sugars and designated for the production of quality wines with attribute may not be chaptalized or enriched in any other way.

Progressive winemakers process **purified must** by adding pure wine yeast cultures. Traditional winemakers prefer the spontaneous genera of original yeast microflora which re-ferments **unclarified must**. However, wines made in this way require one hundred percent grape quality, a sufficient amount of fermentable sugars in the must and more consistent adherence to hygiene and the checking of processes in progress with the fermentation, creation and maturing of the wine. Wines made by spontaneous microflora are more prone to disease and secondary fermentation by residual sugars in the must, and more sensitive to the oxygen effect in the individual phases of production. In order to preserve their positive sensory qualities, they require a more thorough approach from the winemaker. This is particularly true in the years with less ripeness and an average grape quality, when the process of fermentation by spontaneous microflora is unrestrained, frequently uneven and slowed down, and young wines won't ferment up to the dry level of residual sugars.

As opposed to white and rosé wines, the release of red anthocyanin pigments and tannins from berry skins in the must is an important part of the pre-fermentation processing of **red wines**. This is done by fermenting red grape mash, applying enzymes, a combination of both of methods, or thermovinification, i.e., a brief heating up of the grape mash prior to alcoholic fermentation in adjusted vinificators. **Alcoholic fermentation** can take place in stainless steel vessels (steel tanks) or wooden barrels. In less favorable vintages, **malolactic fermentation**, which eliminates unpleasant and tart malic acid in red wine, is important after the fermentation of young wine. Cellar masters continuously check all of the processes mentioned above. In addition to ensuring suitable genuses of yeast or bacteria, they must adjust the physical conditions and regulate the temperature.

The producers' requirements for the quality of red wine constantly grow with the improvements in red wine production technology. To begin, the quality is determined by the right red color corresponding with the variety, adequate tannin content with respect to low astringency, higher post-fermentation alcohol content, lower acid content for a more acceptable harmony of taste with respect to the alcohol and tannins and low residual sugar content. Therefore, in comparison with white and rosé wines, red wines require longer maturing time, controlled oxygen access in the use of micro-oxidation and the use of larger wooden barrels. These are frequently combined with smaller, barrique-type barrels made of new wood.

Creation of Wine

Other processes affecting the sensory quality and physical stability of the final product must be ensured during the **creation of the wine** – in the case of young wines, it begins with fermentation and is completed by racking or siphoning from gross and fine lees. The basic processes accompanying the creation and maturing of wine include the following:

1. oxidation and reduction (oxidation vs reduction wine making methods),
2. esterification (reaction of alcohols and acids),
3. crystallization of tartaric acid salts and polysaccharides,
4. flocculation (adsorption) of proteins,
5. malolactic fermentation (conversion of malic acid into lactic acid caused by the lactic acid bacteria Oenococcus oeni).

In this phase, the winemaker regularly checks the development of the young wine and its sensory and analytical qualities. Wine vessels are regularly replenished and, depending on the desired outcome, the temperature and reductivity of the environment are also adjusted by appropriately applying liquid sulfur dioxide or nitrogen.

Maturing of Wine

The racking of the young wine from the lees in clean vessels of various types is followed by another significant phase – the maturing of the wine, during which the wine's physical and chemical and biochemical balances are stabilized. At this stage, the secondary bouquet begins to show more distinctively in the aroma, while the varietal tones supported by the extract, products of alcoholic fermentation and the already mentioned processes of wine creation towards the required outcome are fully developing in the taste. At the designated phase of maturity before bottling, the clarified and sufficiently stabilized and clear wine is filtered through a thick layer of pads made from diatomaceous earth, cellulose fibers, perlite or a cross-flow filter. Some wines can even be bottled without filtration. This information is indicated on the back label. The producer may also emphasize that any sediment found at the bottom of the bottle is not a sign of poor quality; it is simply a result of the crystallization of tartaric acid salts (potassium sodium tartrate) and red coloring after bottling.

Slovak white, rosé and red wines are classified as dry, medium dry, medium and sweet according to the residual sugar content. Residual sugar represents the part of fermentable sugars that were not processed by yeast during fermentation. Its content is listed on quality wine labels. This information facilitates the decision-making of customers when selecting their favorite taste. When indicating the residual sugar content in wine, we have to keep in mind the fact that the extent of the feeling of dryness in the taste depends not only on the residual sugar content, but also on the acid content.

Pursuant to our legislation, dry wine contains a maximum of 4 g/l of residual sugar. However, winemakers may label wine as dry if the residual sugar content does not exceed 9 g/l, and the difference between the total acid content, quantified in g/l of tartaric acid and the residual sugar content is not less than 2 grams.

Classification of still wines according to residual sugar content

Still wine labeling	Residual sugar content [g/l]
dry (suché)	0 – 4
medium dry (polosuché)	4 – 12
medium sweet (polosladké)	12 – 45
sweet (sladké)	45+

SPARKLING WINES

More than three centuries have passed since of the creation of the first sparkling wine by the classical method of fermentation in bottles. This traditional method is named after the wine region of Champagne, the place of its birth.

The name Champagne may only be used for sparkling wines which were made according to established production methods from grapes cultivated in the Champagne region from the noble red varieties Pinot Noir, Pinot Meunier and white Chardonnay. The production of sekt vinohradníckej oblasti (Sekt V. O. - Sparkling wine of the wine region) in Slovakia requires that the grapes, must and wine and all of the components used for its production come from the declared wine region. (Sect is the German term for some sparkling wine.) The criteria for pestovateľský sekt are even stricter – the grapes, must or wine and all of the components used for this type of sparkling wine must come from the winemaker's vineyard in the declared wine region.

Sparkling wines (sekts) are made by the secondary fermentation of the original still wine and the addition of a selected culture of wine yeast, sugar and a mixture of vitamins that

1– Residual sugar content (compulsory for aerated sparkling and sparkling wines), 2 – Sparkling wine category and name of the protected indication of origin (V.O. - Sekt vinohradníckej oblasti), 3 – Production method (optional), 4 – Producer, 5 – Winemaker, 6 – Name of wine, 7 – Wine category with name of protected indication of origin, 8 – Residual sugar content (compulsory for aerated sparkling and sparkling wines), 9 – Production method (optional), 10 – Production method (optional), 11 – Category and color of wine, 12 – Residual sugar content (compulsory for sparkling wines), 13 – Name of the protected indication of origin (viticultural region), 14 – Vintage (optional for sparkling wine), 15 – Producer and bottler, 16 – Production batch, 17 – Indication of origin (provenience), 18 – Alcohol content, 19 – Volume

protect and nourish yeast cells during growth and amitosis. The carbon dioxide created naturally as a product of the secondary fermentation of wine gradually dissolves in the wine thanks to the isobaric conditions in the closed bottle or other fermentation vessel. The lowest pressure of carbon dioxide for sparkling wines is 350 kPa at a temperature of 20 °C. As a result, sparkling wine features an intensive sparkling of millions of small bubbles when poured. The production method determines the difference in the persistence of foam as well as the refreshing aroma and delicate taste.

Method of Production of Sparkling Wines

Méthode Traditionnelle also known as **Méthode Classique** was first used in our territory with the CHATEAU PALUGYAY in 1825 and HUBERT J.E. sparkling wines in 1845, and after appearing on the market, both brands of this at first aristocratic beverage won generations of fans. According to the classical method, the secondary fermentation of the original wine with added yeasts, sugar and nutrients takes place in the same bottle, which the customer buys after a the demanding process of clarification (remuage), removal of deposits (dégorgement) and adding of sugar syrup known as liqueur d'expédition- expedition liqueur (dosage).

At the beginning of the 19th century, Eugen Charmat improved and successfully patented the sparkling wine production method which enables secondary fermentation in a closed tank under isobaric conditions. **Méthode Charmat** became a success in winemaking practice since it reduced the operational costs and the requirements for a qualified labor force. A bottle of sparkling wine made by the classical method must be handled by the winemaker eighty times on average before it makes its way to the customer. The manual shaking of yeast deposits in the bottle neck, their subsequent freezing, the removal of this shaken and frozen yeast deposit from the bottle neck, manual dosage (adding) of expedition liqueur and the resealing of the bottle with a cork (bouchon) and a wire basket (muselet) are the most demanding acts. The volume of original "manual" manipulating was reduced to one tenth thanks to the Charmat method and the more recent Méthode Transvals (transfer method).

The initial **Méthode Transvals** processes are similar to the classical method. But, as opposed to the Charmat method, the original wine (cuvée) undergoes secondary fermentation in bottles. It is filtered and bottled in new bottles after the fermentation is completed. Sparkling wine with brilliant clarity and fine bubbles is the result. At first sight, most consumers cannot distinguish it from exclusive and more costly "classical" sparkling wine.

Méthode Rurale, which is also used for the production of aromatic sparkling wines, does not use secondary fermentation, but the initial fermentation of the must of aromatic varieties in closed vessels. After careful filtration and bottling, aromatic sparkling wines are surprising because of their pure floral and fruity aroma, impulsive sparkling and slightly larger bubbles of carbon dioxide. Hubert De Luxe, a quality sparkling wine, is a successful example of the application of this method.

HOW WINE IS MADE IN OUR COUNTRY

Classification of sparkling wines according to residual sugar content

Sparkling wine rating	Residual sugar content [g/l]
Brut Natur	0 – 3
Extra Brut	0 – 6
Brut	0 – 12
Extra Dry, Extra Sec, Extra Seco (Extra suché)	12 – 17
Dry, Sec, Seco (Polosuché)	17 – 32
Demi-Sec, Demi-Seco (Polosladké)	32 – 50
Doux, Sweet, Dulce (Sladké)	50+

In addition to listing the production method and other elements important for the classification of wines, sparkling wine labels provide information regarding the residual sugar content, used varieties and sometimes the original wine vintage. The residual sugar content is stated in grams per liter after fermentation or the dosage (adding) of expedition liqueur. Winemakers use it in order to adjust "the complexity" of the sparkling wine's taste qualities with respect to total acid content – based on the requirements of customers, naturally.

The best white wine grape varieties such as Grüner Veltliner, Italian Riesling, Pinot Blanc, Chardonnay, and Müller-Thurgau are used in Slovakia for the production of quality sparkling wines, sparkling wines of the wine region, sekt vinohradníckej oblasti and pestovateľský sekt. Rhein Riesling, Furmint and Feteasca Regala are used sporadically. The elegant red Saint Laurent and Pinot Noir varieties are suitable for sparkling rosé wine in our viticultural conditions.

Aromatic varieties such as Irsai Oliver or Muscat Ottonel constitute the main share of cuvée (blend) in aromatic sparkling wines. Like the region of Champagne, in our country, the secret of success is concentrated in the hands of winemaking masters. However, preparing the blend and use of selected yeast geneses is the foundation. To put it simply, the art of "mixing" musts or finished still wines, along with the selection of the "most suitable" yeast genus, are the most important keys to the sensory qualities of sparkling wine. If the name Blanc de Blancs is on the label of quality sparkling wine or sparkling wine, the entire blend of the original wine is made from the white Chardonnay variety. On the other hand, the labeling Blanc de Noirs suggests that red Pinot Noir grapes were the basis for the blend. More sophisticated consumers and the naturally curious may reach for vintage sparkling wines, which remained in the bottle after bottling, secondary fermentation, clarification and maturing for a minimum of five years up to the moment of their appearance on the market.

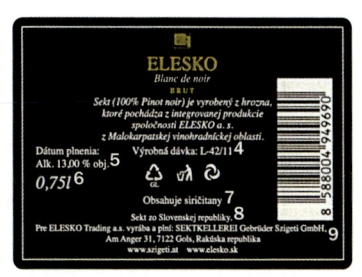

1 – Sparkling wine production method, 2 – The name of the sparkling wine indicates that the must of red varieties (Pinot Noir) was used for its production 3 – Residual sugar content, 4 – Production batch, 5 – Alcohol content, 6 – Volume, 7 – Allergens, 8 – Category of wine and indication of origin (provenience), 9 – Producer and bottler

TOKAJ WINES

For centuries, generations of winegrowers and winemakers have improved the tradition and global fame of the Tokaj brand while using traditional oxidative methods of production. The careful processing of healthy grapes from permitted varieties of Furmint, Lipovina (Hárslevelü) and Yellow Muscat, which are harvested manually at the best stage of ripeness, the spontaneous fermentation and the slow maturing of Tokaj samorodne wine with or without the adding of essence from nobly rotten (Botrytized) raisins are the keys to the production of Tokaj wine. The moderate access of oxygen plays a significant role in the production of classical Tokaj wine. Samorodne wines and Tokaj selections mature in barrels with a volume of 136 up to 250 l in tuff cellars with walls covered by the noble cellar mold *Cladosporium cellare* at a stable temperature of 10 °C and a relative humidity of approximately 95 %. They are also referred to as yellow wines because of their golden-yellow to amber color. The specific microflora of the film forming yeast which participates in the creation and maturing of wine led to the further unique classification of Tokaj wines in the category of "wine from under a film." Regardless, Tokaj wine is unique in the world and occupies an important place in wine cabinets and gastronomy. Therefore, its production is managed by special enological procedures.

Classical Tokaj Wines

The collection of classical wines from the Tokaj viticultural region starts with **Tokaj samorodne wines**. They are golden-yellow with a shade of brown and have a fine bready taste. This taste is created by slow oxidation in classical wooden barrels in Tokaj tuff cellars. We distinguish between dry and sweet types according to their residual sugar content. The average sugar content of must in samorodne dry wines is 21 °NM. Tokaj samorodne sweet wines contain a minimum of 10 g/l of natural sugar and additional extractive substances. They are made by processing ripened Tokaj varieties which are collected and processed along with a smaller portion of sweet nobly rotten (Botrytized) raisins. The sugar content of the must in samorodne sweet wines is at least 24 °NM. Both types of samorodne wines may be introduced to the market after at least two years of aging in Tokaj cellars, one year of which must be in wooden barrels.

HOW WINE IS MADE IN OUR COUNTRY

Tokaj selection wines can feature 3,4,5 or 6 tubs (putnove). The number of tubs indicates the amount of raisins used for production. One Tokaj tub (bucket) represents 25 to 28 kilograms of raisins. Juice acquired from these raisins (Tokaj essence) is added according to the relevant number of tubs to the samorodne dry wine of the same vintage with a volume of one Tokaj barrel (136 l).

The traditional production of Tokaj selection is as follows: a corresponding amount of raisins (given by the number of Tokaj tubs) is added to Tokaj must with a sugar content of at least 21 °NM or to Tokaj samorodne dry wine of the same quality and vintage which comes from qualified vineyards of the Tokaj viticultural region. The volume of Tokaj must or Tokaj samorodne wine mixed with raisins is 136 l and is identical to the volume of a Gönc cask. Tokaj selection may be introduced on the market after its fermentation and sufficiently long maturing in Tokaj tuff cellars after 3 years of aging, of which, at least 2 years must be in Gönc casks. The intensity of the shades of selection from golden-yellow up to dark amber-golden increases with the number of tubs. The content of the exotic honey-fruity, bready-almond up to raisin-date tones of aroma and the taste with a rich extract and minerality are similarly concentrated. The long and persistent aftertaste of the selections is supported by its piquant acid content with residual sugar – a minimum of 60 g/l in 3 tubs, 90 g/l in 4 tubs, 120 g/l in 5 tubs and 150 g/l in 6 tubs (according to the quality and amount of raisins).

Maturing leads to harmony and beauty; this applies to the quality of the Tokaj selection regardless of the number of tubs.

Tokaj máslás (derived from the word copy in Hungarian) and Tokaj fordítás (meaning turning over in Hungarian) are younger siblings of the "great classical Tokaj wines. **Máslás** is made by the fermentation of Tokaj must or wine which was poured over the yeast deposits of Tokaj samorodne wine or Tokaj selection. In the case of **fordítás**, the must or wine from the Tokaj viticultural region poured over the grape marc of raisins is fermented. After fermentation, both wines must mature for at least one year in a wooden barrel, and at least for two years in Tokaj cellars.

Tokaj essence is the sweetest, richest and most expensive product made of raisins. **Selection essence** is made by the alcoholic fermentation of raisins which, after processing, were immersed in sweet Tokaj must or Tokaj wine of the same vintage with a minimum natural sugar content of 180 g/l and 45 g/l of sugar-free extract. The precious **Tokaj essence is** made from the slow fermentation of free-run must from

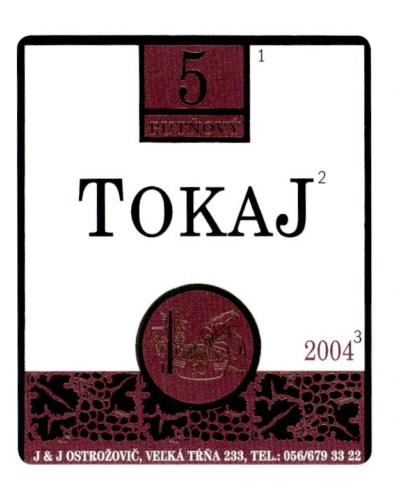

1 – Name of wine, 2 – Name of wine and protected geographical unit (viticultural region), 3 – Vintage, 4 – Producer, 5 – Name of wine, 6 – Category of wine with protected indication of origin, 7 – Indication of geographical unit (vineyard – compulsory for Tokaj wines), 8 –Allergens, 9 – Producer and bottler, 10 – Volume, 11 – Vintage, 12 – Production batch, 13 – Alcohol content

HOW WINE IS MADE IN OUR COUNTRY

specially selected raisins from classified vineyards. One liter of this essence contains 450 g/l of natural sugar and 50 g/l of sugar-free extract. Selection and Tokaj essence have to mature for a minimum of three years in Tokaj tuff cellars, of which at least two years must be in wooden barrels before being put on the market.

Tokaj Furmint is made by the alcoholic fermentation of Furmint grapes with an admixture of the Lipovina (Hárslevelű) and Yellow Muscat varieties (maximum of 15% in total) cultivated in Tokaj vineyards. The same applies to **Tokaj Lipovina (Hárslevelű) and Tokaj Muškát žltý (Yellow Muscat)**, where the admixture of other permitted Tokaj varieties may not exceed 15 %. Grapes for the production of quality Tokaj wines must have a sugar content of at least 17 °NM when harvested. The chaptalizing of must up to 22 °NM for white wines is permitted in the years with a deficit of sunny days.

Tokaj grapes must be harvested in full ripeness and certified at the harvest for the production of **quality wines with attribute**. Quality wines with attribute made in Tokaj, as in other viticultural regions of Slovakia, may not be enriched or chemically conserved with the exception of the use of permitted doses of sulfur dioxide.

All classic Tokaj wines made by the oxidative method are bottled in cylindrical Tokaj bottles with a long neck and a volume of 0.50 l (alternative volumes of 0.375 l and 0.250 l and 0.100 l) made of clear glass. The ratio of the height of the cylindrical bottle neck to the total height of the bottle is 1: 2.7.

---

1 - Vintage, 2 - Producer, 3 - Name of wine 4 - Traditional term (attribute of quality wine), 5 - Date related to origin (provenience), 6 - Name of protected indication of origin (geographical unit), 7 - Term for protected indication of origin, 8 - Traditional data (category of quality wine with attribute), 9 - Color of wine and residual sugar content, 10 - Smaller geographical unit (vineyard), 11 - Allergens, 12 - Vintage, 13 - Production batch, 14 - Alcohol content, 15 - Volume, 16 - Producer and bottler

INNOVATIVE METHODS IN WINE PRODUCTION

Winegrowing and winemaking technologies have progressed to applications of more careful, pure and effective methods just as the taste habits and interest of consumers in certain types of wines are developing. This refers to the integrated protection of grapevines, the elimination of pesticides and fungicides, the ecological cultivation of grapevines and the production of bio-grapes. Sur lie, cryo-maceration and carbonic maceration are among the most frequently used innovative methods in Slovak viticulture.

According to the Sur lie method, which originated in France, wine that has finished its fermentation of young wine is left to rest on its own healthy yeast deposits - lees. This is followed by the gradual decomposition (autolysis) of yeast and important substances such as amino acids, vitamins and polysaccharides released from cell membranes and cell content in the wine which positively affects the fullness of taste and intensity of flavor. More piquant bouquet substances are created in sur lie wines which are important especially with white wines in vintages with higher acid content and low extract in clarified musts. The minimum period of time for the contact of the wine with yeast is three months. During this time, the winemaker mixes fine lees on the bottom of the vessel once a week. Mixing (batonnage) is done manually with a longer stick in the case of the maturing of wine on lees in oak barrels and with a mixer in stainless steel tanks. The Sur lie method works well for the production of wines from our Burgundy varieties such as Pinot Blanc, Pinot Gris, with fruity clones of Chardonnay, and with Grüner Veltliner, Italian Riesling and many other white wine grape varieties.

Cryomaceration is the method of fermenting destemmed and finely ground grapes at low temperatures. It takes place in closed tanks (vinificators) frequently in combination with carbon dioxide. The grape mash is cooled down to the temperature of 4 – 10 °C by using solid carbon dioxide or a cooling agent. All biochemical processes, in particular, the activities of oxidation enzymes, are slowed down with a temperature close to zero, while spontaneous microflora activity is eliminated. This method enables the maceration process without adding sulfur dioxide. The slow mixing of cooled mash causes the careful release of aromatic substances from the berry skins and reduces the release of overall phenols which negatively affects the bitterness and color of the future wine.

Wines made in this way are more intensive and have a richer primary aroma supported by a higher monoterpene content. In aroma and flavor they can extend the varietal nature and pleasant herbal spicy and even fruity bouquet. The successful use of cryomaceration has been confirmed by awards presented to Slovak single varietal wines made of aromatic varieties such as Moravian Muscat, Pálava and Yellow Muscat and the semi-aromatic Sauvignon Blanc and Tokaj Lipovina (Hárslevelű). The Karpatská perla winery employs the cryomaceration of red Alibernet with great results.

Carbonic maceration is based on the fermentation of untouched and unground grapes in the atmosphere of carbon dioxide. Similar to cryomaceration, fermentation takes place in closed vinificators. After harvesting, grapes are carefully destemmed and berries are fermented without touching them. Carbone dioxide prevents the effect of oxygen and the decomposing activities of oxidation enzymes during fermentation. It also allows the mash to keep its natural freshness and intensity of varietal aromas in the must and future wine. It also reduces the need for the use of sulfur dioxide in the pre-fermentation phase. This method works well with the production of young light red wines. Many young wines from varieties such as Saint Laurent, Blauer Portugieser and Zweigeltrebe undergo carbonic maceration and thus acquire a unique fruity aroma of sour cherries, cherries, raspberries and pears. In comparison with the classical fermentation of mashed grapes, the content of harsher tannins is positively reduced in their fresh taste.

WHAT DO THE LABELS OF SLOVAK WINES REVEAL?

Wine labeling is one of the oldest viticultural marketing elements. The first paper labels appeared on wine bottles in the 18th century in France and Germany. Other wine countries of Europe, including winemakers from the territory of present day Slovakia, soon followed their lead.

Labeling of Slovak Wines	62
Wine without Geographical Indication	63
Wine with Protected Geographical Indication	64
Wine with Protected Indication of Origin	65
Quality Wines with Attribute	67
Other Traditional Indications	69

WHAT DO THE LABELS OF SLOVAK WINES REVEAL?

Wine labels are the first reliable help in searching for a good wine. They provide the consumer with important information regarding the origin and quality of the wine. In comparison with twenty years ago, the design and composition of today's labels is of a high quality.

Labels on the bottles of Slovak wines provide important information regarding the variety or varieties from which the wine has been produced. They define the quality classification of the wine, vintage and category according to the residual sugar and the origin, including the producer or bottler. They also provide information about the volume of the bottle, the alcohol content, and the allergens. In the case of branded wine, they list the original formula of the brand and frequently the premium wine of the winery.

LABELING OF SLOVAK WINES

The traditional names derived from the German system of wine classification, and upon which our legislation is based, represent a particular element in the labeling of Slovak wines. The **German classification system** places the greatest emphasis on the variety used in wine making. To a decisive extent it considers the grape quality and amount. When determining the maturity of grapes, it also reflects its sugar content, more precisely, the content of natural sugars in the must. The natural grape sugar content at the time of the harvest in connection with the grape yield calculated per 1 hectare of bearing vineyards is crucial in determining the quality of the future wine.

After entering the common European market, our original system of wine labeling was complemented by elements of Roman nomenclature. As a result, the origin of the wine was emphasized on the labels of Slovak wines and we reached agreement with the wine labeling policy of other Member States of the European Union.

The Roman wine classification system is based on the requirement of grape origin declaration, in particular, the geographical unit where the grapes for wine production came from, where the harvest was processed and where the wine was produced. In Slovakia, the geographical units are the state, country, viticultural/wine regions, viticultural sub-regions, viticultural sites, vineyards and wine villages.

Although the German and Roman systems are based on different points of view, their requirements for wine labeling meet at certain places. The name of the appellation (country, region) usually does not present the names of the varieties. Despite this, wines from the regions of Languedoc, Alsace and Alto Adige carry the names of varieties used for their production on their labels. On the other hand, in addition to the varietal composition, the German labeling of wine from Austria, Germany, the Czech Republic and Slovakia also presents the name of the wine region, village and sometimes even vineyard.

How to Recognize Quality?

The rule for the recognition of the quality of a Slovak wine according to geographical indication is simple: the smaller the geographical unit listed on the label, the better the quality of wine in the bottle.

Slovak wines are classified in three ascending categories:
1. Wine without geographical indication (Wine)
2. Wine with protected geographical indication (CHZO)
3. Wine with protected indication of origin (CHOP), Districtus Slovakia Controllatus (abbreviation D.S.C. or DSC) is the international synonym for CHOP Slovakia.

Sugar Content

Saccharimeters (grape must densimeters) and refractometers are used for measuring sugar content. The degrees of the standardized grape must densimeter [°NM] indicate the kilograms of fermentable sugar per 100 l of grape must. Refractometers serve more for the approximate detection of the ripeness of grapes in the vineyard and the must thickness is expressed in degrees of refractory dry matter [°Brix].

WINE WITHOUT GEOGRAPHICAL INDICATION (WINE / VÍNO)

The basic category of wines in Slovakia is wine without geographical indication (hereinafter referred to as "Wine"). The label may not indicate a geographical unit smaller than the state. However, the grapes may come from any state of the European Union. In addition to must varieties, table varieties may also be used for the production of wine without geographical indication, as well as varieties that are not registered in Slovakia and whose maximum yield per hectare is not established and whose minimum level of sugar content is 13 °NM. The producer must indicate on the label the category of the wine product (e.g., wine, semi sparkling wine, wine from over-ripe grapes), the actual alcohol content, and the name and address of the bottler. Labels of aerated or sparkling wines indicate the name and address of the bottler and the name and address of the producer. Labels also indicate the color, allergens, production batch, evaluation of packaging, bottle volume and data regarding origin (Wine from Slovakia, Sparkling wine from Slovakia, Made in the Slovak Republic, Wine from the European Union, etc.). In most cases, vintage and variety are optional data; however, for aerated sparkling and semi sparkling wines, the data regarding residual sugar content and production method are obligatory.

1 – Name of wine (brand); name of variety is optional, 2 – Indication of the origin of the wine (a geographical unit smaller than the state may not be indicated), 3 – Name of wine (brand); name of variety is optional, 4 – Vintage (optional), 5 – Wine category, 6 – Producer (if identical to bottler, indication of bottler is sufficient), 7 – Indication of the origin of the wine (smaller geographical unit than the state may not be indicated), 8 – Alcohol content, 9 – Production batch, 10 – Volume, 11 – Allergens

WHAT DO THE LABELS OF SLOVAK WINES REVEAL?

WINE WITH PROTECTED GEOGRAPHICAL INDICATION (CHZO)

The labels of CHZO wine may not indicate a geographical unit smaller than a country. The producer declares the category of viticultural product and the name of the protected indication of origin (e.g., Wine with protected geographical indication, Slovak wine, Slovak viticultural unit, Slovak country wine, Country wine). If the winemaker indicates the traditional name **Regionálne víno** (country wine) on the label, the abbreviation CHZO may be omitted from the labeling. The other rules for labeling CHZO wine are identical to those for labeling wine without geographical indication. CHZO wine must be made exclusively of grapes from the Slovak viticultural country and the wine must be made in Slovakia. In terms of quality, grapes must reach at least 13 °NM of sugar content at harvest and the maximum yield per hectare may not exceed 20,000 kg (18,000 kg for country wine). Grapes or wine may be enriched, at most up to 12 % of alcohol volume in the case of white wines and up to 12.5 % of alcohol volume in the case of red wines. The name of the variety from which the wine was made may be indicated on the label if the percentage of other blended varieties does not exceed 15 % of the weight and it is registered in the **List of Registered Varieties**. The traditional name Branded wine, and the production methods which are given by the producer's formula and registered in the production batch, are indicated otherwise. **Burčiak (vernache, Federweißer)** also falls within the category of CHZO.

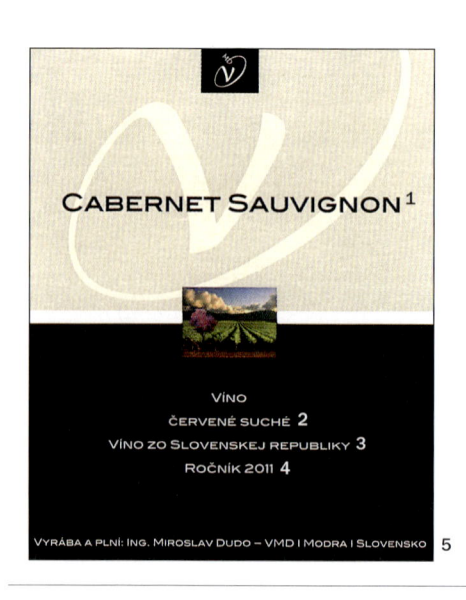

1 - Grapevine variety (optional), 2 - Category of wine, 3 - Wine without geographical indication (a geographical unit smaller than the state may not be indicated), 4 - Vintage (optional), 5 - Producer and bottler, 6 - Volume, 7 - Alcohol content, 8 - Color of wine (compulsory) and residual sugar content (optional), 9 - Wine category and indication of origin (provenience), 10 - Producer and bottler, 11 - Production batch, 12 - Allergens

WINE WITH PROTECTED INDICATION OF ORIGIN (CHOP)

The highest category of wines in the Slovak Republic includes such wines as quality wines and quality wines with attribute. For this category of wine, grapes must achieve a sugar content of at least 16 °NM and the maximum yield may not exceed 18,000 kg per hectare when harvested. After pressing, the grapes or grape must can be enriched with beet sugar or concentrated grape must from the grapes of the same harvest, in the case of white wines up to 22 °NM and in the case of red wines up to 24 °NM.

In the Roman classification system, wine with protected geographical indication (CHOP) is labeled as Small Carpathian Wine if 100 % of the grapes for its production originate from the Small Carpathian wine region. A smaller geographical unit (village, vineyard) or higher geographical unit (Slovak Republic, Slovakia or Slovak) can also be indicated as an alternative. CHOP wine labels must indicate the category of the viticultural product (e.g., sparkling wine, young wine, etc.), the name of the protected origin indication (e.g., Viticultural Region of Central Slovakia) and other compulsory and optional data similar to that in the Wine category. If the producer includes the traditional term Country Wine on the label, the term CHOP need not be indicated as in the previous case.

1 – Producer, 2 – Name of wine (and variety if the amount of other varieties blended in does not exceed 15 % in weight), 3 – Name of protected geographical indication, 4 – Name of wine and vintage, 5 – Indication of origin (provenience), 6 – Name of geographical unit, 7 – Wine category, name of protected indication of origin with indication of the color of the wine (compulsory) and the residual sugar content, 8 – Producer and bottler, 9 – Allergens, 10 – Alcohol content, 11 – Volume, 12 – Production batch

WHAT DO THE LABELS OF SLOVAK WINES REVEAL?

In the production of quality wine with a protected indication of origin (CHOP) the lowest average sugar content in must varies depending on the viticultural region. A minimum of 17 °NM is required in the warmest viticultural regions of Southern Slovakia and Tokaj, 16.5 °NM in the viticultural regions of the Small Carpathians and Eastern Slovakia and 16 °NM in the colder viticultural regions of Nitra and Central Slovakia. The enriching of grapes or must, up to 22 °NM with white wines and up to 24 °NM with red wines is possible. The maximum yield per hectare, which may not exceed 17,500 kg in any region (except for the Tokaj region), is an important quantitative requirement for the production of quality wine. The maximum yield per hectare for quality wines with a protected indication of origin in the Tokaj wine region may not exceed 14,000 kg of grapes. In addition to the name of the wine region, the protected indication of origin of quality single varietal or quality branded wine may also indicate smaller geographical units, including the name of the vineyard.

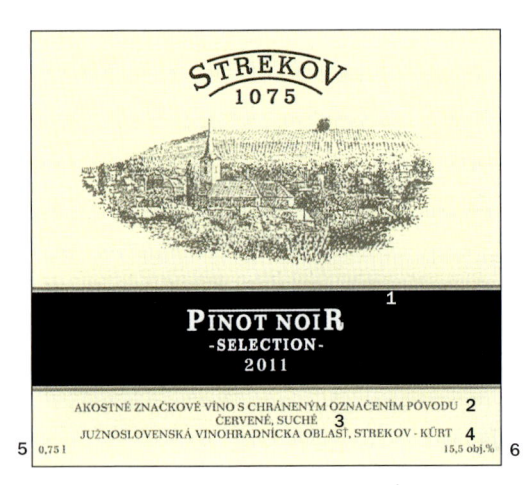

1 - Name of wine (brand), 2 - Traditional term and category of wine with protected indication of origin, 3 - Color of wine and residual sugar content, 4 - Name of protected indication of origin (wine region, wine village), 5 - Volume, 6 - Alcohol content, 7 - Production batch, 8 - Allergens, 9 - Producer and bottler, 10 - Indication of origin (provenience)

QUALITY WINES WITH ATTRIBUTE (CHOP OR DSC)

Quality wine with attribute is a traditional term in labeling Slovak wines according to their quality. For the production of quality wine with attribute, grapes must be harvested in full ripeness and their quality must be certified by an authorized employee of the control institute when harvested. The grapes, must and wine may not be enriched and the wine may not be chemically conserved in a way other than by use of sulfur dioxide. The maximum yield per hectare of quality wine with attribute may not exceed 12,000 kg, and 9,500 kg in the Tokaj wine region.

Slovak wines with attribute are found in the categories kabinett, late harvest, grape selection, selection of berries, raisin selection, nobly rotten raisin selection or Botrytis selection, ice wine and straw wine. The originality of these attributes is certified by allocated **state control numbers** which must be used by winemakers for classified wines when introduced to the market. In addition to the name of the wine region, the CHOP label of a quality single variety wine with attribute or a quality branded wine with attribute may also indicate smaller geographical units, including the name of the vineyard.

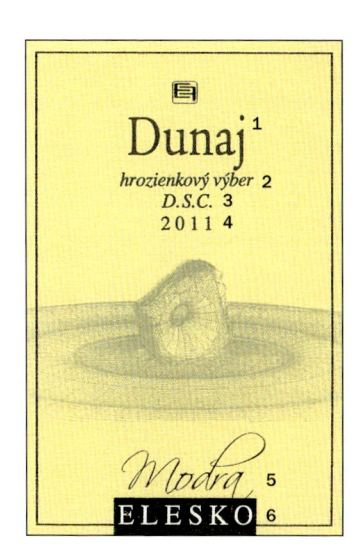

1 – Name of wine (and name of variety, if the amount of other varieties blended in does not exceed 15 % of the weight), 2 – Traditional name (quality attribute of wine), 3 – Name of protected indication of origin D.S.C. (Districtus Slovakia Controllatus), 4 – Vintage, 5 – Smaller geographical unit (Viticultural village or vineyard), 6 – Winemaker, 7 – Name of wine (and name of variety, if the amount of other varieties blended in does not exceed 15 % of the weight), 8 – Name of protected indication of origin, 9 – Wine category and color (along with the traditional term which indicates the attribute of wine and residual sugar content), 10 – Geographical unit (viticultural region, viticultural area, site and vineyard), 11 – Production batch, 12 – Alcohol content, 13 – Volume, 14 – Allergens, 15 – Producer and bottler, 16 – Indication of origin (provenience)

WHAT DO THE LABELS OF SLOVAK WINES REVEAL?

Quality Requirements for Slovak Quality Wine with Attribute

Attribute	Minimum sugar content of must	Quality Requirements
Kabinett wine	19 °NM	Made of fully mature grapes.
Late harvest	21 °NM	Made of fully mature grapes.
Grape selection	23 °NM	Made of fully mature grapes from carefully selected bunches.
Selection of berries	26 °NM	Made of manually selected overripe grape bunches from which immature and impaired berries have been removed manually.
Raisin selection	28 °NM	Made of manually selected overripe natural grape berries.
Nobly rotten raisin (Botrytis) selection	28 °NM	Made of manually selected overripe grape berries refined by effect of Botrytis cinerea Persoon.
Ice wine	27 °NM	Made of grapes harvested at the temperature of minus 7 °C (19 °F) and lower, the grapes must remain frozen during the harvesting and processing
Straw wine	27 °NM	Made of well ripened grapes, stored on straw or reed matting before processing, or left hanging in a well ventilated room on strings for at least three months.

State Control Number

1 – Order number of bottle, 2 – State coat of arms of Slovakia in white field, 3 – Wine classification vintage, 4 – Order number of batch, 5 – Bottle volume

OTHER TRADITIONAL INDICATIONS

Slovak wine bottles also carry other traditional names related to the making of wine. Young Wine is bottled before the end of the calendar year of harvest of the grapes used for its production. Winemakers may put Young Wine on the market starting on the first Monday in November of the harvest year and offer it for sale with the label Young Wine not later than the end of the same calendar year. The labelling Saint Catherine Wine appeared on the bottles of young wine after 2010, but this is not a traditional term. However it is also the labeling of young wines made in Slovak Wine Country from traditional must varieties which winemakers put on the market with the same requirements as young wines with a common logo and marketing. First Fruits indicates wine made of grapes from a vineyard's first harvest. The first harvest must take place in the third or fourth year after planting. Winemakers may begin to sell Archive Wine not earlier than three years after harvesting the grapes used for its production.

1 – Traditional term (optional), 2 – Vintage, 3 – Name of wine (and name of variety, if the amount of other varieties blended in does not exceed 15 % of the weight), 4 – Traditional term (château), which is also the name of the producer and bottler, 5 – Wine category and color with the name of protected indication of origin, 6 – Vintage, 7 – Volume, 8 – Geographical unit, 9 – Winemaker (if identical to bottler, the name of the bottler is sufficient), 10 – Allergens, 11 – Indication of origin (provenience), 12 – Alcohol content and production batch (printed when bottled)

OVERVIEW OF THE BEST WINES IN THE MARKET

Are you looking for white wines made of traditional varieties or red wines made of new clones? Are you interested in Tokaj wines or do you prefer sparkling wines? In this chapter I present an overview of the best Slovak wines in the market which caught my interest by their quality. The order is determined by the registered grapevine varieties according to the significance of their cultivation in Slovakia and the wine categories in terms of consumer demand.

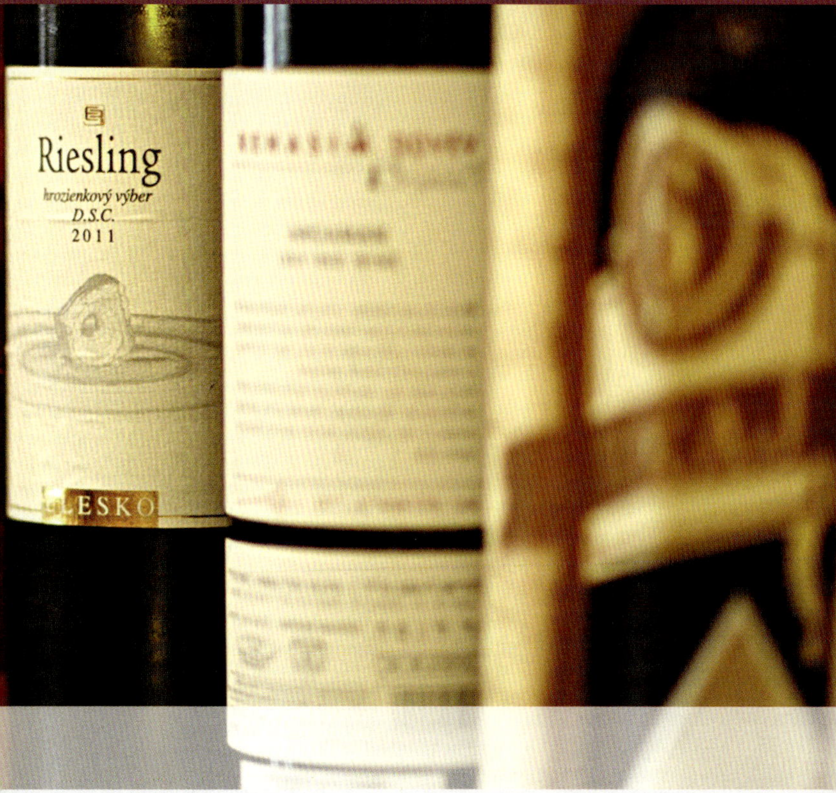
Riesling
hrozienkový výber
D.S.C.
2011

OVERVIEW OF THE BEST WINES IN THE MARKET

Wines Made of Traditional White Varieties	73
Grüner Veltliner	73
Italian Riesling	75
Müller Thurgau	75
Pinot Gris	76
Rhein Riesling	78
Irsai Oliver	82
Traminer	82
Feteasca Regala	84
Chardonnay	84
Grüner Silvaner	86
Sauvignon Blanc	86
Muscat Ottonel	87

Wines Made of Traditional Red Varieties	88
Lemberger (Blaufränkisch)	88
Saint Laurent	90
Cabernet Sauvignon	91
Pinot Noir	93
Blauer Portugieser	96

Wines Made of Tokaj Varieties	98
Furmint	98
Lipovina	98
Yelow Muscat	99

Wines Made of New White Clones	100
Moravian Muscat	100
Devín	100
Pálava	103
Noria	104
Milia	105

Wines Made of New Red Clones	106
Odessa Red (Alibernet)	106
Dunaj	108
Hron	110
Rimava	110
Rudava	110
Rosa	110

Rosé Wines	111
Terroir-respecting Wines	113
Innovative Wines (barrique / kryo / sur lie)	118
Cuvée / Blends	122
Classical Tokaj Wines	127
Bio Wines	129
Sparkling Wines	131

GRÜNER VELTLINER

WINES MADE OF TRADITIONAL WHITE VARIETIES

Veltlínske zelené 2013
Varieto, grape selection, dry — **KARPATSKÁ PERLA**

Wine with protected indication of origin
VRoSC, Modra, Noviny Vineyard

An attractively full and comprehensively balanced Grüner Veltliner of a beautiful golden-yellow color and an intensive smell of a basket of freshly picked apples and butter pears, and which after opening takes on a lovely linden-floral note of dry honey drops on sponge cake. Its distinctive, fresh fruity taste will create an effect of exotic fruit mixed with notes of kiwi, passion fruit and gooseberries. The finish belongs to pineapple and green almonds and has a well-balanced overall sensation.

[13,000 l] • 0.75 l • €€ • LB 1313 • 13.0 % vol. • ① • ○ • ◐ • ★★★★★

Veltlínske zelené 2012
quality varietal wine, dry — **PIVNICA ORECHOVÁ**

Wine with protected indication of origin D.S.C.
VRoES, Orechová, Sekerová Vineyard

This wine has a clear yellow-green color, and after pouring there is higher viscosity connected with the rich, honey-fruity smell of sponge cake filled with yellow plums and linden blossoms. An autochthonous genus of yeasts isolated from its own vineyard was used for must fermenting. The fresh and delicious aftertaste on the tongue is accompanied by higher alcohol content and a distinctive minerality, the finish of which reveals traces of nutmeg, acacia and bitter green almonds.

[6,500 l] • 0.75 l • €€ • L1413 • 14.0 % vol. • ② • ○ • ◐ • {8} • ★★★★1/2

Veltlínske zelené 2013
quality varietal wine, dry — **CHÂTEAU RÚBAŇ**

Wine with protected indication of origin
VRoSS, Strekov, Nový vrch Vineyard

This crystal clear, golden-yellow Grüner Veltliner will immediately catch your eye. Its honey up to almond bouquet is spiced up by a pinch of nutmeg and orange peels, while the rich taste leaves a feeling of fullness which is expressively complemented by tones of honey and black pepper. A hint of bitter almond can be found in the aftertaste.

[1,500 l] • 0.75 l • €€ • L01 • 12.5 % vol. • ① • ○ • ★★★★1/2

GRÜNER VELTLINER

Veltlínske zelené 2013
quality varietal wine, dry   FEDOR MALÍK & SYN.

Wine with protected indication of origin D.S.C.
VRoSC, Modra, Noviny Vineyard

Grüner Veltliner, light, straw-greenish in color with a sparkle of white gold. The apricot-muscat smell with tones of sponge cake covered in acacia honey is inviting. Its fresh, medium-full taste with piquant fruit acid shows traces of summer tropical fruit, meadow herbs and cut dandelions. The bitter note of green almonds leaves a lively overall impression on the tongue.

[1,000 l] • 0.75 l • €€ • L-103/0614 • 12.5 % vol. • 🍷 • ① • ⬮ • {6} • ▢ • 🖌 •
★★★★1/2

Veltlínske zelené 2013
grape selection, dry   VÍNKO KLIMKO MODRA

Wine with protected indication of origin
VRoSC, Modra, Pažite Vineyard

The light green shade of this Grüner Veltliner also has golden tones. It has a fuller and pleasantly spicy smell with Muscat tones and a juicy, fresh taste which creates a balanced and pleasant impression. Its lovely, citrus acid is nicely wrapped in a light, earthy extract which carries a hint of ripe grapes and fallen leaves in the aftertaste. A pure wine of interesting variety with its own Modra identity.

[700 l] • 0.75 l • €€ • L0114 • 12.5 % vol. • 🍷 • ① • ▢ • 🖌 • ★★★★

Veltlínske zelené 2014
late harvest, dry   MARTIN POMFY - MAVÍN

Wine with protected indication of origin
VRoSC, Vinosady

A bright, yellow-green Grüner Veltliner with a pleasant fruity and floral smell of ripe apples with nuances of yellow melon pulp and linden. The taste like the smell is pure, attractively perfumed, medium long and harmonious. It features tones of vineyard peaches and ripe grapes. The finish of this opulent taste is complemented by green almonds.

[2,625 l] • 0.75 l • €€ • L4 • 12.0 % vol. • 🍷 • ①-② • ▢ • 🖌 • ★★★★

Veltlínske zelené 2012
Retro, late harvest, dry   CHÂTEAU TOPOĽČIANKY

Wine with protected indication of origin D.S.C.
VRoSS, Modrany

This Grüner Veltliner of a bright green-yellow color was made of grapes manually harvested from a 26 year old vineyard. The sandy-loam soil with moderate skeleton content and reductive processing helped to captivate the fresh fruity nature of the wine's smell with tones of red grapefruit and nutmeg. The taste impression of this vintage is underlined by its delicious, gentle acidity and relatively full extract reminiscent of citrus fruit with an expressive bitterness and a pinch of bergamot in the after-taste.

[1,500 l] • 0.75 l • €€€ • L358 • 13.0 % vol. • 🍷 • ① • ⬮ • ▢ • 🖌 • ★★★★

ITALIAN RIESLING • MÜLLER THURGAU

Rizling vlašský 2011
ice wine, sweet   CHÂTEAU TOPOĽČIANKY

Wine with protected indication of origin D.S.C.
VRoN, Jelenec, vineyard Jelenecká

The intensive golden-yellow color of this Italian Riesling with a sparkle of amber has an impressive smell of overripe bananas with a honeyed trace of sun-dried figs. 170 g/l of residual sugars dominate its natural sweet taste. The multi-layered structure of 6.5 g/l of fruit acids, charming honey tones and the persistent after-taste of overripe pear compote and sweet tropical fruit meshes elegantly with its smell. The grapes were harvested on January 27, 2012 at an average air temperature of -8.5 °C.

[2,800 l] • 0.375 l • €€€ • L496 • 10.0 % vol. • ♇ • ④ • ◯ • ✑ • ★★★★1/2

Rizling vlašský 2013
late harvest, dry   VÍNO MRVA & STANKO

Quality wine with attribute
VRoSS, Kosihovce

This yellow and green Italian Riesling has a lively, fruity up to piquant floral smell suggesting a basket of freshly picked citrus fruit and apples complemented by a handful of gooseberries. The medium long, earthy body is accompanied by a piquant fruit acid, while the aftertaste, which is full of grapefruit tones and a trace of honey comb, is balanced out by a tender herbal note in the finish.

[500 l] • 0.75 l • €€ • L-02 • 12.5 % vol. • ♇ • ① • ◯ • ✑ • ★★★★

Rizling vlašský 2012
grape selection, medium sweet   RODINNÉ VINÁRSTVO ĎURÍK

Wine with protected indication of origin
VRoCS, Želovce

A sparkly, clear Italian Riesling, yellow-green in color, it has a delicate fruity and honey smell reminiscent of the pulp of overripe apricots with honey. Its balanced taste features proper acid and natural residual sugar which in combination with the extract leaves a round overall impression with a trace of nutmeg and walnuts. The vintage is gradually developing in bottle maturity.

[1,500 l] • 0.75 l • €€ • L-8 • 12.5 % vol. • ♇ • ③ • ◯ • ✑ • ★★★★

Müller Thurgau 2013
Prestige, late harvest, dry   VÍNO MATYŠÁK

Wine with protected indication of origin
VRoSC, Hlohovec, Šomoď Vineyard

A light, golden-yellow wine with green hues on the edges. Its medium full, fruity structure will please by its spicy citrusy note perfumed by nutmeg. The taste is juicy, refreshed by a pleasant fruit acid. In addition to tropical fruit, we can find traces of vineyard peaches in the finish with an elegant hint of lemon drops and kernels of summer apple seeds.

[7,500 l] • 0.75 l • €€ • L05 • 12.0 % vol. • ♇ • ① • ◯ • ✑ • ★★★★1/2

MÜLLER THURGAU • PINOT GRIS

Müller Thurgau 2014
quality varietal wine, dry
VELKEER

Wine with protected indication of origin
VRoSS

The light, straw-yellow shade of this wine along with the fresh smell of citrus fruit, gooseberries and ripe artichokes creates an intensive first impression. Its taste with a pleasant acid content features traces of mango and nutmeg. The medium-long aftertaste leaves a fruity note of plums and green apples in the finish with a fashionable, spicy bouquet which changes from hazelnuts to butter vanilla.

[1,450 l] • 0.75 l • €€ • L0114 • 12.0 % vol. • ① • ○ • ★★★★

Müller Thurgau 2013
quality varietal wine, dry
PIVNICA ORECHOVÁ

Wine with protected indication of origin D.S.C.
VRoES, Orechová, Sekerová Vineyard

This nutty Müller from Orechová keeps its features even in the 2013 vintage. A brilliantly clear, yellow-green wine, it has the smell of citrus fruit and hazelnuts complemented by traces of muscat, white pepper and vanilla. The live gentle acidity dominates in a lighter fruity and spicy taste and is accompanied by a more distinct note of gooseberries and lemon zest. Its aftertaste leaves an apple-nutty impression, as if hazelnuts and freshly sliced apples were its firm component.

[9,000 l] • 0.75 l • € • L914 • 12.5 % vol. • ① • ○ • ★★★1/2

Pinot Gris 2013 Varieto
late harvest, dry
KARPATSKÁ PERLA

Wine with protected indication of origin
VRoSC, Šenkvice, Suchý vrch Vineyard

A light, golden-yellow wine with greenish hints. We can find a handful of ripe garden fruit with tones of pears, plums, apricots and meadow flowers in late summer in its distinctive bouquet smell, thoroughly covered by walnut notes. The full taste of dried fruit is laced with noble cloves on bread crust. The long vanilla aftertaste is enhanced by a lively gooseberry skin and a precise overall impression.

[10,000 l] • 0.75 l • €€ • LB 0613 • 12.5 % vol. • ① • ○ • ❄ {2} • ★★★★★

Rulandské šedé 2013
grape selection, medium dry
VÍNO MRVA & STANKO

Quality wine with attribute
VRoSC, Čachtice

This attractive yellow Pinot Gris with golden hues will please you with its concentrated, fruity-honey aroma of exotic mango, apricots and tones of ripe plums up to candied pineapple in its lovable taste. The aroma of its bouquet keeps up with the opulent, medium dry aftertaste which, along with freshly peeled apricots, is complemented by traces of honey comb and vanilla. An attractive and even extroverted representative of this popular vintage.

[800 l] • 0.75 l • €€ • L-10 • 13.0 % vol. • ② • ○ • ★★★★★

PINOT GRIS

Pinot Gris 2013 "1"
late harvest, dry ELESKO

Wine with protected indication of origin D.S.C.
VRoSC, Vištuk, Iveta and Mária Vineyard

A lively, yellow-green wine with golden sparkles. The smell is interesting due to its multilayered palette of fruit with a hint of yellow melon, cloves and sage, all complemented by traces of gooseberries and pears, which is also confirmed by the full taste after swallowing. The taste is harmonious and very fresh thanks to the acids and tender residual sugar, which however does not leave any trace of sweetness but rounds up the final overall impression.

[26,250 l] • 0.75 l • €€ • L-1/13 • 13.5 % vol. • ① - ② • 90 % + 10 % • ★★★★1/2

Rulandské šedé 2013
grape selection, dry PIVNICA ZSIGMOND

Wine with protected indication of origin
VRoCS, Vinica viticultural area

This is a clear, straw-yellow Pinot Gris with a medium full aroma of ripened grapes with herbal tones of cut meadow flowers complemented by traces of beeswax. The fruity taste profile is balanced with a smell of intensity or perception and purity. It is reminiscent of the pulp of yellow melon, gooseberries and grated lemon zest, and its aftertaste presents a sweet hint despite the more distinct trace of alcohol. This technologically precise bouquet wine is just beyond maturity and has the gentility of an attractive attribute.

[1,500 l] • 0.75 l • €€ • L-04 • 13.0 % vol. • ② • ★★★★1/2

Rulandské šedé 2013
grape selection, dry PIVNICA ORECHOVÁ

Wine with protected indication of origin D.S.C.
VRoES, Orechová, Sekerová Vineyard

This Pinot Gris with shades of yellow amber and golden hints, and its higher glycerol content and magical, sweet tones of grape-honey aroma with a note of bread crust makes an attractive impression. It has a fruity, earthy taste, that is slightly more distinctive than the smell thanks to the acids and higher alcohol concentration and full varietal extract. It contains exotic traces of marinated pineapple with a pinch of cloves and curry.

[9,795 l] • 0.75 l • €€ • L1814 • 14.0 % vol. • ① • {8} • ★★★★

Rulandské šedé 2014
Vinitory Premium, grape selection, dry VVD

Wine with protected indication of origin D.S.C.
VRoSS, Dvory nad Žitavou, Viničný vrch Vineyard

A golden Pinot Gris with onion-yellow hues. Its full, fruity smell is a result of the extreme ripeness of the grapes and their pure reductive processing. We find in it tones of bread crust, gooseberries and sage. The distinctive extractive taste features well-balanced acids and leaves traces of gooseberries, open nuts and a fine spicy note of cloves in gingerbread on the palate.

[5,000 l] • 0.75 l • €€ • L-37 • 13 % vol. • ① • ★★★★

PINOT GRIS • RHEIN RIESLING

Rulandské šedé 2014
quality varietal wine, dry SVV VINANZA
Wine with protected indication of origin
VRoN, Veľké Lovce

This light yellow and green Pinot Gris has the smell of ripened grapes with tones of meadow flowers. The taste is pleasant and has a well-balanced smell that is medium long with juicy fruit acid. It will please you with its honey grape bouquet emphasized by a trace of tropical fruit with tones of mango and banana in its finish. A stylish product from the Fermedza vineyard, it is a continuation of the successful history of this excellent variety in the Vráble area.

[2,000 l] • 0.75 l • € • L-98 • 12.0 % vol. • ★★★★

Rizling rýnsky 2011
ice wine, sweet CHÂTEAU BELÁ
VRoSS, Štúrovo viticultural area, Mužla

This light straw-yellow Rhein Riesling with the honey-fruity smell of candied tropical fruit with a note of sweet caramelized almonds and dried apricots marinated in linden honey has an aristocratic appearance. Its rich taste with higher content of fruit acids and redundancy of natural sugar leaves a long piquant impression on the tongue. The intensity of the smells and tastes will become finer as the wine slowly matures in the bottle. A wine with long aging potential.

[400 l] • 0.50 l • € € € • L 11 • 8.0 % vol. • ★★★★★

Rizling rýnsky 2013
nobly rotten raisin selection, sweet CHÂTEAU BELÁ
VRoSS, Štúrovo viticultural area, Mužla

A light golden-yellow elixir made from manually picked, nobly rotten Rhein Riesling raisins which left the vineyard on October 29, 2013. The smell of a hundred year old linden tree blossom overlaps with an oil concentrate of rose petals that abundantly fell into a basket of peaches, grapefruits and apricots. The taste in love with the smell is reluctant to end the ritual fading away on the tongue. Impulsive acids grandiosely tame two hundred grams of natural sugar. The energy of the sun deposited in the earth and the grapes finishes off the aftertaste of this vintage in the form of a mineral Botrytised extract with a citrus and honey impression.

[50 l] • 0.50 l • € € € • L 08 • 10.5 % vol. • ★★★★★

Rizling rýnsky 2012 Premium
grape selection, medium dry CHATEAU MODRA
Wine with protected indication of origin D.S.C.
VRoSS, Cintorínske Vineyard

A golden-yellow Rhein Riesling with high viscosity on the wall of the goblet that makes a great first impression. The distinct aroma of tropical fruit features fresh notes of grapefruits, white peppers and linden blossoms. The wealth of this extractive vintage is hidden in its high mineralization underlined by a piquant acid content and adequate residual sugar. The long, multilayer aftertaste of this wine creates an unforgettable experience on your tongue. It will attract all fans of Rhein Riesling.

[4,000 l] • 0.75 l • € € • L9 • 12.5 % vol. • ★★★★★

RHEIN RIESLING

Rizling rýnsky 2013
Varieto, late harvest, dry **KARPATSKÁ PERLA**
Wine with protected indication of origin
VRoSC, Šenkvice, Suchý vrch Vineyard

This bright, green-yellow Rhein Riesling with golden hints carries the smell of a distinctive fruity and even spicy note of green limes and fresh citrus. The taste sensation with mineral undertones and fresh acid causes an explosion of juicy tones reminiscent of yellow grapefruit pulp and early winter nectarines, while the linden-honey citrus aftertaste leaves a long feeling of refreshment on the tongue.

[8,000 l] • 0.75 l • €€ • LB 1113 • 13.0 % vol. • ♇ • ①-② • ◯ • 🛢 {2} • 🗡 •
★★★★1/2

Rizling rýnsky 2011
grape selection, medium sweet **CHÂTEAU BELÁ**
Quality varietal wine with attribute, D.S.C.
VRoSS, Štúrovo viticultural area, Mužla

An elegant, bright green and yellow Rhein Riesling with a honey and fruity smell of exotic fruit. Its smell contains the concentrate of ripe grapes, mango, ground yellow pomelo peels and a drop of linden honey. Its juicy taste with a well-balanced content of acids and minerals is rounded out by a residual natural sugar which encircles a massive and long aftertaste. The last drops come back to life in the form of jasmine nectar with candied pieces of summer fruit.

[10,000 l] • 0.75 l • €€€ • L 10 • 14.0 % vol. • ♇ • ③ • ◯ • ▬ •
★★★★1/2

Rizling rýnsky 2014
grape selection, dry **VPS – PAVELKA A SYN**
Wine with protected indication of origin D.S.C.
VRoSC, Pezinok, Hauspereg Vineyard

A distinctive golden-yellow Rhein Riesling with an elegant fruity up to floral smell of grapefruit, linden tree blossoms and dying rose petals. Its background features pieces of citrus peels mixed with gooseberries. The taste sensation is similar to the smell due to the use of pure selected yeasts and maceration on fine lees. After swallowing, this wine leaves a medium-full impression with a distinctive fruity extract and delicate acid.

[1,500 l] • 0.75 l • €€ • L0104 • 12.5 % vol. • ♇ • ① • ◯ {1} • ◯ • 🗡 • ★★★★1/2

Rizling rýnsky 2012
selection of berries, medium sweet **CHÂTEAU BELÁ**
VRoSS, Štúrovo viticultural area, Mužla

This full, straw-yellow wine with greenish hues has the earthy and fruity smell of ripe apricots and gooseberries with a drop of meadow flower honey. Its taste is well balanced with its smell in terms of intensity and is reminiscent of a concentrate of nectarines with a piquant acid and delicious residual sugar on the edge of a sweet wine. After swallowing, the bouquet of dry hay and mountain grass will enchant you.

[6,000 l] • 0.75 l • €€€ • L 07 • 14.0 % vol. • ♇ • ③ • ◯ • ▬ • ★★★★1/2

RHEIN RIESLING

Rizling rýnsky 2013
late harvest, dry   MARTIN POMFY - MAVÍN
Wine with protected indication of origin
VRoSC

This elegant, light golden-yellow wine has a floral linden smell with notes of overripe grapes and ripe citrus. Its full and long taste nicely develops the tones of quince mixed with apricots, spiced up by lemon grass and refreshed by juicy acids. The wine's fashionable finish confirms a hint of grapefruit up to gooseberry pulp in the aftertaste.

[9,750 l] • 0.75 l • € € € • L-06 • 13.0 % vol. • ① • ★★★★1/2

Rizling rýnsky 2013
late harvest, medium dry   VÍNO MRVA & STANKO
Quality wine with attribute
VRoSC, Dolné Orešany

A bright yellow and green Rhein Riesling with the smell of citrus fruit and a hint of a fresh mineral character which, after opening, develops in tones of linden blossoms and dried fruit. The mineral structure is a variable of a distinctively long and rich taste trace. Its earthy character is impressively complemented by pieces of oranges, grapefruit, gooseberries and lemons multiplied by juicy acid in excellent equilibrium with residual sugar.

[3,000 l] • 0.75 l • € € • L-18 • 13.0 % vol. • ② • ★★★★1/2

Rizling rýnsky 2013 Selection
quality varietal wine, sweet   KASNYIK RODINNÉ VINÁRSTVO
Wine with protected indication of origin
VRoSS, Pod vinohradmi Vineyard

This lively, golden-yellow Rhein Riesling has a bouquet of freshly opened apricots with tones of pineapple and scattered with linden blossoms. A complex, rich and long wine in taste, it has a massive extract with 70 grams of residual sugar. The higher mineralization of the soil in combination with the longer maceration of skins of botrytis grapes before the must pressing gave this wine a noble aroma which remains in the aftertaste.

[900 l] • 0.75 l • € € € • L-19 • 12.0 % vol. • ④ • ★★★★1/2

Rizling rýnsky 2012
grape selection, sweet   RODINNÉ VINÁRSTVO ĎURÍK
Quality wine with attribute
VRoCS, Opatovská Nová Ves

This is a noble Rhein Riesling, green-yellow in color with hints of white gold and a higher viscosity. The full, elegant linden-honey smell features tones of gooseberries, yellow plums, and overripe apricots with a bouquet of dried meadow flowers, while the multilayered taste contains more mature fruity tones of esters rounded out by natural residual sugar, which in combination with the extract contributes to the balance of the overall impression of this wine with an aftertaste featuring dried apples pickled in acacia honey.

[5,000 l] • 0.75 l • € € € • L-9 • 10.5 % vol. • ④ • ★★★★1/2

RHEIN RIESLING

Rizling rýnsky 2013
late harvest, dry PIVNICA ZSIGMOND

Wine with protected indication of origin
VRoCS, Vinica viticultural area

A brilliantly clear, yellow-green Rhein Riesling with a golden shade characterized by rich meadow flowers, apricots and ripened grapes, around which honey-lime notes nicely develop with the growth of the bottle bouquet. More sensitive noses will pick up the presence of flaxseed oil up to kerosene. Its taste is mineral and medium full. Traces of dried exotic fruit with a pinch of spice, a distinctive equilibrium of acids and residual sugar close out the excellent overall impression of this vintage.

[3,000 l] • 0.75 l • € € • L-01 • 13.0 % vol. • 🍷 • ①-② • ▭ • 🖌 • ★★★★

Rizling rýnsky 2013
grape selection, dry PIVNICA ORECHOVÁ

Wine with protected indication of origin D.S.C.
VRoES, Orechová, Sekerová Vineyard

The bright yellow-greenish color of this Rhein Riesling is accompanied by a smell of linden trees in bloom and honeycombs along with tones of dried apricots and exotic fruit. Its medium full herbal taste on the palate suggests the presence of quince with a bitter note of nuts and Cayenne pepper. Its aftertaste also belongs to flowers, this time, rose petals with a fine hint of paraffin. Pleasantly drinkable and maturing wine.

[6,000 l] • 0.75 l • € € • L2114 • 13.0 % vol. • 🍷 • ① • ▭ • ◠ • {6} • 🖌 • ★★★★

Riesling 2013
quality varietal wine, dry BOTT FRIGYES

Wine with protected indication of origin
VRoSS, Mužla

This yellow-green wine, which has a nice viscosity and an intensive smell of honey combs and dried fruit, confirms the excellent ripeness and careful processing of grapes. Its mineral taste contains an attractively abundant acid content, and at its core leaves a rich sensation in its herbal honey aftertaste. A full extractive wine with a longer potential of maturing, fermented and matured in oak caskets. The full sensory profile will become finer with its maturing in bottles.

RR • [2,250 l] • 0.75 l • € € € • L05/0514 • 13.0 % vol. • 🍷 • ① • 🛢 • 🖌 •
★★★★

Rizling rýnsky 2013
grape selection, medium sweet VINÁRSTVO BERTA

Wine with protected indication of origin
VRoSS, Gbelce

The lively green-yellow color of this Rhein Riesling, the aroma of honeycomb with a lovable sweet note of pear purée is spiced up by a touch of cinnamon. Its firmer acids nicely refresh the residual sugar and create a feeling of smooth fullness on the tongue. The bouquet gradually releases a concentrate of overripe citrus, garden apricots with a drop of flaxseed oil and pistachios.

[1,500 l] • 0.75 l • € € • L33 • 12.7 % vol. • 🍷 • ③ • ▭ • 🖌 • ★★★★

RHEIN RIESLING • IRSAI OLIVER • TRAMINER

Rizling rýnsky 2013

late harvest, medium sweet SVV VINANZA

Wine with protected indication of origin
VRoN, Veľké Lovce

This is a Rhein Riesling, straw-yellow in color, with honey and traces of ripened apricot with a hint of grape juice and fading linden tree in its nose. The pleasant harmony of residual sugar and fruit acids stand out in its medium-full taste which is just right. The herbal up to candied traces of its delicious aftertaste are supported by a fine bitterness of pomelo peels and lemon grass. This Mosel raisin Riesling is especially pleasing for ladies. However, do not put it in your archive, as it will reach the peak of its maturity in a year or two.

[4,900 l] • 0.75 l • €€ • L-345 • 12.0 % vol. • 🍷 • ③ • ⬜ • {4,5} • 🗡 • ★★★★

Irsai Oliver 2013

Vinum Galéria Bozen, quality wine, dry VÍNO MATYŠÁK

Wine with protected indication of origin
VRoSC

This attractive, golden-yellow wine with a pleasant spicy smell of muscatel mixed with fresh mint leaves and ripe nectarines makes an impression upon the first inhalation. Its delicate, slightly spicy and fruity taste is well balanced with the smell and features harmonious acids which in combination with 6.6 g/l of residual sugar will leave a fresh perfumed aftertaste of yellow melon. A vintage at the peak of its life.

[20,000 l] • 0.75 l • € • L01 • 12.0 % vol. • 🍷 • ①-② • ⬜ • 🗡 • ★★★★

Tramín červený 2012 Premium

grape selection, medium sweet CHATEAU MODRA

Wine with protected indication of origin D.S.C.
VRoN, Pohranice II Vineyard

A green and yellow Traminer of an excellent vintage with higher viscosity in the glass and an enchanting floral-muscatel bouquet. The perfumed notes of rose petals and red spice go arm in arm with the fruity component featuring overripe pineapples and honey comb. The taste is full and long at the same time. It features an interesting equilibrium of 18 grams of residual sugar and 7 grams of organic acids per 1 liter of wine, which causes it to taste "drier" than it is.

[2,000 l] • 0.75 l • €€ • L6 • 12.5 % vol. • 🍷 • ③ • ⬜ • 🗡 • ★★★★★

Tramín červený 2012

straw wine, sweet PIVNICA TIBAVA

Wine with protected indication of origin D.S.C.
VRoES, Tibava, Hrun Vineyard

The oily viscosity, distinctive golden-yellow shade, massive sweet smell of raisins, exotic mango, litchi and fig marmalade along with a full extractive taste reveal a high share of grape drying of this Traminer. After pressing, the must reached a sugar content of 36 °NM. Its residual sugar content is 174 g/l which in connection with fresh fruit acids creates a veritable explosion in the mouth. The long aftertaste releases tones of sweet hazelnuts, honey comb and piquant apricot mash.

[500 l] • 0.375 l • €€€ • L-12/13 • 10.5 % vol. • 🍷 • ④ • ⬜ • 🗡 • ★★★★★

TRAMINER

Tramín červený 2013 Château Palugyay
ice wine, sweet   VILLA VINO RAČA

Wine with protected indication of origin
VRoSC, Rača, Žajdlík Vineyard

The bright, golden-yellow color of this Traminer features a brilliant clarity and intoxicating smell of the overripe pulp of juicy yellow melon in combination with notes of beebread and rose hips in a blossom that enchants our senses at first sight. The captivating supple taste hides in an extract of fruit acids and sweet must slowly pressed from frozen grapes. A complex overall impression suitable for further maturing, however it encourages one to indulge before its time.

[750 l] • 0.50 l • €€€ • L-20 • 9.5 % vol. • ♀ • ④ • ◯ • ✍ • ★★★★1/2

Tramín červený 2014 Privat Exclusive
grape selection, medium sweet   MOVINO

Wine with protected indication of origin
VRoSS, Záhorce, Lomené pod jablonkami Vineyard

This golden-yellow wine has a brightness to it along with charming spicy and floral smells accompanied by a violet and tea rose admixture. They lure us by tones of cinnamon, honey and ripe peaches. The fuller and more extractive taste is spicy with a medium-full body and mature tones of tropical fruit dominated by pineapple. Its juicy acids are nicely complemented by 25 grams of natural sugar.

[5,500 l] • 0.75 l • €€ • L-16 • 11.5 % vol. • ♀ • ③ • ◯ • ✍ • ★★★★1/2

Tramín červený 2014
late harvest, medium dry   VÍNO MIROSLAV DUDO

Wine with protected indication of origin
VRoSC, Modra, Bolflajtna Vineyard

The golden-yellow shade of this Traminer has a crystal clear appearance. Its unique, exotic Muscat character and the lily-of-the-valley up to apricot tones with a fuller spicy aromatic profile catch our interest. The taste copies the smell of this wine. It is equally lively and piquant with a floral-fruity character where the fine residual sugar is complemented by more distinctive fruit acids. No wine gastronomy gourmet will be able to resist Miroslav Dudo's Traminer.

[1,950 l] • 0.75 l • €€ • L187 • 12.5 % vol. • ♀ • ② • ◯ • ✍ • ★★★★1/2

Tramín červený 2013
grape selection, sweet   VELKEER

Wine with protected indication of origin
VRoSS, Svodín, hon Pántúk

This reductive, straw-yellow Traminer bears the sweet, spicy smell of pears marinated in cloves and carnation petals sprinkled with honey. The taste combines juicy, fruity notes of pineapples, peaches and rose oil and reveals white pepper, refreshing acids and a pleasant 67 grams of residual sugar. The overripe grape extract complements the fullness not only in the focus of the taste but also in the never ending perfumed bouquet.

[1,500 l] • 0.5 l • €€€ • L-0613 • 11 % vol. • ♀ • ④ • ● • ⌐ • ★★★★1/2

TRAMINER • FETEASCA REGALA • CHARDONNAY

Tramín červený 2013
grape selection, medium sweet   VÍNO MRVA & STANKO

Quality wine with attribute
VRoSC, Čachtice

This lively, golden-yellow Traminer with a distinctive, honey-spicy smell is interesting due to its note of Muscat leaves, white flowers and rose petals in combination with a fruity perfumed undertone of overripe mangoes, pears and a pinch of white pepper. The full spicy taste with a fine mineral character on the root of the tongue features an intoxicating combination of ripe peaches, cinnamon and carnations. The intensity of the ester smell does not vanish after swallowing; on the contrary, it appears even after the residual sugar aftertaste fades away.

[2,500 l] • 0.75 l • €€ • L-37 • 13.5 % vol. • 🍷 • ③ • ⬜ • 🗝 • ★★★★

Pesecká leánka 2014
quality varietal wine, medium dry   FEDOR MALÍK & SYN.

VRoSC, Modra, Firigle vineyard

The greenish shade of this Feteasca Regala has a brilliant sparkle with light, straw-yellow hints. A charming, fresh smell of a handful of ripe citrus fruit and freshly picked green apples. The young generous taste with fine sparkles of carbon dioxide is supported by merry acids with a generous portion of gooseberries which are overshadowed by a mischievous pomelo in the aftertaste. If the role of the residual sugar is to complete the overall impression of the wine, then it is the master of thrills in this Feteasca. This lively "pebble" wine from the Firigle vineyard is approved by the winemaker and calls for another glass.

[1,000 l] • 0.75 l • €€ • L-124 • 12.0 % vol. • 🍷 • ② • ⬜ • 🗝 • ★★★★★ 1/2

Chardonnay 2012
grape selection   VÍNO MRVA & STANKO

Quality wine with attribute
VRoSC, Čachtice

A bright yellow-green wine with a tender, fruity-creamy smell of peanut butter spiced up by bee pollen and juicy pieces of exotic mango. The elegant, full taste of fruit is balanced out by a smell which suggests freshly ripe pomelo with a pinch of wild medlar and tender vanilla. It leaves a medium-long, grape aftertaste on the root of the tongue emphasized by a piquant touch of peanuts. A harmonious wine worthy of genuine connoisseurs.

[600 l] • 0.75 l • €€€ • L-05 • 13.5 % vol. • 🍷 • ① • ⬜ + 🛢 • 🗝 • ★★★★★

Chardonnay 2014
grape selection, dry   VPS – PAVELKA A SYN

Wine with protected indication of origin D.S.C.
VRoSC, Pezinok, Dolné Kogle Vineyard

This wine has a lively, golden-yellow color, and a fresh, fruity up to honey smell with a trace of ripe peaches, honeycomb and Mediterranean tangerines. The distinctively juicy character of the taste shows a passionate relationship with the smell which is supported by tones of yellow melon and pieces of caramelized walnuts and fragile egg biscuits.

[1,500 l] • 0.75 l • €€ • L0105 • 12.0 % o • 🍷 • ① – ② • ⬭ {1} • 90 % ⬜ + 10 % 🛢 • 🗝 • ★★★★★

84

CHARDONNAY • PINOT BLANC

Chardonnay 2013
Premium, grape selection, medium dry   CHATEAU MODRA
Wine with protected indication of origin D.S.C.
VRoSS, Šamorín, Cintorínske Vineyard

A darker, straw-yellow wine with golden hues on the edges. Its perfumed floral and fruity smell features a combination of compote peaches and yellow melons with traces of beeswax. The lower alcohol content suits the softer, medium-long and medium sweet taste, while its citrus finish shows hazelnut and pistachio notes.

[10,125 l] • 0.75 l • €€ • L2 • 11.5 % vol. • 🍷 • ② • ⬯ {7} • 🍾 • ★★★★1/2

Chardonnay 2014
grape selection, medium dry   MARTIN POMFY - MAVÍN
Wine with protected indication of origin
VRoSS, Jasová

The intensive yellow-green shade and the elegant smell of juicy, overripe nectarines and peaches is emphasized by an appropriate medium long taste with tones of whipped cream and tangerines. The slightly bitter aftertaste of this vintage nicely harmonizes with the residual sugar and tender fruit acid. Overall, a pure and balanced wine with a delicious, primary fruity structure.

[4,500 l] • 0.75 l • €€€ • L6 • 13.0 % vol. • 🍷 • ② • ⬯ • 🍾 • ★★★★

Chardonnay 2014
medium dry   TAJNA VINEYARDS AND WINERY
Wine with protected indication of origin
VRoN, Tajná

This bright, yellow-green wine reveals aromas of ripening pears with a note of acacia blossoms complemented by a taste with a delicate trace of sponge biscuits and juicy grapefruit accompanied by popcorn. This fresh floral taste will slowly mature into a creamy fruity taste with an aftertaste of homemade butter on fresh bread in a finish with nuances of juice made of ripe oranges and pineapples.

[1,980 l] • 0.75 l • €€€ • L-04 • 13.0 % vol. • 🍷 • ◯ • ② • ⬯ • 🍾 • ★★★★

Pinot blanc 2014
grape selection, dry   VPS – PAVELKA A SYN
Wine with protected indication of origin D.S.C.
VRoSC, Pezinok, Tále Vineyard

This is a rich, elegant, and charming up to spicy Pinot with a multilayered structure that is fresh and creamy fruity in its bouquet and smell. If features the tones of a meadow in blossom, leaves of medicinal herbs, and the rare equilibrium of residual sugar, acids and alcohol. The long velvet taste reflects the extract of *genius loci* which, thanks to an excellent vineyard and professional processing, reaches the potential of maturing.

[1,500 l] • 0.75 l • €€ • L0103 • 12.5 % vol. • 🍷 • ① - ② • ◯ {1} • ⬯ • 🍾 •
★★★★★

PINOT BLANC • GRÜNER SILVANER • SAUVIGNON BLANC

Rulandské biele 2014

Vinitory Premium, late harvest, dry   VVD

Wine with protected indication of origin D.S.C.
VRoSS, Dvory nad Žitavou, Viničný vrch Vineyard

A bright, golden-yellow Pinot Blanc with a distinctive aroma of pears, bananas and yellow tropical melons in the nose and the mouth. The taste is greater and more intense than the smell. It contains a higher concentration of alcohol and a distinctive extract complemented by fruit acid. As a result, the taste lingers on the root of the tongue after swallowing. The aftertaste is reminiscent of a mixture of citrus fruit and apples.

[5,000 l] • 0.75 l • € € • L-34 • 13.5 % vol. • 🍷 • ① • ◯ • 🗡 • ★★★★

Silvánske zelené 2013

Gold Prestige, grape selection, dry   VÍNO MATYŠÁK

Wine with protected indication of origin
VRoSC, Pezinok, Chrastina Vineyard

This crystal clear Grüner Silvaner has a light, yellow-green color with golden hues. In smell it reminds one of apple puree with a drop of acacia honey and a pinch of cinnamon; in taste it reminds of the ripened pulp of Williams pears and freshly peeled clementine. The harmonious and pleasantly spicy, long aftertaste with a fine trace of cloves and exotic spice leaves an impressive tone with a hint of pome fruits and a trace of honeycomb in the background.

[5,000 l] • 0.75 l • € € € • L 14 • 13.0 % vol. • 🍷 • ① • ◯ • 🗡 • ★★★★★

Sauvignon 2014

kabinett, dry   MARTIN POMFY - MAVÍN

Wine with protected indication of origin
VRoSS, Belá

This wine's watery green shade with a delicate reductive sparkling of carbon dioxide, and piquant intensive smell with a spicy and even herbal character will enchant New Zealand fans of Sauvignon. The aroma is full of tones of white currants and mowed grass which transforms through the notes of pineapple to fine yeast lysates. The fresh taste is spiced up by impressive acids and closes up a wonderful note of gooseberries. Pomfy's kabinett is however fuller and more lively than the majority of great "New Zealanders."

[2,625 l] • 0.75 l • € € • L1 • 10.5 % vol. • 🍷 • ① • ◯ • 🗡 • ★★★★★

Semillon Sauvignon Blanc 2014

dry   TAJNA VINEYARDS AND WINERY

Wine with protected indication of origin
VRoN, Tajná

This sparkly clear wine with greenish-yellow shades has a pleasant herbal up to fruity smell which suggests tones of mowed meadows and honey and citrus. Its medium-full taste is unique thanks to the tones of green tea and a hint of a jasmine bouquet with a tender wine-fruity aftertaste which will show pieces of yellow melon pulp as it matures.

SE 60 %, SB 40 % • [1,800 l] • 0.75 l • € € € • L-01 • 13.0 % vol. • 🍷 • ① - ② • ◯ • 🗡 • ★★★★

SAUVIGNON BLANC • MUSCAT OTTONEL

Sauvignon 2014
Exclusive, late harvest, medium sweet   ČAJKOVIČ WINERY
VRoN

This bright, green-yellow wine with golden hues features the expressive smell of forest raspberries against a background of ripe vineyard peaches with a nectar note of elderberry blossoms. The peach and honey, fruity taste is slightly finer in its intensity and more mature than the smell. A well balanced combination of residual sugar and acids rounds out the overall sensory impression.

[2,000 l] • 0.75 l • 9.00 EUR • L 39 • 12.5 % vol. • ②-③ • ★★★★

Sauvignon 2014
kabinett, dry   VÍNO MIROSLAV DUDO
Wine with protected indication of origin
VRoSS, Dvory nad Žitavou, Viničný vrch Vineyard

This bright yellow-green wine has a sparkly clarity and a piquant smell of elderberry blossom which reigns over its fresh taste that also features white currants, young nettle leaves and an abundance of garden peaches. A merry acid wrapped in a spicy aftertaste nicely closes down the overall impression with notes of gooseberries and lemon grass. This New Zealand style competitor will not disappoint any fan of Sauvignon.

[1,950 l] • 0.75 l • €€ • L185 • 12.0 % vol. • ① • ★★★1/2

Muškát Ottonel 2013
quality varietal wine, medium dry   SOŠVO MODRA
Districtus Slovakia Controllatus
VRoSC, Modra

The yellowish shade of this Muscat Ottonel and its elegant, full smell of nutmeg and white jasmine flowers are complemented by impressive tones of exotic citrus fruits. Its dry fruit taste keeps up with the intensity of the smell. A 2013 vintage, it surprisingly keeps pleasant acids which after swallowing leave a harmonious overall impression in the mouth. Pieces of green lime and ginger appear in the juicy aftertaste.

[700 l] • 0.75 l • €€ • L 02 • 13.0 % vol. • ② • ★★★1/2

LEMBERGER (BLAUFRÄNKISCH)

WINES MADE OF TRADITIONAL RED VARIETIES

Frankovka modrá 2011
Oak Wood, grape selection, dry   VÍNO MATYŠÁK

Wine with protected indication of origin
VRoSC, Hlohovec, Šomoď Vineyard

This dark, ruby-red Lemberger (Blaufränkisch) with higher viscosity on the edges will immediately catch your attention. It has a harmonious, rich smell reminiscent of the tones of sour cherries, ground black pepper and vanilla, while its full robust taste stimulates the palate by its piquant note of dried stone fruit, chocolate and licorice. A nobly maturing wine with a plum and coffee aftertaste and a complex overall impression.

[11,700 l] • 0.75 l • € € € • L 18 • 13.5 % vol. • ♀ • ① • 🛢 {24} • 🖌 • ★★★★★

Frankovka modrá 2012
Château Palugyay, grape selection, dry   VILLA VINO RAČA

Wine with protected indication of origin
VRoSC, Rača, Žajdík Vineyard

This is an attractive dark ruby-red Lemberger (Blaufränkisch) with purple edges. We can detect a mixture of fruit, balsamic and spicy aromas in its deeper fruity smell. The intensive bouquet of overripe mulberries, hazelnuts and burnt wood is well balanced by a full and fresh taste with higher tannin content supported by delicate fruit acids. The attractive late rose hip aftertaste with a trace of plum marmalade and black pepper lingers on the tongue.

[1,500 l] • 0.75 l • € € • L-90 • 13.0 % vol. • ♀ • ① • 🌀 • 🛢 {6} • 🖌 • ★★★★1/2

Frankovka modrá 2012 "S"
Terroir Rača, quality varietal wine, dry   MILOŠ MÁŤUŠ

Wine with protected indication of origin
VRoSC, Bratislava – Rača

An attractive, ruby-red wine with a fiery smell and a taste of intensive tones of plums, cinnamon and black pepper. The hot blood of Rača's full temperament shows its face. After decanting, the wine features candied cherries mixed in dark chocolate with vanilla and wrapped in oak wood. The mature tannins, higher alcohol content and rich structure of acids contribute to a long, seemingly never ending taste trace.

[900 l] • 0.75 l • € € € • L-04/014 • 14.0 % vol. • ♀ • ① • 🌀 • 🛢 {14} • 🖌 •
★★★★1/2

LEMBERGER (BLAUFRÄNKISCH)

Frankovka modrá 2013

grape selection, dry VPS – PAVELKA A SYN

Wine with protected indication of origin D.S.C.
VRoSC, Pezinok, Štvrce Vineyard

The robust temperamental vintage of this ruby-red Lemberger (Blaufränkisch) features a rich varietal bouquet of baked plums on pie with hazelnuts and sprinkled with cinnamon. Ten days of fermentation on skins and slow maturing in oak casks, one third of which was barrique style, refined the piquant and fresh taste of this wine, which opened the way for the development of a sweet rose-hip and cherry aftertaste wrapped in roasted coffee tones and black raspberry compote.

[1,500 l] • 0.75 l • € € € • L0110 • 13.0 % vol. • ♀ • ① • ◎ • 30 % • ▤ • ✎ •
★★★★1/2

Frankovka modrá 2012

grape selection, dry RODINNÉ VINÁRSTVO MAGULA

Wine with protected indication of origin
VRoSC, Orešany viticultural area, Suchá nad Parnou

A dark, ruby-red Lemberger (Blaufränkisch) whose intensive bouquet of sweet caramelized stone fruits, leather and roasted coffee confirms its slow maturing in oak caskets with the presence of a small dose of oxygen. The taste of this wine is velvety smooth with a sweet tannin and a long aftertaste. An unfiltered, lively wine with longer maturing potential and a low overall sulphur dioxide, its content will also surprise orthodox fans of Bordeaux varieties by its wealth.

[1,500 l] • 0.75 l • € € € • L 0127 • 13.5 % vol. • ♀ • ① • ▤ {24} • ↓SO₂ • ✎ •
★★★★

Frankovka modrá 2013

Selection, quality varietal wine, dry KASNYIK RODINNÉ VINÁRSTVO

Wine with protected indication of origin
VRoSS, Strekov, Góré Vineyard

A darker, violet-red Lemberger (Blaufränkisch) with an opulent smell of dried plums, licorice and black sour cherries. This serious wine with a smooth structure is complex and well balanced in all aspects. The sweet taste supported by alcohol, slow micro oxidation with the perfect effect of the wooden cask enabled the development of varietal qualities in the course of maturing and revealed a pleasant marmalade fruitiness in the aftertaste.

[1,460 l] • 0.75 l • € € € • L-20 • 14.0 % vol. • ♀ • ① • ◎ • ◯ {9} • ▤ • ⚭ •
★★★★

Račianska frankovka 2011

Exclusive Collection, quality branded wine, dry VILLA VINO RAČA

Wine with protected indication of origin
VRoSC, Rača, Rača Vineyard

This ruby-red Rača Lemberger (Blaufränkisch) with sparkles and a darker violet hint features tones of stone fruit with a predominance of plums, cherries and dried rose hips and a pinch of black pepper are present in a spicy, fruity smell. The medium-full mineral taste with a well-balanced content of cinnamon tannins and juicy acids is rounded out by a trace of residual sugar. It achieves harmony by maturing and micro-oxidation in 3,000 liter oak caskets. The classical fruity style of this original Lemberger from the heart of Rača will please all fans of this variety.

[3,000 l] • 0.75 l • € € • L-25 • 13.0 % vol. • ♀ • ① • ◎ • ▤ {8} • ✎ • ★★★★

LEMBERGER (BLAUFRÄNKISCH) • SAINT LAURENT

Frankovka modrá 2013
quality varietal wine, dry **BOTT FRIGYES**
Wine with protected indication of origin
VRoSS, Mužla

This ruby-red Lemberger (Blaufränkisch) with purple hints has an attractive, red beet-almond smell in the background with a note of plum pie baked on oak wood. The taste is suitable for its smell. It contains nicely combined fruit acids with more distinctive tannins and warmer alcohol which leaves a medium-full overall impression on the tongue. Its finish is complemented by an interesting spectrum of stone fruits, bitter almonds and cocoa beans.

[1,875 l] • 0.75 l • € € € • L16/08 • 13.5 % vol. • ⚱ • ① • 🛢 • 🗝 • ★★★★

Frankovka modrá 2011
Oaked, grape selection, dry **REPA WINERY**
Wine with protected indication of origin D.S.C.
VRoN, Drženice, Baričky Vineyard

This dark crimson Lemberger (Blaufränkisch) with violet hues has a fuller fiery smell that combines notes of cranberries, stone fruit and vanilla with a pinch of ground black pepper. The taste perfectly complements the smell, while maturing in oak casks and slow micro oxidation has left a distinctive trace. It will enchant you by the full structure of tannins and higher alcohol content. The finish of the aftertaste opens the way for exotic spices dominated by juniper.

[2,000 l] • 0.75 l • € € • L16 • 13.5 % vol. • ⚱ • ① • ◎ {0,8} • 🛢 {12} • 🗝 •
★★★★

Frankovka modrá 2011
straw wine, sweet **CHÂTEAU TOPOĽČIANKY**
Wine with protected indication of origin D.S.C.
VRoN, Topoľčianky, Nad kostolom Vineyard

This ruby-red Lemberger will impress all your senses with its brilliant clarity and smell of cherry jam on butter brioche with chunks of caramel and traces of roasted coffee. The sweet concentrated taste of the wine nicely dissolves the note of candied stone fruit dominated by cherries, plums and raspberries. The fine aftertaste reveals bits of sweet red watermelon. The grapes were dried for 104 days on strings under the roof of the winery before pressing.

[2,450 l] • 0.375 l • € € € • L498 • 9.0 % vol. • ⚱ • ④ • ◯ • 🗝 • ★★★★

Svätovavrinecké 2012 Classic
quality varietal wine, dry **STREKOV 1075**
Wine with protected indication of origin
VRoSS, Strekov, Góré Vineyard

A Saint Laurent of a nice, ruby-red color with light violet shades. The smell reveals light micro-oxidation and maturing in wooden casks. The sweet tones of macerated plums and cherries are exotically complemented by a fine note of incense and smoke supported by a higher alcohol content. The taste confirms the cooperation of oxide in wooden casks, thanks to which the wine shows notes of baked bread crust and bitter sour cherries in the aftertaste.

[1,600 l] • 0.75 l • € € € • L6 • 12.7 % vol. • ⚱ • ① • ◎ • ◯ {5} + ❄ {2} • 🗝 •
★★★★

SAINT LAURENT • CABERNET SAUVIGNON

Cisárske Svätovavrinecké 2013

grape selection, dry   VILLA VINO RAČA

Wine with protected indication of origin
VRoN, Vinohrady nad Váhom, Ružová hora Vineyard

The dark, ruby-red color of Imperial Saint Laurent accompanied by a distinctive and even spicy smell with tones of stone fruit, cinnamon and a balsamic hint of roasted coffee and oak barrel. The alcohol and extract combine with a concentrated tannin in a long and well-balanced taste which leaves a firm finish on the palate. Rustic rough tannins are sought after.

SL [6,000 l] • 0.75 l • € € • L-28 • 13.0, % vol. • 🍷 • ① • ⊚ • 🛢 {7} + 🛢 {7} • 🗡 • ★★★★

Svätovavrinecké 2012

quality varietal wine, medium dry   PIVNICA ORECHOVÁ

Wine with protected indication of origin D.S.C.
VRoES, Orechová, Sekerová Vineyard

The darker raspberry shade of this Saint Laurent wine and its fruity and medium full smell reminds of a basket full of May cherries complemented by notes of marmalade of overripe, dark, sour cherries. The nicely maturing trace of forest raspberries and blackberries forms part of the wine's bouquet which is complemented on the palate by a reductive and pleasantly smooth taste of sweet tannins affected by the maturing of wine in oak casks. Its harmonious impression is refreshed by an appropriate fruit acid content.

[10,000 l] • 0.75 l • € • L4814 • 12.0 % vol. • 🍷 • ② • ⊚ • 🛢 {18} • 🍾 • ★★★1/2

Cabernet Sauvignon barrique 2012

Winemaker´s Cut, grape selection, dry   VÍNO MRVA & STANKO

Quality wine with attribute
VRoSS, Belá

The dark, purple-red shade of this wine and its higher viscosity attract attention at first sight. The intensive, fruity and mineral aroma of juniper, blackberries, elderberries and graphite is enriched by distinctive tones of tobacco leaves, burnt cedar wood and white pepper. Its rich body and long comprehensive aftertaste will enchant you by the depth of its mature tannins, the hot trace of alcohol and a juicy acid content which is complemented by a note of licorice and vanilla in the finish.

[700 l] • 0.75 l • € € € • L-31 • 13.5 % vol. • 🍷 • ① • 🛢 {18} • 🗡 • ★★★★★

Cabernet Sauvignon Barrique 2012

grape selection, dry   CHÂTEAU BELÁ

Quality varietal wine with attribute, D.S.C.
VRoSS, Štúrovo viticultural area, Mužla

A dark, violet-red wine with a distinctive aroma of juniper, dark chocolate and black pepper. The balsamic traces of oak wood and tobacco have fiery support in the higher alcohol which is in harmony with the swift tannins and lively fruit acid. The distinctive and full wooden character of the taste is the result of a complex overall impression created by 16 months of maturing in casks.

[1,200 l] • 0.75 l • € € € • L 09 • 13.5 % vol. • 🍷 • ① • 🛢 {16} • ★★★★★

CABERNET SAUVIGNON

Cabernet Sauvignon 2011
ice wine, sweet   CHÂTEAU BELÁ

Quality varietal wine with attribute, D.S.C.
VRoSS, Štúrovo viticultural area, Mužla

Lively pink-orange in color with a garnet-red shade, this wine has higher viscosity and a concentrated fruity smell of red currents and raspberry marmalade, mint leaves and lemon peels. The distinctive taste is interesting not only because of its high acid content, but its residual sugar (240 g/l). It features tones of dried citrus, honey, current mash and forest fruit on sweet whipped cream. The full and rich aftertaste has a persistence that is not easily forgotten. Women in particular will appreciate this wine with a progressive glass cap.

[600 l] • 0.50 l • € € € • L 13 • 8.0 % vol. • 🍷 • ④ • ☐ • ▭ • ★★★★★

Cabernet Sauvignon blanc 2014
late harvest, dry   MARTIN POMFY - MAVÍN

Wine with protected indication of origin
VRoSS, Jasová

This light, golden-greenish wine was made by using the blanc de noir method. The fruity and fresh aroma is reminiscent of gooseberries and tropical limes, with nettle undertones in the background. The distinctive citrus note is the part of the taste where we recognize it in lemon-grapefruit up to orange-pineapple tones. However, the distinctive acid fails to cover the refined residual sugar. It nicely complements the herbal aftertaste of a wine of green pods of white currants.

[4,500 l] • 0.75 l • € € € • L10 • 12.0 % vol. • 🍷 • ①-② • ☐ • 🖌 • ★★★★1/2

Cabernet Sauvignon 2013
grape selection, dry   VÍNO MIROSLAV DUDO

Wine with protected indication of origin
VRoSS, Dvory nad Žitavou, Viničný vrch Vineyard

This dark, sour-cherry-red wine has an open smell of juicy berries mixed with black currants, raspberries and coffee and is balanced by a delicious medium-long up to long taste with tones of red beet and coriander. It's a Mediterranean style wine with sweet tannins and a cassis aftertaste with a hint of cocoa beans. It is sincere, tempting and fascinating.

[1,850 l] • 0.75 l • € € • L180 • 13.0 % vol. • 🍷 • ① • 🛢 • 🖌 • ★★★★1/2

Cabernet Sauvignon 2013
dry   TAJNA VINEYARDS AND WINERY

Wine with protected indication of origin
VRoN, Tajná

This dark, violet-red vintage with terracotta hues will catch your interest with its rich smell comprised of cassis, ferns, blackberry compote and black mulberries. Its firm, concentrated taste has mild tannins and an elegant fruity structure of black fruit. Its aftertaste bears traces of tobacco, burnt wood, green coffee beans and dark chocolate.

[800 l] • 0.75 l • € € € • L-02 • 14.5 % vol. • 🍷 • ① • ⑤ • 🛢 • {12} • 🖌 • ★★★★1/2

CABERNET SAUVIGNON • PINOT NOIR

Cabernet Sauvignon 2013
Privat Exclusive, grape selection, dry   MOVINO
Wine with protected indication of origin
VRoSS, Bušince, Hatalec Vineyard

This wine is ruby-red with a dark carmine sparkle and violet hues. The full berry-fruity smell of the mixture of ripe elderberries, forest strawberries and green poppy heads with a blueberry note is nicely complemented by a complex of empyreumatic tones of wood and tobacco. The taste is nicely balanced with its smell. It contains more tannins which, in combination with the long, plum-coffee aftertaste, leaves a dry and slightly bitter overall impression on the tongue.

[18,500 l] • 0.75 l • € € • L-57 • 13.0 % vol. • 🍷 • ① • 🛢 {6} • 🔑 • ★★★★1/2

Cabernet Sauvignon 2013
straw wine, sweet   CHÂTEAU BELÁ
Quality varietal wine with attribute, D.S.C.
VRoSS, Štúrovo viticultural area, Mužla

This bright raspberry-red wine has a wonderful smell of sweet red berries. The winnowed part of the quality raisin selection was dried until March 4, 2014 when the grapes were pressed. Fermentation resulted in a unique wine which combines the freshness of a white, the intensity of a red and the artfulness of a rose wine. The bouquet of marmalade raspberries, red currants and citrus harmonizes with the fresh and long aftertaste which fully opens a great potential for maturing.

[100 l] • 0.50 l • € € € € • L 13 • 9.5 % vol. • 🍷 • ④ • ○ • ▱ • ★★★★1/2

Cabernet Sauvignon 2013
grape selection, dry   PIVNICA ZSIGMOND
Wine with protected indication of origin
VRoCS, Vinica viticultural area

A purple-red wine with claret shades on the edges. Tones of juniper and poppy heads appear in the pure concentrated smell against a background of a drop of cassis liqueur. Maturing velvety tannins in the taste nicely wrap the medium long body with a higher extract covered by ripe grape berries, coffee beans and late forest strawberries.

[1,500 l] • 0.75 l • € € • L-13 • 13.0 % vol. • 🍷 • ① • 🛢 {8} • 🔑 • ★★★★

Pinot noir Special Selection 2012
grape selection, dry   MARTIN POMFY - MAVÍN
Wine with protected indication of origin
VRoSS, Belá

The light, brick-red color with cherry sparkles and viscose edges will instantly catch your attention. Its bouquet has a rich and elegant profile with tones of dried plums, strawberry marmalade and delicate vanilla pods. The taste is in balance with the smell. It features traces of coffee beans, licorice and candied sour cherries and leaves a touch of leather with a sweet note of alcohol on the palate. Its potential and noblesse will develop after several years of maturing in the bottle.

[3,600 l] • 0.75 l • € € € • L-18 • 13.5 % vol. • 🍷 • ① • ○ • 🛢 • 🔑 • ★★★★★

PINOT NOIR

Pinot Noir 2013
quality varietal wine, dry   BOTT FRIGYES
Wine with protected indication of origin
VRoSS, Mužla

Bright, garnet-red color, smell of forest berries. The first positive impression hides a rich structure of smell harmoniously complemented by tones of wood and almond chocolate. Pieces of dried plums covered by licorice and traces of blueberry mash are present in the concentrated taste of this wine. The alcohol content nicely falls into a balsamic note of tannins and fresh fruit acids. This noble wine with an earthy aftertaste is ready for maturing in bottles.

[1,500 l] • 0.75 l • € € € • L11/0614 • 13.0 % vol. • ▼ • ① • 🛢 • ✦ • ★★★★1/2

Rulandské modré Barrique 2011
grape selection, dry   CHÂTEAU BELÁ
Quality varietal wine with attribute, D.S.C.
VRoSS, Štúrovo viticultural area, Mužla

A garnet-red Pinot Noir with violet hues, a fine fruity aroma of plums and blackberries with a note of roasted chestnuts. The medium-full taste suits its smell, which features marmalade tones of forest strawberries and cedar wood which after swallowing shows in a bouquet of a sweet and pleasantly complex harmony on the root of the tongue, while the aftertaste reveals the presence of peeled almonds with traces of forest raspberries and a sweet note of fresh mash in the maceration of the ripe grapes of this variety.

[2,300 l] • 0.75 l • € € € • L 14 • 13.0 % vol. • ▼ • ① • 🛢 {6} • ✦ • ★★★★1/2

Pinot noir Special Selection 2011
grape selection, dry   MARTIN POMFY - MAVÍN
Wine with protected indication of origin
VRoSS, Svodín

A garnet-red wine with hues of dark sour cherry on the edges. Its fiery smell of alcohol and macerated stone fruit is wrapped in tones of oak wood with a distinctive dominating vanilla. The impressive launch of aroma in the mouth is balanced by a rich structure of taste sensations reminiscent of plum compote and forest strawberries with an admixture of cassis and chocolate. The delicious, concentrated aftertaste is further emphasized by notes of new oak wood.

[300 l] • 0.75 l • € € € € • L-25 • 13.5 % vol. • ▼ • ① • ◎ • 🛢 • ⊷ •
★★★★1/2

Pinot noir 2013
grape selection, dry   VPS – PAVELKA A SYN
Wine with protected indication of origin D.S.C.
VRoSC, Pezinok, Pod Urbánkou Vineyard

A garnet-red wine with elegant viscosity and brick-red hues on the edges. The distinctive bouquet of black raspberries and forest strawberries with a pleasant note of marinated cherries is affected by the impressive character of a new oak barrel. Its fresh fruity body with velvet tannins opens up in a charming sour cherry and balsamic style where concentrated tones of ripe berries appear in the aftertaste.

[1,000 l] • 0.75 l • € € • L0108 • 12.5 % vol. • ▼ • ① • ◎ • 30 % 🛢 • ✦ • ★★★★

PINOT NOIR

Pinot Noir 2012
grape selection, dry
VÍNO MRVA & STANKO

Quality wine with attribute
VRoSC, Čachtice

This light, brick-red wine with an attractively sweet, fruity smell of blackberries, mulberries, and forest raspberries will immediately catch your attention. The distinctive, medium-long taste of stone fruit is impressively complemented by cunning tones of tannins with a noble focus on the tongue, while the velvety and slightly spicy aftertaste is complemented by notes of dried plums, leather and powdered black pepper. Slow maturing in bottles will multiply its elegance.

[3,300 l] • 0.75 l • €€€ • L-378 • 13.5 % vol. • ★★★★

Pinot Noir 2012
grape selection, dry
RODINNÉ VINÁRSTVO ĎURÍK

Wine with protected indication of origin
VRoCS, Opatovská Nová Ves

This darker, brick-red wine with garnet-red shades has the sweet smell of cherries. When inhaling, we can smell tones of compote strawberries and blackberries. The harmonious combination of mature tannins and acids complemented by tones of plum marmalade leaves a direct, pleasant taste on the palate. The elegant, impressive and pure style of Pinot Noir maturing in contact with oak wood is finished by a bitter aftertaste of cocoa beans.

[5,000 l] • 0.75 l • €€€ • L-6 • 14.0 % vol. • {6} • ★★★★

Pinot Noir 2013
dry
TAJNA VINEYARDS AND WINERY

Wine with protected indication of origin
VRoN, Tajná

A lively, garnet-red wine with transparent coral-red hues on the edges and nice viscosity that is immediately attractive. Its smell is reminiscent of red fruit, plums and red currants with a hint of noble wood, leather and truffle. The taste is piquant and elegant with a warming trace of alcohol, mild tannins and a juicy, fruity flavor. Medium long finish.

[550 l] • 0.75 l • €€€ • L-03 • 13.5 % vol. • + {12} • ★★★★

Rulandské modré 2009
grape selection, dry
PIVNICA RADOŠINA

Quality varietal wine with attribute
Wine with protected indication of origin D.S.C.
VRoN, Radošina

A lively crimson Pinot Noir, its full, mature smell of dark sour cherries and licorice are complemented by a velvety medium-long taste in developing bottle maturity. The rounded tannins, appropriate juicy acid and piquant alcohol content with noble tones of leather mature in equilibrium with a finished dry earthy aftertaste. The potential of the 2009 vintage continues towards elegance and noblesse.

[1,200 l] • 0.75 l • €€€ • L 905 • 14.0 % vol. • {24} • ★★★★

BLAUER PORTUGIESER

Modrý Portugal barrique 2012
quality wine, dry   RODINNÉ VINÁRSTVO MAGULA
Wine with protected indication of origin
VRoSC, Orešany viticultural area, Suchá nad Parnou

The elegant, scarlet-red shade of this Blauer Portugieser has raspberry-red edges and a fascinating smell of forest strawberries mixed with tones of cherries and raw leather which appears in the first impression and after breathing in the wine's taste. Its medium-full, fruity-herbal taste is in perfect balance with the smell. In addition to stone fruits, it is elegantly complemented by notes of oak wood, fennel and tobacco.

[825 l] • 0.75 l • € € € • L 0122 • 12.0 % vol. • 🍷 • ① • 🛢 {24} • ↓SO_2 • ⚔ •
★★★★★

Modrý Portugal 2012
Classic, quality varietal wine, dry   STREKOV 1075
Wine with protected designation of origin
VRoSS, Strekov, Stredný vrch Vineyard

A rich, ruby-red color with garnet-red hues. The elegant smell of ripe May cherries with an admixture of candied plums and creamy buttermilk. This is a drinkable wine with a harmonious, full taste together with marmalade tones of stone fruit and intoxicating licorice. It comes from a 4 year old vineyard. The opulent overall impression is supported by higher extract and alcohol which however does not stand out; on the contrary, it protects its ripe, sweet-earthy aftertaste.

[800 l] • 0.75 l • € € € • L2 • 13.2 % vol. • 🍷 • ① - ② • ◎ • 🛢 {6} • 🍾 •
★★★★1/2

Modrý Portugal Barrique 2009
quality varietal wine, dry   TERRA PARNA
VRoSC, Suchá nad Parnou, Trnavské vrchy Vineyard

Blauer Portugieser is a sparkling clear wine of dark ruby-red color with higher viscosity. Its smell is reminiscent of a mixture of stone and berry fruits with a predominance of sour cherries and blackberries enriched by notes of cold smoke and cocoa. The fuller medium long taste of stone fruits is fresh and spicy-fruity. Tones of bitter almond and dried plums with a pinch of green pepper appear in the wine's aftertaste. This wine will especially please those who like lighter barrique-type wines with a more distinct identity of the variety of which the wine was made.

[5,000 l] • 0.75 l • € • L14 • 13.5 % vol. • 🍷 • ① • ◎ {1} • 🛢 {24} • ⚔ • ★★★★

Modrý Portugal 2013
dry   VÍNO MRVA & STANKO
Quality wine
VRoSC, Dolné Orešany

A ruby-red Blauer Portugieser with a pleasant bouquet of sour cherries, cherries and blackberries. Traces of stone fruit are present even in its juicy, fruity taste supported by proper acid and a distinct tone of firmer tannins which are typical for this traditional Small Carpathian variety. Its robust, earthy aftertaste of plum chutney and cinnamon has a slightly bitter hint of walnuts and balsamic wood.

[2,400 l] • 0.75 l • € € • L-16 • 12.5 % vol. • 🍷 • ① • 🛢 • ⚔ • ★★★★

BLAUER PORTUGIESER

Modrý Portugal barrique 2011

Retro, quality varietal wine, dry   CHÂTEAU TOPOĽČIANKY

Wine with protected indication of origin
VRoN

This Blauer Portugieser is garnet-red with hints of mahogany. Its mature, fruity smell is reminiscent of a basket of blackberries and blueberries against a balsamic wood background. After maturing for six months in new oak barrels and subsequent maturing in bottles, this wine takes on a fullness in addition to harmony. The mature velvet taste hides tones of candied cherries and sour cherries wrapped in notes of bitter chocolate and licorice.

[800 l] • 0.75 l • €€€ • L404 • 12.0 % vol. • 🍷 • ① • 🌀 • 🛢 {6} • 🍾 • ★★★★

WINES MADE OF TOKAJ VARIETIES

Furmint 2013 Anniversary Edition
nobly rotten raisin selection, sweet — J. & J. OSTROŽOVIČ

Wine with protected indication of origin
VRoT, Malá Tŕňa, Makovisko Vineyard

This exclusive wine with a sparkly golden color has the intensive, inviting smell of overripe berries, and an exotic hint of acacia honey, juicy mango and pineapple. A respectable portion of nobly rotten raisins brought into the sensory profile traces of botrytis whose rich and long taste is complemented by a distinctive mineral content and residual sugar in harmony with sufficient acids and alcohol.

[1,900 l] • 0.75 l • €€€€ • L34 • 14.0 % vol. • 🍷 • ④ • 🍇 • ⚪ {3} • ⎯ •
★★★★★

Furmint 2011
grape selection, medium dry — ELESKO TOKAY

Wine with protected indication of origin D.S.C.
VRoT, Malá Tŕňa, Makovisko Vineyard

A crystal clear, green-yellow wine with a distinctive herbal and honey aroma and a pleasantly drinkable medium long fruity taste. The bouquet of mountain flowers mixed with pink pomelo and citruses is extremely inviting. The acacia-honey taste is supported in its elegance by balanced residual sugar and developing bottled maturity which refines the mineral nature of this wine supported by higher acids.

[11,400 l] • 0.75 l • € • L-4/11 • 12.5 % vol. • 🍷 • ② • ⚪ • 🔑 • ★★★★

Lipovina NATUR Special Collection 2011
grape selection, medium dry — J. & J. OSTROŽOVIČ

Wine with protected indication of origin
VRoT, Malá Tŕňa, hon Makovisko Vineyard

This is a golden-yellow, crystal clear wine featuring the pure, honey-herbal smell of meadow flowers, Melissa, lychee and ripe exotic fruit. The taste is fuller in comparison with its smell, suggesting a mixture of garden gooseberries, yellow grapefruit up to exotic papaya. A medium full-bodied extractive wine, it has great potential for maturing in the bottle. It was made from grapes of integrated production that were grown without the use of any herbicides or fungicides. NATUR guarantees the purity of origin and careful processing of grapes.

[4,500 l] • 0.75 l • €€€ • L17 • 13.5 % vol. • 🍷 • ② • ⚪ • 🔑 • ★★★★ 1/2

LIPOVINA • YELOW MUSCAT

Lipovina 2011

straw wine, sweet   ELESKO TOKAY

Wine with protected indication of origin D.S.C.
VRoT, Malá Tŕňa, Makovisko Vineyard

The grapes for this wine were manually harvested early in the morning on November 14, 2011 at a temperature - 8 °C. After the pressing of the frozen berries, the must reached a sugar content of 27 °NM. This precious Tokaj straw wine will please you with its golden-yellow color, high viscosity and rich floral and fruity smell with a hint of linden honey and candied fruit. The taste, which is full and sweet with tones of exotic fruit, is supported by 99 g/l of residual sugar.

[1,000 l] • 0.375 l • €€€€ • L-9/11 • 9.0 % vol. • 🍷 • ④ • ◯ • 🗝 • ★★★★

Muškát žltý Saturnia 2010

straw wine, sweet   J. & J. OSTROŽOVIČ

Wine with protected indication of origin
VRoT, Malá Tŕňa, Makovisko Vineyard

A yellow Muscat with an intensive golden shade and dark amber sparkles. This wine's distinctive fruity up to muscatel-spicy smell with a hint of baked sweet dough and ginger bread has an extremely exotic character. Its honey-raisin taste hides notes of peeled sweet almonds, pistachios and cashews. This harmonious, full, naturally sweet wine with 160 grams of residual sugar enhances the expressive nature of dried aromatic berries of the oldest Tokaj variety and leaves a tender citrus sensation on the tongue.

[490 l] • 0.375 l • €€€ • L15 • 9.0 % vol. • 🍷 • ④ • 🛢 {8} • 🗝 • ★★★★1/2

MORAVIAN MUSCAT • DEVÍN

WINES MADE OF NEW WHITE CLONES

Muškát Moravský 2014
Jagnet, dry   KARPATSKÁ PERLA

Wine with protected indication of origin
VRoSC, Šenkvice, Suchý vrch Vineyard

This sparkly, yellow-green Moravian Muscat has an intensive spicy and fruity smell with tones of nutmeg, elderberry flowers and dried pome fruits. Its impressive light bouquet taste with piquant fruit acid, which is well balanced with the smell, contains juicy tones of tropical fruit with a slight trace of meadow flowers. The fine, spicy and fresh aftertaste offers an enchanting experience that will surprise many dry wine aficionados.

[35,000 l] • 0.75 l • €€ • LB 0714 • 12.0 % vol. • ♀ • ① • ○ {6} • ✦ • ★★★★

Muškát moravský 2013
quality varietal wine, medium dry   PIVNICA ORECHOVÁ

Wine with protected indication of origin D.S.C.
VRoES, Orechová, Sekerová Vineyard

A perfumed, elegant Moravian Muscat, yellow-green in color with aromatic tones of jasmine flowers, vanilla, and the juicy taste of mango with a distinctively spicy note of nutmeg. It cannot deny its full Muscat family temperament even in its overall impression. It is attractive, defiant, full-blooded and mysterious at the same time. The residual sugar on the margin of this medium sweet wine balances out the relatively fresh acids.

[2,900 l] • 0.75 l • € • L 2014 • 12.5 % vol. • ♀ • ② • ○ • ⌇ • ★★★★

Devín 2013 Gold Prestige
selection of berries, medium sweet   VÍNO MATYŠÁK

Wine with protected indication of origin
VRoSS, Búč, Vinohrady Vineyard

A shiny, yellow-greenish wine with golden hues. The ethereal smell combines tones of overripe mango, pineapple and yellow melon, and is in perfect harmony with its rich and long taste. It's reminiscent of dried tropical fruit with a honey-soap raisin note. The aftertaste of this unique extractive vintage is emphasized by a balanced content of acids and residual sugars.

[6,000 l] • 0.75 l • €€€ • L 7 • 12.5 % vol. • ♀ • ③ • ○ • ✦ • ★★★★★

DEVÍN

Devín 2013
quality varietal wine, medium sweet   CHÂTEAU RÚBAŇ

Wine with protected indication of origin
VRoSS, Strekov, Ormok Vineyard

A sparkly yellow, crystal clear wine with a perfumed, spicy smell of curry, anise and cloves enhanced by tones of honey and soap. Its rich multilayered taste has a hint of cinnamon and hazelnuts. The residual sugar content is somewhere between that of a medium-dry and medium-sweet wine; however due to its equilibrium with acids, this vintage makes a rather medium-dry impression. The finish on the root of the tongue belongs to rose petals and dried fruit. Excellent choice.

[500 l] · 0.75 l · €€€ · L03 · 14.5 % vol. · 🍷 · ② · ○ · ✒ · ★★★★★

Devín 2014
grape selection, medium dry   MARTIN POMFY - MAVÍN

Wine with protected indication of origin
VRoSS, Jasová

The best phrase to describe all of the qualities of this golden-yellow wine would be a tropical fruit rainfall. Its refreshing, rich, intensive and exotic combination of roses, anise and white pepper is attractively combined with a spicy taste and tones of soap, cloves, freshly peeled orange peels and a finish that carries a pinch of curry and cinnamon.

[3,000 l] · 0.75 l · €€€ · L3 · 13.5 % vol. · 🍷 · ②-③ · ○ · ✒ · ★★★★1/2

Devín 2014
late harvest, medium dry   VÍNO MIROSLAV DUDO

Wine with protected indication of origin
VRoSC, Modra, vineyard Dolný Trávnik

This light, green-yellow wine with golden hues reveals etheric aromas of May flowers of rose and elderberry emphasized by the tropical pulp of passion fruit, pineapple and oriental anise. Honey tones appear even in the taste of this wine where the fruit acids in harmony with delicious residual sugar overlay traces of quince mesh. The rich aroma in the aftertaste doesn't burn at the root of the tongue; the wine creates a concentrated harmonious overall impression.

[1,850 l] · 0.75 l · €€ · L188 · 12.0 % vol. · 🍷 · ② · ○ · ✒ · ★★★★1/2

Devín 2013
selection of berries, sweet   VÍNO MRVA & STANKO

Quality wine with attribute
VRoSS, Búč

This green and yellow wine has a fruity, honey and floral smell which evokes a basket of exotic fruit with white flower petals and a tender Muscat trace. The delicious and elegant taste is dominated by overripe raisins and plums with pieces of tangerine peels, a pinch of cinnamon and lychees. Its graceful overall impression is completed by natural residual sugar with harmonious acid content.

[120 l] · 0.50 l · €€ · L-08 · 12.0 % vol. · 🍷 · ④ · ○ · ✒ · ★★★★

DEVÍN

Devín 2013
dry   ŽITAVSKÉ VINICE

Wine without geographical indication

A distinctive, golden yellow wine with a full, honey-fruity up to spicy taste reminiscent of overripe raisins mixed with anise and cloves. Its robust, fiery taste with higher alcohol content is pure and long. The honey trace of botrytised raisins and the coquettish bouquet finish of dried fruit and rose flowers bring an interesting view of Devín in dry concentrated form.

[2,000 l] • 0.75 l • €€€ • L 03 • 14.5 % vol. • 🍷 • ① • ◯ {6} • 🛢 • 🗡 • ★★★★

Devín 2013
grape selection, medium sweet   VELKEER

Wine with protected indication of origin
VRoSS, Nové Zámky, Pri železnici Vineyard

This sparkly yellow-green wine with golden hues opens its aroma with a mixture of dried fruit, cloves and anise. Its intensive smell, which is followed by a slightly milder and more mature taste with tones of soap, white pepper and forest honey, flows throughout the entire body of the wine. Low fermentation temperatures and slow maturing in fine lees supported the manifestation of a spicy fruity aftertaste with enchanting pieces of cinnamon and mango.

[1,690 l] • 0.75 l • €€€ • L0313 • 12.0 % vol. • 🍷 • ③ • ◯ • ▢ • 🗡 • ★★★★

Devín 2013
grape selection, dry   PIVNICA TIBAVA

Wine with protected indication of origin D.S.C.
VRoES, Tibava, Nad pivnicou Vineyard

The first vintage made of the first fruit harvest of young plantings will surprise by its intensive golden-yellow color and aroma of white roses, cloves and lavender soap. Its exotic taste with tones of anise, cinnamon and passion fruit whispers of the interesting potential of this new clone planted in a heavier soil profile. The temperament of a fragrant young man is refreshed by a modest acid on the palate.

[600 l] • 0.75 l • €€ • L-8/14 • 12.5 % vol. • 🍷 • ① • ▢ • 🍾 • ★★★★

Devín 2014
Exclusive, grape selection, dry   MOVINO

Wine with protected indication of origin
VRoCS, Príbelce

The tender honey, spicy and fruity bouquet of a meadow full of flowers and rose and carnation petals with perfumed soap tones enriched by a note of exotic mangoes and pomelo confirms the ripeness of the grapes and pure reductive processing. A distinctive aromatic style can also be found in the spicy aftertaste of this wine whose freshness is briskly underlined by the right amount of fruit acids.

[30,400 l] • 0.75 l • € • L-19 • 12.5 % vol. • 🍷 • ① • ▢ • 🗡 • ★

PÁLAVA

Pálava 2011
straw wine, sweet   ELESKO

Wine with protected indication of origin D.S.C.
VRoSC, Vištuk, Zoya Vineyard

The wonderfully golden-yellow clear color of this wine features a distinctive viscosity on the edges. Its rich smell bears a clear trace of overripe exotic fruit and apricot compote with a clove undertone in the background. The taste is long, extractive and nicely balanced with its smell. It is inspired by a trace of exotic lychees and candied figs with a persistent honey-spicy aftertaste.

[11,250 l] • 0.375 l • € € € • L-11/11 • 9.0 % vol. • 🍷 • ④ • ◯ • ▭ • ★★★★★

Pálava 2011
Dílemúre, straw wine, sweet   KARPATSKÁ PERLA

Wine with protected indication of origin
VRoSC, Šenkvice, Suchý vrch Vineyard

This distinctive golden-yellow wine has the smell of overripe raisins and tropical fruit enriched by honey-spice notes. Its endless taste is well balanced with the smell. It concentrates tones of passion fruit, overripe tangerines and dried mango supported by a juicy extract with delicious fruit acid wrapped in almost two hundred grams of natural residual sugar. The fresh fruitiness leaves an aftertaste where marmalade of pomelo with a pinch of clove resonate on the palate.

[1,000 l] • 0.375 l • € € € • L 0312 • 9.0 % vol. • 🍷 • ④ • 🛢 • ◯ • ✒ •
★★★★1/2

Pálava 2013 "2"
grape selection, medium sweet   ELESKO

Wine with protected indication of origin D.S.C.
VRoSC, Vištuk, Zoya, Iveta, Mária Vineyard

This full yellow and green wine with golden hues and higher viscosity on the edges has a smell reminiscent of ripe vineyard peaches and pears with a tender trace of roses in blossom. The taste is full, medium-long up to long and extractive, and rich in fruit acids which are in balance with the residual sugar. It features tones of tropical fruit combined with mangoes, kiwi, passion fruit, Williams pears and nutmeg. A temperamental wine with a well-balanced impression.

[28,500 l] • 0.75 l • € € € • L-8/13 • 12.0 % vol. • 🍷 • ③ • ◯ • ✒ • ★★★★1/2

Pálava 2013
grape selection, medium sweet   VELKEER

Wine with protected indication of origin
VRoSS, Nové Zámky, Pri železnici Vineyard

A lively, golden-yellow wine with the smell of exotic passion fruit, soap and dried fruit with a trace of white pepper. The medium- full taste with over twenty grams of residual sugar is in nice harmony with the fuller fruit acids which leaves a harmonious overall impression. The selection of grapes in the aftertaste shows traces of ripe tangerines with lavender honey and thus emphasizes the vintage's distinctive aromatic profile.

[1,050 l] • 0.50 l • € € € • L1113 • 11.5 % vol. • 🍷 • ③ • ◯ • ✒ • ★★★★

PÁLAVA • NORIA • MILIA

Pálava 2012
quality varietal wine, medium dry **SVV VINANZA**
Wine with protected indication of origin
VRoN, Veľké Lovce

This wine has a greenish-yellow shade with a golden sparkle, and its intensive bouquet carries white carnations, cloves in its center and almond soap foam after opening. The spicy taste refined by residual sugar has an exotic hint of passion fruit in the background with a fine hint of rose oil and curry. However, the spicy charge does not end with the taste; it lingers in the mouth in the form of a maturing pear chutney aroma.

[2,400 l] • 0.75 l • €€ • L-94 • 11.5 % vol. • ② • ★★★★

Noria 2013
late harvest, medium sweet **VÍNO-MASARYK**
Wine with protected indication of origin
VRoSS, Strekov

This bright, yellow-green wine features an attractive tropical fruit aroma with tender undertones of soft citrus, mango and linden blossom. The medium-full, honey-sweetish taste is refreshed by proper acid content, while the honey, slightly spicy up to herbal aftertaste is reminiscent of a mowed meadow. The well balanced overall impression is enhanced by a feeling of the ripeness of the grapes from which this wine was made.

[2,600 l] • 0.75 l • €€ • L 11 • 12.0 % vol. • ④ • ★★★★★

Noria 2013
quality varietal wine, medium sweet **CHÂTEAU RÚBAŇ**
Wine with protected indication of origin
VRoSS, Strekov, Pod vinohradmi Vineyard

A distinctive golden-yellow wine with green hues. The aroma calls to mind a bowl of fresh exotic fruit including mango, kiwi, papaya, pineapple with drops of linden honey and the juice of overripe lemons. The taste is extremely full and features tones of dried apricots and orange peels with discreet lemon grass in the background. The unique harmony of smell and taste is appropriately balanced by the alcohol, acid and residual sugar content.

[600 l] • 0.75 l • €€ • L06 • 11.5 % vol. • ③ • ★★★★1/2

Milia 2013
grape selection, dry **VÍNO-MASARYK**
Wine with protected indication of origin
VRoSS, Strekov

The golden-yellow shade along with the acacia-honey and fresh and slightly spicy smell of exotic fruit with tones of muscatel, apricots and litchi after opening make this wine extremely attractive. The light, fruity taste resonates with a noble dose of mango and overripe oranges. The medium-long, dry aftertaste in the finish is enriched by fresh acids. Its distinctive aromatic character will win over lovers of dry wine.

[1,400 l] • 0.75 l • €€ • L 5 • 14.0 % vol. • ① • ★★★★1/2

Milia 2013

Premium, quality varietal wine, dry   CHATEAU MODRA

Wine with protected indication of origin D.S.C.
VRoSS, Galanta, Mlynská cesta Vineyard

A bright yellow and green wine with a magical muscatel and fruity smell with tones of freshly squeezed pink pomelo, pineapple and lime peels. Exotic tones are also present in its juicy taste rich in fruit acids. The dry, more mature aftertaste with fine bitterness is affected by tones of lemons and early fall tangerines.

[1,200 l] • 0.75 l • €€€ • L47 • 12.0 % vol. • ♀ • ① • ▢ • ▪ • ★★★★

ODESSA RED (ALIBERNET)

WINES MADE OF NEW RED CLONES

Alibernet 2009
quality varietal wine, dry

TERRA PARNA

VRoSC, Suchá nad Parnou, Trnavské vrchy Vineyard

This dark, ink-violet wine has claret sparkles on the edges. Its excellent aroma and complex, well-balanced taste are underlined by a rich concentration of blueberries, plums and vanilla. The velvety tannin structure is wrapped in tones of licorice. The wine matured for four years in new barrique barrels made of French oak. The chocolate and juniper marmalade aftertaste is unforgettable.

[1,100 l] • 0.75 l • €€€ • L-B2 • 13.5 % vol. • ♦ • ① • ◎ • 🛢 {48} • ⊶ •
★★★★★

Alibernet Barrique 2011
grape selection, dry

CHÂTEAU BELÁ

Quality varietal wine with attribute, D.S.C.
VRoSS, Štúrovo viticultural area, Mužla

A dark violet and carmine wine with an ink shade on the edges. The massive bouquet of burnt wood, tobacco leaves and gingerbread spices with sweet blackberry mash has a spicy up to empyreumatic character. Its distinct, full taste promises considerable experience during several years of maturing in the bottle. The finish of the aftertaste features dry poppy heads underlined by a rich tannin which the wine acquired during maturing in new barrique casks.

[900 l] • 0.75 l • €€€ • L 06 • 14.0 % vol. • ♦ • ① • 🛢 {26} • ⊶ • ★★★★★

Alibernet 2011
barrique, grape selection, dry

VPS - PAVELKA A SYN

Wine with protected indication of origin D.S.C.
VRoSC, Pezinok, hon Bajzle

The attractive, claret-violet shade of this wine features a full and concentrated smell of red currents and juniper with a distinctive trace of ground poppy seeds and dark chocolate. This is a full-bodied and complex wine whose bouquet is reminiscent of overripe forest strawberries. A long structured taste with charming tannins and poppy head and cocoa bean tones displays fine tones of chili pepper and black pepper on the edges of the tongue after swallowing.

[2,500 l] • 0.75 l • €€€ • L0112 • 13.0 % vol. • ♦ • ① • ◯ • 🛢 {12} • ⊶ •
★★★★★

ODESSA RED (ALIBERNET)

Alibernet 2011 Varieto
grape selection, dry   KARPATSKÁ PERLA

Wine with protected indication of origin
VRoSC, Šenkvice, Suchý vrch Vineyard

This dark ink wine was made by the cryomaceration of grapes and ennobled by maturing in French barrique-type barrels. Its massive smell of blackberry and blueberry marmalade combined with tones of sweet poppy-seed strudel is spiced up by a hint of fennel and the bark of pine trees from the Tatra Mountains. The full, smooth taste of this big wine with a long body leaves traces of dark chocolate, oak barrel, vanilla, exotic anise and caramelized cranberries.

[13,500 l] • 0.75 l • €€€ • L 3513 • 13.5 % vol. • 🍷 • ① • ❄ • 🍽 {18} • ◯ {18} •
🗔 • ★★★★★

Alibernet 2012
ice harvest, sweet   TERRA PARNA

VRoSC, Suchá nad Parnou, Trnavské vrchy Vineyard

The garnet-red and brown shade and the smell of sour cherries in chocolate complemented by rose hip oil and a bouquet of violets will create an unusual degustation experience. The grapes were harvested on December 13, 2015 when the air temperature was less than minus 9 °C. Its taste is reminiscent of kirsch with a delicious residual sugar (174 g/l). It has a gorgeous combination of plum-poppy purée with raisins in its finish.

[500 l] • 0.375 l • €€€ • L-10 • 9.0 % vol. • 🍷 • ④ • ◯ • 🗝 • ★★★★★

Alibernet 2013
ice wine, sweet   PIVNICA RADOŠINA

Quality varietal wine with attribute
Wine with protected indication of origin D.S.C.
VRoN, Radošina

The grapes were harvested on January 27, 2014 at an outside temperature of 9 °C, and after processing they provided brick-red nectar with brown hues and a smell of sweet tones of cranberries and plum marmalade with chocolate shavings and a pinch of Arabic coffee. The sweet taste is dominated by 252 grams of residual sugar and delicious acid. An excellent example of how Mother Nature allows for the processing of precious ice wine in a northern border area.

[150 l] • 0.35 l • €€€ • L 316 • 9.0 % vol. • 🍷 • ④ • ◯ • 🗝 • ★★★★1/2

Alibernet 2012
late harvest, dry   PIVNICA TIBAVA

Wine with protected indication of origin D.S.C.
VRoES, Tibava, Široká medza Vineyard

The dark, claret-violet color of this wine with tones of tint on the edges of the goblet renders it almost opaque. The fruity bouquet with a cabernet note is complemented by traces of mulberry, black currants and new wood. Its medium-full taste has the elegance of green poppy heads and gooseberries. The lively fruity finish of this wine with pleasant acids is of blackberries and bitter almonds.

[3,300 l] • 0.75 l • €€ • L-16/14 • 12.5 % vol. • 🍷 • ① • ◯ • 🗝 • ★★★★

ODESSA RED (ALIBERNET) • DUNAJ

Alibernet 2013
grape selection, dry

VPS – PAVELKA A SYN

Wine with protected indication of origin D.S.C.
VRoSC, Pezinok, Bajzle Vineyard

This wine has an intensive, violet-red color with a purple up to ink shade. The cranberry-current, marmalade-cassis aroma in the core features a fresh fruity maturing and suitably complements the distinctive and long taste with an admixture of blueberries and traces of coffee and dried plums. An elegant, maturing Alibernet with no irritating tannins and alcohol with a fruity character and an aftertaste of bitter sour cherries dipped in dark chocolate.

[2,500 l] • 0.75 l • € € • L0112 • 12.5 % vol. • ⓘ ⓞ • 35 % ▬ • ✎ • ★★★★

Alibernet 2012
ice wine, sweet

CHÂTEAU BELÁ

Quality varietal wine with attribute, D.S.C.
VRoSS, Štúrovo viticultural area, Mužla

This bright garnet red wine was made from grapes harvested and pressed on December 8, 2012. Its smell is reminiscent of canned blackberries and cranberries with traces of open cocoa beans, while its juicy taste with a distinctive redundancy of fruit acids and high natural sugar content (230 g/l) makes for an unusually rich taste experience. The long, citrus-raspberry sweet and bitter aftertaste completes the structured overall impression of this wine.

[200 l] • 0.50 l • € € € • L 11 • 7.0 % vol. • ⓘ ④ • ▭ • ⟿ • ★★★★

Dunaj 2012
grape selection, dry

ELESKO

Wine with protected indication of origin D.S.C.
VRoSC, Vištuk, Iveta Vineyard

A wine, dark ink in color with purple-red edges and higher viscosity. The distinctive bouquet of berries suggests a combination of cassis, juniper and plums complemented by traces of sweet spices, tobacco and dark chocolate acquired by maturing in barrique-type casks. The taste is long and extractive with higher alcohol content and is perfectly balanced by a pleasant tannin. The aftertaste of this wine will surprise you by tones of ripe sour cherries with a hint of cigarette smoke.

[22,500 l] • 0.75 l • € € € • L-35/12 • 14.5 % vol. • ⓘ ⓞ • ▬ {15} • ✎ •
★★★★★

Dunaj 2011
grape selection, dry

VINÁRSTVO BLAHO

Wine with protected indication of origin
VRoSC, Zeleneč, Pri Kríži Vineyard

A temperamental, dark violet-red wine with a rich smell of chassis and caramel and a hint of dried plums and raisins. Its distinctive bouquet does not end at the nose but continues in equally full tones of coffee, sour cherry, and gingerbread with a hint of tobacco smoke after swallowing. The extremely long and full aftertaste creates a honey-juniper impression with a delicious coca-vanilla finish. A reserve with great maturing potential.

[900 l] • 0.75 l • € € € • L-05 • 13.2 % vol. • ⓘ ⓞ • ▭ + ▬ {12} • ⟿ •
★★★★★

DUNAJ

Dunaj 2013
grape selection, medium dry   PIVNICA ORECHOVÁ

Wine with protected indication of origin D.S.C.
VRoES, Orechová, Sekerová Vineyard

This ink dark wine with scarlet shades on the edges has a higher viscosity. Its full concentrated smell presents tones of roasted coffee and cocoa beans enriched by notes of elderberry and juniper mesh. The taste is dominated by the high tannin content and warm traces of alcohol which are followed by traces of sweet plum marmalade with an admixture of poppy seeds and elderberry marmalade on the base of the tongue. A massive, well-balanced and rich wine.

[3,000 l] • 0.50 l • € € • L2013 • 13.0 % vol. • ⚲ • ② • ◯ + 🛢 • 🔪 •

★★★★★

Dunaj 2011
selection of berries, dry   VÍNO-MASARYK

Wine with protected indication of origin
VRoSS, Strekov

The dark crimson color of this wine and rich viscosity in the goblet with violet drops are heralds of an excellent vintage concentrate. The massively fruity smell of current compote and sour cherries with ground coffee beans is accompanied by a sweet and hot note of alcohol at the limit of 15.0 % vol. The taste from the high tannin content and fruit extract create the impression of fullness multiplied by tones of berries and dark chocolate.

[1,000 l] • 0.50 l • € € € • L 12 • 15.0 % vol. • ⚲ • ② • ◯ + 🛢 • ▭ • ★★★★1/2

Dunaj 2013
dry   ŽITAVSKÉ VINICE

Wine without geographical indication

An ink-violet variety with higher viscosity and a wonderful blackberry-chocolate smell against a background of violets followed by burnt wood after opening. The taste is naturally dominated by fullness since the manually picked grapes reached a sugar content of 27 °NM on harvest day. Noble coffee tannins, a higher alcohol content and a distinct trace of burnt wood correspond with the quality and processing of this vintage and finish off the aftertaste with a hot overall impression.

[500 l] • 0.75 l • € € € • L 12 • 14.5 % vol. • ⚲ • ① • 🛢 {8} • 🔪 • ★★★★1/2

Dunaj barrique 2011 Retro
grape selection, dry   CHÂTEAU TOPOĽČIANKY

Wine with protected indication of origin
VRoN, Topoľčianky, Dolné Vineyard

A dark ruby-red wine with purple hues and the smell of berries with a hint of vanilla husk. Its opulent taste corresponds with the intensity of its smell. It suggests tones of ripe stone fruit with dominating sour cherries in chocolate as the pleasant tannin closes down the aftertaste.

[2,000 l] • 0.75 l • € € € • L467 • 12.5 % vol. • ⚲ • ① • ② • 🛢 {6} • 🔪 •

★★★★

HRON • VÁH • RIMAVA • RUDAVA • ROSA

Cuvée Hron Váh Rimava Rudava 2011

Winemaker´s Cut, dry   VÍNO MRVA & STANKO

Quality branded wine, VRoSC, Dolné Orešany

This dark, ruby-red wine with scarlet hues will interest you by its rich spectrum of smells of elderberries, juniper and blueberries which slowly opens up in a spicy up to herbal-mineral note reminiscent of carnations, tobacco and graphite wrapped in a distinctive oak barrel trace. Its massive body holds the senses on "fire" thanks to the higher alcohol content, smooth tannins and brisk acid. The opulently long aftertaste features the refrains of cognac tones accompanied by juniper and dark chocolate.

[300 l] • 0.75 l • € € € • L-46 • 14.0 % vol. • 🍷 • ① • 🛢 {20} • ⊶ •
★★★★★

Hron 2012

quality wine, dry   VINÁRSTVO BLAHO

Wine with protected indication of origin
VRoSC, Zeleneč, Pri Kríži Vineyard

This wine features an intensive scarlet color and an impressive aroma of dark berries with a piquant note of tobacco, cloves, tar and coco pulp. The rich, fiery, slowly maturing taste with a warming alcohol content embodies the harmony of individual components. The aftertaste has a more distinctive concentration of tannins and includes recognizable tones of dark chocolate, nettle, bitter almond and a fine admixture of white pepper.

[1,500 l] • 0.75 l • € € • L-06 • 14.0 % vol. • 🍷 • ① • ◎ • 🛢 {16} • ⊶ • ★★★★★

Rudava 2012

quality wine, dry   VINÁRSTVO BLAHO

Wine with protected indication of origin
VRoSC, Zeleneč, Pri Kríži Vineyard

A scarlet wine full of aromas of forest berries which show tones of raspberries and blueberries complemented by licorice in the background. The juicy medium-long taste is the same in its character and intensity as the smell. The harmonious tones of cranberries and sour cherries are uniquely complemented by a bouquet of poppy heads and freshly baked bread crust.

[1,000 l] • 0.75 l • € € • L-11 • 13.5 % vol. • 🍷 • ① • ◎ • 🛢 {16} • ✦ • ★★★★1/2

Rosa 2012

selection of berries, medium sweet   ELESKO

Wine with protected indication of origin D.S.C.
VRoSC, Vištuk, Mária Vineyard

This intensive, crimson-claret wine with violet shades has a higher glycerol content which can be seen on the walls of the goblet by its higher viscosity. The perfumed smell of mulberries, cranberries and sweet plums competes with attractive tones of rose and viola petals, while its full, rich, fruity taste with a higher sweet tannin content is well balanced with its smell. The aftertaste features tones of cinnamon, plum pie and roasted chestnuts.

[7,125 l] • 0.75 l • € € € • L-23/12 • 13.5 % vol. • 🍷 • ③ • ◯ • ✦ • ★★★★1/2

ROSÉ WINES

Cabernet Sauvignon Rosé 2013
dry VÍNO MRVA & STANKO
Quality wine
VRoN, Vinodol

A salmon-pink wine with a tender butter pear smell featuring juicy tones of red currents, tea rose and forest raspberries. The taste, which is in harmony with the smell, combines fresh citrus fruit with forest strawberries which is emphasized by a nettle and grapefruit aftertaste. This rosé with its pleasant, fruity structure and distinctive juicy note of acids is reaching the culmination of its esprit.

[120 l] • 0.75 l • €€ • L-04 • 12.5 % vol. • ♀ • ① • ◯ • ▮ • ★★★★

Cabernet Sauvignon 2013 Prestige
late harvest, dry VÍNO MATYŠÁK
Wine with protected indication of origin
VR of Southern Slovakia, Búč, Vinohrady Vineyard

This attractive, garnet-red and pink wine has a crystal clear and intoxicating aroma of candied red fruit with a predominance of garden strawberries and sweet sour cherries. The marmalade notes of berries also appear in the taste. Its fruity structure is emphasized by a fresh acid and is adequately rounded by residual sugar. The finishing impression belongs to red currents in white chocolate. A rosé in bloom, do not leave it in the bottle unnoticed.

[10,000 l] • 0.75 l • €€ • L09 • 12.5 % vol. • ◡ • ♀ • ①-② • ◯ • ▮ • ★★★★

ROSÉ Cuvée 2014
late harvest, dry VPS – PAVELKA A SYN
Wine with protected indication of origin D.S.C.
VRoSC, Pezinok

The garnet-pink color and the smell of red garden fruit with tones of May cherries, raspberries and strawberry marmalade create a pleasant impression. The fruity taste of this wine with adequate acid content is well balanced with its smell. It leaves a trace of juicy citrus peels with a note of pink grapefruit on the palate. A pleasantly drinkable wine with refreshingly a pure finish and lively reductive trace.

CS, BF • [6,500 l] • 0.75 l • €€ • L-0114 • 12.0 % vol. • ♀ • ① • ◯ • ▮ • ★★★★

ROSÉ WINES

Cabernet Sauvignon rosé 2014

late harvest, dry   MARTIN POMFY - MAVÍN

Wine with protected indication of origin
VRoSS, Jasová

This wine with a more marked raspberry-red shade, along with its smell of overripe garden strawberries and raspberries, will please fans of fruity rosé wines. In comparison, the taste is appropriate, light and smooth with a juicy acid and fine residual sugar. The aftertaste features traces of red and white currants and tender undertones of cherry marmalade with pieces of macerated lemon peels.

[5,250 l] • 0.75 l • € € • L9 • 12.0 % vol. • ① - ② • ★★★1/2

TERROIR-RESPECTING WINES

Chardonnay 2012
Winemaker´s Cut, grape selection, dry   VÍNO MRVA & STANKO
Quality wine with attribute
VRoSC, Čachtice

This attractive, bright yellow and green wine has a rich smell of butter toast with a hint of dried tropical fruit markedly complemented by traces of vanilla, roasted hazelnuts and wood. The full, intensive mineral taste features a complex of fresh acids and extract and its full aftertaste is emphasized by tones of oak wood and beeswax. The promising development of the bottle bouquet adds notes of dried meadow flowers and cedar wood with pieces of walnuts to the background.

[800 l] • 0.75 l • €€€ • L-27 • 13.0 % vol. • 🍷 • ① • ◯ • 🛢 • ✦ • ★★★★★

Rizling rýnsky 2013
Terroir Rača, quality varietal wine, medium sweet   MILOŠ MÁŤUŠ
Wine with protected indication of origin
VRoSC, Bratislava – Rača

This crystal clear Rhein Riesling, golden-yellow in color with viscosity on the edges, has a rich, lively smell of linden blossoms, citrus and apricot pie with honey. Its medium-sweet concentrated taste with a medium-long body is dominated by wonderful tones of juicy grapefruits flavored by linden tea which after swallowing gain an herbal and even mothball undertone. The taste of rose petals dipped in lime juice with a slightly spicy finish is extremely inviting.

[1,350 l] • 0.75 l • €€€ • L-16/014 • 11.5 % vol. • 🍷 • ◯ • ③ • ◯ {14} • ✦ • ★★★★★

Frankovka modrá 2012
Unplugged, quality wine, dry   RODINNÉ VINÁRSTVO MAGULA
Wine with protected indication of origin
VRoSC, Orešany viticultural area, Suchá nad Parnou

This wine has an attractive, bright, ruby-red shade with a hint of purple on the edges. The extract of overripe raisins harvested only after the first frost leaves traces of rose hip marmalade, mulberry and fig chutney in the smell. The spicy, ethereal, sweet and extremely attractive concentration of taste underwent a procedure worthy of royalty (pressing by bare feet, maceration and fermentation in an open tank by spontaneous microflora, etc.).

[190 l] • 0.75 l • €€€ • L 0126 • 13.5 % vol. • 🍷 • ① - ② • 🌀 {1,5} • ◯ {15} • 🛢 {26} • ↓SO₂ • ▭ • ★★★★★

TERROIR-RESPECTING WINES

Rizling rýnsky 2012
Winemaker´s Cut, grape selection, dry   VÍNO MRVA & STANKO
Quality wine with attribute
VRoSC, Dolné Orešany

A pretty, yellow and green Rhein Riesling with full golden hues; the distinctive smell of quince, overripe raisins and lemon grass is complemented by mineral tones of wet soil with a balsamic trace of eucalyptus. The taste is full and structured with an elegant and rich body and a long honey aftertaste. It features notes of citrus fruit and butter brioche, while its piquantly fresh finish features the presence of gooseberries and dried pome fruit thanks to maturing on fine lees. This vintage has the potential for further maturing.

[2,000 l] • 0.75 l • € € € • L-18 • 13.0 % vol. • 🍷 • ① • ⌒ • 🖌 • ★★★★★

Cabernet Franc 2011
Oak Wood, quality wine, dry   VÍNO MATYŠÁK
Wine with protected indication of origin
VRoSS, Rúbaň, Nový vrch Vineyard

A dark, claret-red wine with garnet-brick-red shades. Its full fruity aroma is dominated by an intensive note of cassis leaves. Thanks to longer maturing in oak casks, it has a noble smell of wood. The marmalade taste sensation is supported by a sweet tannin and an excellent development of bottle maturity. Traces of spices, tobacco, candied cherries and plums in dark chocolate develop in the finish. A unique Cabernet Franc from an excellent terroir.

[7,950 l] • 0.75 l • € € € € • L 89 • 14.5 % vol. • 🍷 • ① • 🛢 {30} • 🖌 •
★★★★★

Silvánske zelené 2013
quality varietal wine, dry   FEDOR MALÍK & SYN.
Wine with protected indication of origin D.S.C.
VRoSC, Modra, Téglik Vineyard

This Grüner Silvaner with a pale green sparkle has a straw-yellow complexion around the edges. After contact with the goblet wall, it leaves sticky traces of glycerol whose drops do not want to slide down. This is a generous, playful, piquantly vivid mineral wine of medium-full intensity with a white pepper, gooseberry skin and fresh basil bouquet. It leaves traces of pomelo with green tomato pulp on the base of the tongue.

[500 l] • 0.75 l • € € • L-98/0514 • 13.0 % vol. • 🍷 • ① • ⌒ {6} • ⌒ • 🖌 •
★★★★★

Pinot Gris 44 2012
sweet   ŽITAVSKÉ VINICE
Wine without geographical indication

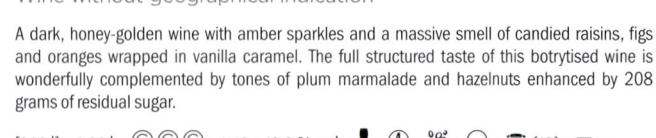

A dark, honey-golden wine with amber sparkles and a massive smell of candied raisins, figs and oranges wrapped in vanilla caramel. The full structured taste of this botrytised wine is wonderfully complemented by tones of plum marmalade and hazelnuts enhanced by 208 grams of residual sugar.

[200 l] • 0.20 l • € € € • L 12 • 12.0 % vol. • 🍷 • ④ • 🍇 • ⌒ • 🛢 {12} • •
★★★★★

TERROIR-RESPECTING WINES

Aurelius 2013

Dílemúre, raisin selection, sweet — KARPATSKÁ PERLA

Wine with protected indication of origin
VRoSC, Šenkvice, Suchý vrch Vineyard

Amber-golden in color with a bouquet of blooming apricots and pears up to grapefruit in the goblet. The selection of nobly rotten raisins of this rare new clone will please you with its proper dose of acacia honey. The rich extract of taste is enhanced by its juicy, fruit acids and high residual sugar content. The aftertaste confirms the non-traditional fusion of pineapple and linden tones with pieces of orange peel. Its pleasant, sweet taste is reminiscent of acacia honey.

[2,000 l] • 0.50 l • € € € • L 1513 • 10.0 % vol. • 🍷 • ④ • 🍇 • 🛢 • ⬭ • 🖌
★★★★1/2

Radošinský Klevner 2013

Terroir, late harvest, medium dry — PIVNICA RADOŠINA

Wine with protected indication of origin D.S.C.
VRoN, Radošina

A straw-yellow wine with golden hues. Its delicious, impressively fruity-spicy smell evokes the aroma of ripe pomelo with cloves on butter brioche baked with vanilla sugar. The dry and delicate taste is ennobled by contact with autochthonous yeasts and half a year of fermentation in barrique casks. It has an interesting herbal honey note and bread-like character with pieces of butter pear and the tender trace of wooden barrel in the aftertaste.

PG, PB • [1,000 l] • 0.75 l • € € € • L 314 • 12.0 % vol. • 🍷 • ② • ⬭ • {3} • 🛢 • {6} •
🖌 • ★★★★1/2

Interval100 2012

medium sweet — SLOBODNÉ VINÁRSTVO

Wine without geographical indication
VRoSC, Zemianske sady

This wine is dark golden up to amber with tender sparkles after opening and smells of overripe raisins, pistachios and dried apricots. It creates a great impression due to the excellent balance of 15 g of residual sugar and acids. The bouquet that develops after swallowing opens herbal notes of meadow flowers, honey comb and paraffin. A nicely maturing Rhein Riesling that is approaching its culmination.

RR • [400 l] • 0.75 l • € € € • L41 • 12.5 % vol. • 🍷 • ③ • 🌀 • 🛢 {18} • 🖌 •
★★★★1/2

Hankove Special Collection 2012

grape selection, medium dry — J. & J. OSTROŽOVIČ

Wine without geographical indication
Wine from Slovakia

The light golden shade of this wine with straw-yellow sparkles and the honey-raisin smell with tones of dried bananas, raisins and star anise creates a unique impression in combination with the round mineral taste. Old Furmint and Lipovina plants from the 1947 planting drew a rich concentrate of minerals from the depths of the tuff bedrock of the Makovisko vineyard and gave unique potential to the taste of this wine. Its piquant finish featuring pieces of fresh pulp of overripe pears is irreplaceable.

F, L • [4,000 l] • 0.75 l • € € • L3 • 12.5 % vol. • 🍷 • ② • 🛢 {7} • 🖌 • ★★★★

TERROIR-RESPECTING WINES

Frankovka modrá 2013
Classic, quality varietal wine, dry STREKOV 1075
Wine with protected designation of origin
VRoSS, Strekov, Údolie Márie Vineyard

This wine from an ecological vineyard with yields of 0.7 kg per plant has a dark, ruby-red color. The spicy bouquet and mineral taste which also features fresh acid are affected by the alcohol and firm tannin. Its temperament was not tamed even by "treatment" in wooden casks. It leaves traces of peat, black raspberries and plums cooked in cooper pot on the palate.

[800 l] • 0.75 l • € € € • L7-1 • 13.5 % vol. • ♀ • ① • ◉ • 🛢 {13} • ↓SO₂ • 🔌 •
★★★★

MONO Furmint 2014
quality varietal wine, dry TOKAJ MACIK WINERY
Wine with protected indication of origin
VRoT

Straw-yellow with golden hues. The full, spicy smell of this wine with tones of pome fruits and citrus is emphasized by the piquant taste of mineral acids and full extract. After opening, the goblet reveals a bouquet of mowed meadow with pieces of lime and grapefruit. It leaves a trace of mint leaves and white currents on the root of the tongue. A fresh wine with a personality and potential for maturing, it will speak to advanced fans of more complex and dry wines.

[5,000 l] • 0.75 l • € € • L 25/15 • 14.0 % vol. • ♀ • ① • ◯ • {6} • ◯ • 🔌 • ★★★★

Dunaj 2012
Selection II, quality varietal wine, medium dry STREKOV 1075
Wine with protected designation of origin
VRoSS, Strekov

A robust wine of intensive and ink-ruby-red color with dark purple sparkles and nice viscosity. The aroma will astonish you by its concentrate of balsamic tones of Cyprus and eucalyptus with assistance from the high concentration of alcohol. Its primary and secondary aromas feature small berries accompanied by sour cherries in chocolate. The long, hot taste of plum marmalade with cocoa leaves a distinctive overall impression on the root of the tongue.

[1,800 l] • 0.75 l • € € € € • L1-2 • 16.7 % o • ♀ • ② • ◉ • 🛢 {9} • 🔌 •
★★★★

Cabernet Sauvignon 2011
quality wine, dry PIVNICA CSERNUS
VRoCS, Vinica

The intensive claret-red shade and rich smell of forest fruits, black currants and cranberries with undertones of wood will please lovers of robust cabernets. Its full tannin taste carries traces of juniper, tobacco and dark chocolate. It is underlined by lively acids and in connection with a higher alcohol content, it leaves a deep up to complex impression in the mouth. Spicy tones appear only at the end of tasting. A vintage with maturing potential.

[105 l] • 0.75 l • 12.00 EUR • L-13 • 13.5 % vol. • ♀ • ① • ◉ • 🛢 {20} + 🛢 {3} • 🔌 •
★★★★

TERROIR-RESPECTING WINES

Červený Klevner 2012

Terroir, late harvest, dry   PIVNICA RADOŠINA

Quality branded wine with attribute
Wine with protected indication of origin D.S.C.
VRoN, Radošina

This claret-red cuvée is a mixture of Pinot Noir and Dunaj varieties and has the smell of stone fruit and black raspberries. The spicy undertone of the clove aroma shows wood traces, while its full structured taste leaves a hint of cranberry mash on the tongue and a fine vanilla and chocolate trace in the finish.

PN, DU • [1,500 l] • 0.75 l • €€ • L 219 • 13.0 % vol. • 🍷 • ① • 🛢 • 🔪 • ★★★★

Rizling vlašský 2013

dry   TIBOR MELECSKY

Wine without geographical indication
VRoSS, Strekov

The orange-yellow color and the fine opalescence in this Italian Riesling are the first signs of the oxidative processing of unfiltered grape wine. The return to traditional production methods with limited use of sulfites also had an impact on the smell, which is tea-herbal and slightly balsamic with a pleasantly earthy background. Spontaneous microflora and slow maturing in acacia barrels created an interesting mixture of bread, dried apples and exotic spices in the aftertaste.

[225 l] • 0.75 l • €€€ • L 3 • 12.0 % vol. • 🍷 • ① • ◯ • {3} • 🛢 • ↓SO_2 • ⎯ •
★★★ 1/2

INNOVATIVE WINES
(BARRIQUE / CRYO / SUR LIE)

Frankovka modrá 2012
Varieto, grape selection, dry   KARPATSKÁ PERLA

Wine with protected indication of origin
VRoSC

This opulent Lemberger (Blaufränkisch) is claret-red and bears a cultivated smell of dark berries reminiscent of the pulp of plums, and cherries with a herbal note of tobacco leaves in the background. The velvet taste reveals the sensible harmony of mature tannins and fruit acid. It is made of a reduced harvest after cryomaceration and maturing in American, French and Slovak barrels and leaves a distinctive trace of bitter almonds and dark cherries with a spicy-oak finish.

[12,500 l] • 0.75 l • € € • L 2913 • 13.0 % vol. • 🍷 • ① • ❄ • 🛢 + 🛢 {8} • ✒ •
★★★★★

Cabernet Sauvignon Barrique 2011
grape selection, dry   CHÂTEAU BELÁ

Quality varietal wine with attribute, D.S.C.
VRoSS, Štúrovo viticultural area, Mužla

An intensive violet-red wine with a rich spectrum of aromas of cassis and blackberries. The high alcohol concentration does not cause a burning sensation after opening in the goblet; on the contrary, the impression is sweet and fiery. The wine's rich and firm taste is affected by the massive extract which leaves a full, fruity-balsamic impression in the mouth. The aftertaste features a mixture of smoke, green coffee beans and baked dark chocolate. It is worth longer maturing in the bottle.

[2,000 l] • 0.75 l • € € € • L 15 • 14.5 % vol. • 🍷 • ① • 🛢 {12} • ✒ • ★★★★★

Frankovka modrá 2012
Winemaker´s Cut, grape selection, dry   VÍNO MRVA & STANKO

Quality wine with attribute
VRoN, Drženice

A dark, claret-red Lemberger (Blaufränkisch) in the goblet with an attractive viscous necklace of glycerol on the surface and a rich smell of baked stone fruits, cinnamon and a pinch of cayenne spice. The broad aromatic profile of this wine with long persistence is multiplied by sour cherry and macadamia nut tones thanks to the maceration of the mash, while the aftertaste features tannins wrapped in a crust of freshly baked bread sprinkled with ground Arabic coffee beans and black pepper.

[2,400 l] • 0.75 l • € € € • L-32 • 13.5 % vol. • 🍷 • ① • 🛢 {12} • ✒ • ★★★★1/2

INNOVATIVE WINES (BARRIQUE / CRYO / SUR LIE)

Portito Rosso

4 years old, sweet   VÍNO MATYŠÁK

Liquor wine
VRoSC

A massive, fortified, dark garnet-red wine with a lively brick-red and mahogany sparkle. The distinctive smell of ginger bread spices and anise show tones of candied cherries, plums and chocolate. The quality wooden casks and the slow micro oxidation process have left a distinctive trace in the aromatic profile of this wine. Its sweet taste opens up by a fiery note of alcohol and a nice caramelized basket of roasted chestnuts and dried raisins in chocolate.

OR, BF • [7,000 l] • 0.50 l • €€ • L 67 • 19.0 % vol. • 🍷 • ④ • 🛢 • {48} • ⌐ •
★★★★1/2

BOTRIS Late Harvest 2013

quality branded wine, sweet   TOKAJ MACIK WINERY

Wine with protected indication of origin
VRoT, Malá Tŕňa, Podcestie Vineyard

This attractive, full yellow wine with golden hues has the smell of candied fruit with tones of overripe raisins and honey pear, which is intensive and spicy at the same time. Volcanic soil has a distinctive impact on the taste of this vintage and gives this wine a fresh fruity and mineral character. Its long maturing is supported by an extract of overripe nobly rotten raisins and a more piquant acid. A stylish, nobly rotten raisin Tokaj wine in modern reductive style.

F 50 %, L 50 % • [5,000 l] • 0.50 l • €€€ • L 23/15 • 12.5 % vol. • 🍷 • ④ • 🍇 • ◎
• ○ • ⌐ • ★★★★1/2

Merlot 2009

Oak Wood, dry   VÍNO MATYŠÁK

Wine with protected indication of origin D.S.C.
VRoSS, Mužla

This wine's lively, brick-red color combined with an elegant aroma of overripe forest fruit and smooth, full taste reveals meticulous enological processing and noble development in bottles. The well balanced harmony of smell and taste indicates that this vintage is culminating. Its elegant sweet bouquet shows tones of blackberries and rose hip marmalade, while the taste is affected by traces of small raspberries mixed with a sweet matured tannin.

[10,000 l] • 0.75 l • €€ • L 45 • 14.0 % vol. • 🍷 • ① • 🛢 + 🛢 • {18} • ⚔ •
★★★★1/2

Pinot Noir – Blanc 2012

late harvest, dry   REPA WINERY

Wine with protected indication of origin D.S.C.
VRoSS, Dvory nad Žitavou, Viničný vrch Vineyard

This wine is orange up to amber in color and has a fuller, fruity bouquet of forest strawberries with a note of Mediterranean figs, and a taste featuring piquant citrus peels of pink pomelo and green limes. Its wider aromatic spectrum and fresh fruity aftertaste provides genuine refreshment due to its delicious aftertaste and nice equilibrium of acids and noble fruit tannins.

PN • [2,000 l] • 0.75 l • €€ • L06 • 13.0 % vol. • 🍷 • ① • ◐ • ○ • ⚔ •
★★★★1/2

INNOVATIVE WINES (BARRIQUE / CRYO / SUR LIE)

Pinot Noir – Blanc 2012
Oaked, late harvest, dry REPA WINERY

Wine with protected indication of origin D.S.C.
VRoSC, Doľany

A yellow-green wine with golden hues and the intensive aroma of overripe tropical fruit with a full balsamic note of vanilla and coconut. Its robust full taste with a firm body and higher extract attracts by its empyreumatic tones of butter toast and licorice. The fresh aftertaste features a fuller fruit acid tone supported by a note of dried pears and mountain flowers.

PB • [1,300 l] • 0.75 l • €€€ • L11 • 12.5 % vol. • ▯ • ① • ◎ • ⌣ • ⬛ {4} • ⚏ •
★★★★1/2

Heion 2013
Special, dry STREKOV 1075

Wine without geographical indication
VRoSS, Strekov, Kalvária Vineyard

An orange wine fermented on skins in an open tank for 15 days and maturing for 9 months in old casks, unfiltered, unclarified, bottled with the use of gravitation, will raise your interest by its fruity-balsamic smell with tones of dried raisins, apples, apricots and meadow grasses with an undertone of wood and hazelnut. Its full structured taste is in balance with the smell. This wine with proper acid content, fermented to total dryness will leave an impressive complex of sensations on the palate.

IR • [450 l] • 0.75 l • €€€ • L-4-1 • 12.5 % vol. • ▯ • ① • ⌣ • ⬛ {9} • ↓SO₂ • ✦ •
★★★★1/2

Petit Merlau 2013
quality branded wine, dry VINÁRSTVO BERTA

Wine with protected indication of origin
VRoSS, Pribeta

This crystal clear wine has an elegant ruby shade, with an obviously higher glycerol content. The note of stone fruit blends with a hint of gingerbread spices in its smell. The pure taste is medium full with a distinctive tone of black sour cherries and abundant tannins. The aftertaste is enhanced by aromas of juicy grape skins after cryomaceration which emphasizes the overall piquant profile of the wine with a fine spicy note at the finish.

ME • [1,000 l] • 0.75 l • €€ • L28 • 12.7 % vol. • ▯ • ① • ❄ • ⬛ {2} • ✦ •
★★★★

Chardonnay 2013
Slovak regional wine, dry GEORGINA – RODINNÉ VINÁRSTVO

Wine with protected indication of origin
VRoSS, Strekov

The brilliantly clear golden color of this wine will catch your interest by its intensive, honey-fruity smell of peaches and hazelnuts with a pinch of vanilla. Thanks to the use of the sur lie method, the rich, distinctive alcohol taste is firmly wrapped in tones of butter brioche with an aftertaste of roasted almonds and bits of refreshing yellow melon in the background. Those who are patient will be rewarded with the opportunity to discover its new and heretofore undescribed qualities.

[600 l] • 0.75 l • €€ • L-5 • 14.0 % vol. • ▯ • ① - ② • ⌣ • ⬛ {12} • ✦ • ★★★★

INNOVATIVE WINES (BARRIQUE / CRYO / SUR LIE)

BLANC FIZZ 2014

sparkling wine, medium dry   TOKAJ MACIK WINERY

Slovak Wine
VRoT

The golden and decently refreshing and fine sparkling of this wine will immediately catch your attention, and the smell of linden tree blossoms and sweet apricot pulp is charming. Its light fruity taste with tones of yellow melon and mango is well balanced in this 2014 vintage, and along with 10 grams of residual sugar, it rounds out the body of this elegant sparkling wine. The aftertaste features the pulp of pink grapefruit and lilies of the valley.

L • [5,000 l] • 0.75 l • €€ • L 20/15 • 12.5 % vol. • ♀ • ❋ • ② • ◯ • ♀ • ★★★1/2

CUVÉE / BLENDS

Camerlon 2011
Oak Wood, quality wine, red, dry   VÍNO MATYŠÁK

Wine with protected indication of origin
VRoSS

This darker purple red wine with garnet-red shades on the edges has a noble aroma of forest fruit, berries and black pepper cunningly covered by toast with plum marmalade. The full, mature taste is in harmony with the smell and features a rich mixture of sweet tannins, grape extract, and a spicy hot trace of alcohol. It leaves an aftertaste of oak wood, coffee biscuits and chocolate muffins with cassis.

CS, ME, CF • [7,000 l] • 0.75 l • €€ • L 92 • 13.5 % vol. • ♆ • ① • ▦ • ✦ •
★★★★★

4 ŽIVLY 2009
late harvest, red, dry   KARPATSKÁ PERLA

Wine with protected indication of origin
VRoSC, Šenkvice, Suchý vrch Vineyard

The lively claret-crimson color and fine viscosity will immediately catch your attention. This FOUR ELEMENTS cuvee made of four varieties of an excellent vintage from one vineyard will impress you with its full, fiery smell and taste which combines special features. The massive aromatic profile is a reflection of the mastery of its creators. We can find baked plums, overripe cherries, mulberries and the ash of noble wood and myrrh here. The rich long taste is impressively balanced with the smell.

PN, OR, AN, CS • [6,000 l] • 0.75 l • €€ • L 5913 • 13.0 % vol. • ♆ • ① • ◯ {1} •
▦ {24} • ✦ • ★★★★★

Veterlín 2011
quality branded wine, red, dry   ELESKO

Wine with protected indication of origin D.S.C.
VRoSC, Vištuk, Zoya and Iveta Vineyard

The intensive, dark ink color of this wine has violet edges with dense viscosity. Its deep balsamic smell is dominated by tones of eucalyptus, cypress and vanilla, while the massive bouquet is complemented by fruit marmalade made of cassis and plums, which after opening changes to caramel and cocoa. Maturing in barrique casks supported the smoothness and equilibrium of the rich taste which is in perfect balance with the smell and completed by long persistence.

DU, OR, ME • [3,000 l] • 0.75 l • €€€ • L-33/11 • 13.5 % vol. • ♆ • ① • ◉ •
▦ {13-15} • ⚒ • ★★★★★

CUVÉE / BLENDS

Tokaj cuvée Saturnia 2011
straw wine, sweet J. & J. OSTROŽOVIČ

Wine with protected indication of origin
VRoT, Malá Tŕňa, Makovisko Vineyard, Chotár Vineyard

An elegant golden wine with olive-yellow hues whose viscosity (density) will attract immediate attention. The honey-fruity up to floral smell is reminiscent of a concentrate of dried raisins, apricots and tropical fruit marmalade. The secret of the aromas fully develops side by side with the taste which explodes thanks to its multilayer structure in which the rich residual sugar (168 g/l), minerals and organic acids meet.

F, L, YM • [1,500 l] • 0.375 l • € € € • L21 • 9.5 % vol. • 🍷 • ④ • ☞ •
★★★★★

PAVES CUVÉE 2012
quality branded wine, red, dry VPS – PAVELKA A SYN

Slovak Wine D.S.C.
VRoSC, Pezinok

The unique smell of candied berries with a fresh note of juniper, plums and cherries in dark bitter chocolate. The aroma of this blend reaches a sweetish profile of burnt oak wood with massive equilibrium of the extract and more matured tannins, which leave a bitter feeling of dryness on the tongue after swallowing. The aftertaste of this wine brings together distinctive perceptions of wood, smoke, green pepper and coffee with a pinch of cinnamon and vanilla.

CS, BF, NE • [4,000 l] • 0.75 l • € € € • L500 • 13.0 % vol. • 🍷 • ① • ◐ • ▦ {12} •
☞ • ★★★★★

4 ŽIVLY 2013
late harvest, white, dry KARPATSKÁ PERLA

Wine with protected indication of origin
VRoSC, Šenkvice, Suchý vrch Vineyard

This straw-yellow Cuvée of FOUR ELEMENTS with nice golden hints and oily edges will catch your attention by its distinctive fruity-balsamic smell of dried exotic fruits, vanilla and an impressive herbal note of meadow herbs and small flowers. The long taste is well balanced with the smell of the wine in its intensity with tones of candied citrus, grapefruit and limes. The spicy finish of the fresh aftertaste shows traces of cloves and coriander.

PG, GV, RR, AU • [3,000 l] • 0.75 l • € € € • LB 1913 • 13.0 % vol. • 🍷 • ① – ② • ◯
• 🛢 • ▦ • ◯ • ☞ • ★★★★1/2

Móže byt 2012
quality branded wine, red, dry VÍNO MIROSLAV DUDO

Wine with protected indication of origin
VRoSC, Modra

A purple-red wine with higher viscosity in the goblet and a sweet smell of stone fruit and oak cask in a pleasant extraction will create a positive first impression. The taste is consistent, long nature and woody up to mildly balsamic on the root of tongue. The fruit acids harmonize with the slightly piquant tannin content. The finish of this wine allows the development of a spicy note of tannins reminiscent of May cherries, anise with coffee and licorice.

SL, ZW, CS • [2,000 l] • 0.75 l • € € • L106 • 12.0 % vol. • 🍷 • ① • ▦ {9} • ✒ •
★★★★1/2

CUVÉE / BLENDS

Enem 2014
quality branded wine, red, dry   VÍNO-MASARYK

Wine with protected indication of origin, VRoSS

This dark claret-red wine has a full, fruity smell with tones of cranberries, cassis and dark chocolate. Its distinctive medium-long taste with a smooth balance of alcohol and spicy tannins makes an impressive and more mature impression. The taste bears traces of black raspberries and mulberry. Live acids multiply the profile of the unique blend of Alibernet, C40 and Cabernet Franc varieties. This new clone with the working name C40 was bred by Prof. Vilém Kraus in Moravia from the following varieties (Malinger x Chasselas Blank x Corint Rosa) x Alibernet.

OR, C40, CF • [4,000 l] • 0.75 l • €€ • L 20 • 12.5 % vol. • ① • ○ • ▢ •
• ★★★★1/2

Rizling cuvée 2012
quality wine, white, dry   REPA WINERY

Wine with protected indication of origin D.S.C. VRoSC, Dubová and Pezinok

A light yellow and green Riesling blend with a fresh fruity smell that is reminiscent of ripening summer apples with pieces of hazelnuts and a tender linden blossom admixture. Its medium-full up to full mineral taste is well balanced by tones of citrus fruit underlined by light notes of honeycomb with a harmonious residual sugar and pleasant acid content. After fermentation, this wine matures on fine lees in a stainless steel tank without filtration for 6 months.

RR, IR • [2,815 l] • 0.75 l • €€ • L08 • 12.5 % vol. • ① • ○ • {6} • ▢ •
★★★★1/2

Naše cuvée zo starých viníc 2013
quality branded wine, white, dry   VINO MIROSLAV DUDO

Wine with protected indication of origin VRoSC, Modra

This sparkly golden-yellow wine with a spicy, honey-fruity smell is ennobled by delicate tones of older wooden casks. Its piquant taste is more robust in comparison with its smell. It contains well-balanced fruit acids with a slightly balsamic finish. The longer contact of the young wine on clean fine lees did wonders for its rich structure. The expressive herbal aroma of this wine in the aftertaste is supported by a fresh bouquet, thanks to which it will mature nicely in bottles.

FA, PB, GS, FR, FRV • [3,300 l] • 0.75 l • €€ • L182 • 12.0 % vol. • ① • ○ • ▢ •
• ★★★★1/2

PAVES CUVÉE 2011
quality branded wine, white, dry   VPS – PAVELKA A SYN

Slovak Wine D.S.C. VRoSC, Pezinok

This wine has an intensive shade of 24-carate gold with amber hues. Its oily viscosity and brilliant clarity promise a rich taste experience. The firm structure of vanilla and fruity impulses of the massive aroma are accompanied by tones of dried exotic fruit with a distinctive effect of wood in barrique casks which is balanced by the high extract and a distinctive fresh acid. A long-structured wine with a citrus aftertaste and a note of apricot brioche dripped in linden honey.

CH, RR, MT • [1,000 l] • 0.75 l • €€€ • L18 • 12.5 % vol. • ① • ○ • {1} • ▣ • {12}
• ★★★★1/2

CUVÉE / BLENDS

Super Granum 2013
quality varietal wine, white, dry   BOTT FRIGYES
Wine with protected indication of origin
VRoSS, Mužla

Golden-yellow with amber hues, this wine's fruity-floral up to herbal bouquet combines notes of orange peels, acacia flowers, oak wood, green tea and cinnamon. Its taste features a higher alcohol content and herbal tones supported by a sufficient amount of acids and tannins from a wooden barrel. The maturing of this vintage in bottles will bring harmony and support the creation of a honey-spicy bouquet.

J, F, L • [1,500 l] • 0.75 l • €€€ • L15/08 • 13.5 % vol. • ★★★★

Rizling vlašský Tramín 2014
white, dry   TAJNA VINEYARDS AND WINERY
Wine with protected indication of origin
VRoN, Tajná

A light yellow-green Italian Riesling Traminer that is crystal clear. It will please you with its lively, fruity up to honey-spicy bouquet and firm juicy taste with hazelnut tones in a basket of freshly picked apples. The piquant fruity aftertaste reveals tender elderberry up to Muscat notes with a pinch of white pepper. This blend of 80 % Italian Riesling and 20 % Gewürztraminer was given the name Cuvée Tajna to emphasize the origin of these traditional varieties from the place of their birth in the vineyard above the village of Tajná.

IR, T • [2,130 l] • 0.75 l • €€€ • L-02 • 13.0 % vol. • ★★★★

TOKAJ GRAND Macik cuvée 2013
grape selection, white, medium sweet   TOKAJ MACIK WINERY
Wine with protected indication of origin
VRoT, Malá Tŕňa, Podcestie Vineyard

This wine bears the smell of butter pear and quince marmalade with tones of meadow honey and exotic fruit. The light yellow and green shade with a hue of the setting sun and the rich aftertaste of yellow melon with pieces of ripening peaches create an extremely pleasant experience. The multilayered structure of the blend is nicely complemented by forty grams of natural sugar which is in balance with the wine extract and acid.

L 60 %, F 40 % • [6,000 l] • 0.75 l • €€ • L22/15 • 12.5 % vol. • ★★★★

Cuvée Cabernet 2012
quality wine, red, dry   GEORGINA – RODINNÉ VINÁRSTVO
Wine with protected indication of origin
VRoSS, Strekov

The high level of ripeness of the grapes and their maturing in oak casks reflect the firm rustic structure of this rich red wine. Dark ink in color, the concentrated smell of juniper, chocolate and cassis is enhanced by a higher alcohol content. The non-filtered medium leaves a bittersweet feeling of fullness with tones of blueberries, burnt wood and coffee.

CS, OR • [600 l] • 0.75 l • €€€ • L-1 • 14.5 % vol. • {18} • ★★★★

CUVÉE / BLENDS

Pinoter 2013
white, dry
SLOBODNÉ VINÁRSTVO
Wine without geographical indication
VRoSC, Zemianske sady

Golden-yellow with thicker edges and an elegant honey-fruity smell of linden tea, apples and lemons with a hint of fallen leaves. The taste corresponds with the smell in its intensity and structure. It contains traces of acacia blossom, pear pulp, nuts and green almonds. Refreshing acids make an impression on the palate before gradually fading.

PG, GV • [675 l] • 0.75 l • €€ • L31 • 13.0 % vol. • ▼ • ① • ◯ • ✦ • ★★★★

Partisan Cru 2011
red, dry
SLOBODNÉ VINÁRSTVO
Wine without geographical indication
VRoSC, Zemianske sady

A raspberry-red Cuvée with purple shades on the edges and the smell of cranberries mixed with cassis, it offers interesting notes of plum marmalade and coffee up to dark chocolate after airing. It has an opulent, juicy taste with a smooth body veiled in a silk tannin which confirms that it has already reached the peak of its maturity. As a result, this vintage provides a rich concentrate of overripe berries with a pleasant note of licorice.

BF, CS, OR • [1,000 l] • 0.75 l • €€€ • L39 • 13.0 % vol. • ▼ • ① • ◎ • 🛢 {18} • ✦ • ★★★★

Schiller Cuvée 2014
quality wine, claret, dry
PIVNICA CSERNUS
VRoCS, Vinica

This wine acquired its bright claret shade with purple and rose hues thanks to 72 hours of maceration of the grape mash on skins with the presence of oxygen. Its edges are complemented by a ruby sparkle. Its smell speaks to us with tones of raspberry, white currants and gooseberry compote, while its higher acidity in the mineral taste results in a pleasant refreshing tone of fresh pink grapefruit, cut meadow grass and butter pears.

AN, ZW, OR, BF • [335 l] • 0.75 l • €€ • L-09 • 12.5 % vol. • ▼ • ① • ◎ • ◯ • ✦ • ★★★★

Sv. Juraj 2009
barrique, red, medium dry
RODINNÉ VINÁRSTVO ĎURÍK
Quality branded wine, VRoCS, Želovce

A garnet-red shade with brick-pink hues on the edges. The higher alcohol content is reflected in the robust barrique smell and taste of this wine. Its balsamic-fruity bouquet is combined with tones of sour cherries marinated in dark chocolate, juniper, and sweet plums against a background of burnt wood. The intensive and long taste with a distinctive impact of tannins enriches the finish with traces of roasted coffee, green pepper and tobacco leaves.

PN, CS • [1,000 l] • 0.75 l • €€ • L-1 22 • 14.0 % vol. • ▼ • ② • ◎ • 🛢 {5} • ✦ • ★★★★

CLASSICAL TOKAJ WINES

Tokajská výberová esencia 2003
TOKAJ & CO

Slovak Tokaj Wine, VRoT, Veľká Bara, Ružičky Vineyard

This Tokaj selection essence features a crystal clear, dark amber color with high viscosity. The exploding smell of forest honey, pear chutney, figs in coffee liqueur, roasted hazelnuts and massive tones of orange marzipan in contrast with roasted coffee and dark chocolate with coconut are only a slice of the abundant spectrum of smells which is beyond compare with any wine made on this planet. The fiery mineral taste was created during the alcohol fermentation of raisins from the most precious harvest of botrytized grapes.

F 65 %, L 25 %, YM 10 % • [5,000 l] • 0.50 l • €€€ • L 3/2010 • 12.0 % vol. • ⏦ • ④ • 🍇 • 🌑 • 🛢 {84} • ▭ • ★★★★★

Tokajský výber 6 putňový 2006
TOKAJ & CO

Slovak Tokaj Wine, VRoT, Malá Tŕňa, Čierna hora Vineyard

This six-tubs Tokaj selection has an intensive golden amber color, crystal clarity and higher density, and enchantment at first sight is the result. Its rich, concentrated bouquet of fig marmalade, dried oranges, maple syrup, botrytized grapes and rose oil is in perfect harmony with the full endless body. The highly extractive taste with a hint of walnuts marinated in Tokaj essence provides an outstanding multilayered charge to the overall finish.

F 65 %, L 25 %, YM 10 % • [10,500 l] • 0.50 l • €€€ • L 15/12 • 10.0 % vol. • ⏦ • ④ • 🍇 • ◐ • 🛢 {72} • ▭ • ★★★★★

Tokajský výber 5 putňový 2004
J. & J. OSTROŽOVIČ

Slovak Tokaj Wine, VRoT, Malá Tŕňa, Makovisko Vineyard

A five-tubs selection with a dark amber golden color and a rich fruity-balsamic smell featuring tones of overripe Tokaj raisins, exotic figs, dates and honey drop multiplied by an intensive note of noble botrytis. The aroma is harmoniously complemented by the flavor of volcanic minerals. Thanks to 4 years of maturing in a classical Tokaj cellar in the presence of oxygen, this royal wine preserves its uniquely attractive yet delicate character multiplied by 36 g/l of extract and 120 g/l of residual sugar.

F, L, YM • [9,990 l] • 0.375 l • €€€ • L26 • 13.0 % vol. • ⏦ • ④ • 🛢 {48} • 🍇 • ▭ • ★★★★★

CLASSICAL TOKAJ WINES

TOKAJ SELECTION Tokajský výber 5 putňový 2006

TOKAJ MACIK WINERY

Slovak Tokaj Wine, VRoT, Malá Tŕňa

A more reductive five-tubs Tokaj wine from the oxidative wine of the TOKAJ SELECTION collection attracts by its dark golden-yellow color with amber hues and higher density. It matured in barrique type casks in tuff cellars for 3 years. The bouquet is reminiscent of an avant-garde mixture of raisins, hazelnuts, dried pears and oranges. Later, it features drops of honey brandy wrapped in noble Botrytis. The long, fruity and balsamic taste is sweet, sour and refreshing.

F 60 %, L 35 %, YM 5 % • [2,000 l] • 0.50 l • €€€€ • L 12/11 • 11.0 % vol. • ⚜ •
④ • ⚘ • 🛢 {36} • ⟶ • ★★★★★

TOKAJ CLASSIC Tokajský výber 5 putňový 2002

TOKAJ MACIK WINERY

Slovak Tokaj Wine, VRoT, Malá Tŕňa

A classic five-tubs oxidative Tokaj wine with an attractive dark-orange color. It has the smell of nobly rotten grapes with honey and nutmeg and mace. The aroma of caramelized fruit, licorice and the Tokaj cellar micro-climate suit its rich taste. This is a wine with a long and full spicy aftertaste which combines the richness of grape extract, an excitable mineral character and a distinctively Botrytic nature.

F 60 %, L 35 %, YM 5 % • [3,000 l] • 0.50 l • €€€€ • L 08/08 • 10.5 % vol. • ⚜ •
④ • ⚘ • ◯ • 🛢 {72} • ⟶ • ★★★★★

Tokajský výber 5 putňový 2003

TOKAJ & CO

Slovak Tokaj Wine, VRoT, Malá Tŕňa, Lastovičie Vineyard

The dark orange amber shade of this five-tubs Tokaj selection shows fiery hues in the goblet and the smell of botrytized grapes with nutmeg and mace. The taste features tones of caramelized fruit, licorice and Tokaj bread. Tastes starting with baked pear pie with raisins up to coffee liqueur with ginger were combined in it thanks to its intensive oxidation.

F, L, YM • [20,850 l] • 0.50 l • €€€ • L 09 • 11.0 % vol. • ⚜ • ④ • ⚘ • ◯ • 🛢
{84} • ⟶ • ★★★★1/2

TOKAJ SELECTION Tokajský výber 4 putňový 2006

TOKAJ MACIK WINERY

Slovak Tokaj Wine, VRoT, Malá Tŕňa

This four-tubs Tokaj wine is golden-brown and has a higher density with a visible glycerol content and bright clarity which confirms the perfect combination of an extract of ripe grapes, a nobly rotten raisin essence and slow micro-oxidation in wooden casks. The smell of Christmas ginger bread with a pinch of cloves and cinnamon is attractive. The piquant taste with a firm mineral structure, acid and residual sugar content leaves a distinctive trace on the tongue.

F 60 %, L 35 %, YM 5 % • [3,000 l] • 0.50 l • €€€€ • L 11/11 • 11.0 % vol. • ⚜ • ④
• ⚘ • 🛢 {24} • ⟶ • ★★★★1/2

BIO WINES

BIO WINES

Cabernet Sauvignon 2009

grape selection, dry   NATURAL DOMIN & KUŠICKÝ

Wine with protected indication of origin D.S.C.
VoSS, Modrý Kameň and Vinica viticultural area

A dark claret wine with a full intensive smell and a persistent and well-balanced taste. Its bouquet is reminiscent of tones of cassis and new oak wood. The higher alcohol content does not burn the tongue; on the contrary, it complements the extract of this vintage supported by fresh acids and delicious residual sugar. The rich aftertaste with a dry trace of tannins and a hint of the rare fruit of the checkerberry tree only confirms the exceptional terroir.

[7,500 l] • 0.75 l • €€€ • L8.12 • 14.0 % vol. • ⚘ • ① - ② • ◉ • ▦ {18} • ⚔ •
★★★★★

Rizling rýnsky 2013

Bio, quality varietal wine, dry   MÁTYÁS – RODINNÉ VINÁRSTVO

Wine with protected indication of origin
VRoSS, Strekov viticultural area, Nová Vieska

The lighter straw-yellow shade of this Rhein Riesling and its delicious, honey-fruity smell continue in the attractive qualities of its predecessor, the 2012 vintage. The aroma features tones of dried exotic fruit, overripe raisins, linden tree and vanilla, while the medium full taste is affected by mineral acid. The tangerine and lime zest aftertaste is in harmony with the aroma; this wine has a potential for maturing in bottles.

[1,200 l] • 0.75 l • €€€ • L 79 • 13.0 % vol. • ⚘ • ① • ▦ {9} • ◯ • ↓SO₂ • ▭ •
★★★★★

Rulandské modré 2009

grape selection, dry   NATURAL DOMIN & KUŠICKÝ

Quality wine with attribute
VRoCS, Veľký Krtíš, Viničky Vineyard

This is a red brick-garnet Pinot Noir with higher viscosity on the edges. Maturing in new oak casks enriched the pleasant plum-marmalade tone by notes of oak wood and African roiboos bark. The taste sensation is well balanced with the smell. It contains the profile of a mature vintage with well-matured tannins, a nicely rounded combination of acids and alcohol and an aromatic, balsamic and animal trace of Cyprus spices and leather in the aftertaste.

[4,000 l] • 0.75 l • €€ • L 07 • 13.5 % vol. • ⚘ • ① • ▦ {8} • ⚔ • ★★★★★1/2

BIO WINES

Tramín červený 2011
grape selection, dry   NATURAL DOMIN & KUŠICKÝ

VRoCS, Veľký Krtíš, Vinička Vineyard, Pustatina Vineyard

The wonderful yellow and green shade of this Traminer shows golden hues on the edges and has the rich, perfumed smell of mountain herbs with notes of wild roses, acacia honey, horsetail, lavender and wild thyme. The brisk, spicy taste is as full as the smell, but the high alcohol content does not create a burning sensation on the tongue. The pleasant fading of the taste with a fine peat undertone leaves a complex impression. An exceptional bio wine from an exceptional terroir.

[7,500 l] • 0.75 l • €€ • L 4 • 14.0 % vol. • 🍷 • ① • ⬯ • ✐ • ★★★★1/2

Chardonnay 2011
late harvest, dry   NATURAL DOMIN & KUŠICKÝ

Wine of Central Slovakia, Modrý Kameň, Katovka Vineyard

This bright, golden-yellow wine features an aroma combining meadow flowers and the pulp of fresh apples. Its full, fruity taste wonderfully expresses its mineral character, the reduction of the yield and the natural ripening of grapes in a dry sub-tropical vintage with a colder autumn. The ethereal bouquet opens in the mouth tones reminiscent of hazelnut and butter cream which are joined in the finish by a note of balsa wood and dried orange peels.

[7,500 l] • 0.75 l • €€ • L 7 • 13.0 % vol. • 🍷 • ① • ⬯ • ✐ • ★★★★1/2

SPARKLING WINES

Cuvée Brut 2011
Méthode Traditionnelle   VÍNO MRVA & STANKO

Sparkling wine from the Slovak Republic

The lively golden-yellow color and crystal clearness accompanied by dense foam and delicate sparkling after pouring are identical to the great vintages of sparkling wines from Champagne. This blend of Chardonnay (85 %) and Pinot Noir (15 %) varietal wines is a guarantee of a firm multilayered structure of fresh, fruity smells emphasized by tones of butter pears with lemon peels. The juicy, delicious taste features pieces of pears, citrus fruit and a dry honey drop. Moreover, the decent creamy-lysate note emphasizes the complexity of this premium sparkling wine.

CH, PN • [1,200 l] • 0.75 l • € € € • L-47 • 13.0 % vol. • 🍷 • ❄ • ① • ⦿ {20} • 🗡 • ★★★★★

Sekt Pálffy Brut
Méthode Classique

White sparkling wine V.O.   VÍNO NITRA

Sparkling wine of the VRoSS

The mature, golden-yellow color, the intense creation of foam with fine sparkles along with the delicate creamy and fruity smell confirm the longer maturation of this sparkling wine in contact with yeasts. The fruity bouquet is complemented by tones of autolysis emphasized by traces of nuts, butter and citrus peels. This sparkling wine was prepared without dosage after clarification, which resulted in an extremely "hard" and drinkable sparkling wine in the super-dry category.

CH, PB • [750 l] • 0.75 l • € € • L657/11 • 12.5 % vol. • 🍷 • ❄ • ① • 🗡 • ★★★★★

Johann E. Hubert Extra Dry 2009
Méthode Traditionnelle   HUBERT J.E.

Quality white sparkling wine, VRoSS

The sparkling wine from this vinicultural area was made by secondary fermentation in bottles. Chardonnay and Grüner Veltliner from the excellent 2009 vintage create the basis of this blend. It will enchant you by its intensive golden-yellow color, massive and persistent sparkling and attractive bouquet. The full biscuit smell is dominated by honeycomb with pieces of ripe exotic fruit against a background of cream with traces of dried meadow herbs, linden blossoms, bitter almonds and walnuts.

CH, GV • [10,000 l] • 0.75 l • € € € • L-121601 • 12.0 % vol. • 🍷 • ❄ • ② • ⦿ {12} • 🗡 • ★★★★★

SPARKLING WINES

Rulandské modré Brut 2011
Méthode Classique — HACAJ

Winegrower's sparkling wine
VRoSC, Pezinok, hon Zumberg-Urbánka

This sparkling wine of the supreme appellation category was made of Pinot Noir grapes from their own vineyards from the basic wine up to its finalizing in sparkling wine by the same winemaker and bottler. The persistent sparkling of carbon dioxide, the light, straw-yellow and pink shade and the smell of forest strawberries will create an unforgettable experience. It has a full and dynamic taste that explodes with a fruity intensity and a rich spectrum of aftertastes.

PN • [300 l] • 0.75 l • € € € € • L04/13 • 12.5 % vol. • 🍷 • ② • ● • ❄ {18} • 🖌 • ★★★★★

Sekt 1933 Brut
Méthode Traditionnelle — CHÂTEAU TOPOĽČIANKY

Sparkling wine
VRoN

An avalanche of tiny bubbles of carbon oxide accompanies the rich foam creation after pouring. Its golden-yellow color with a hint of green and the charming smell of dried exotic fruit with citrus and honey promises to refresh. This well matured cuvee of 2010 vintage creates a harmonious overall impression in combination with its smell which is emphasized by tones of butter pear, dry meadow flowers and hazelnuts.

CH 80 %, PN 20 % • [3,000 l] • 0.75 l • € € • L-610 • 12.0 % vol. • 🍷 • ① - ② • ● {9} • ❄ • 🖌 • ★★★★1/2

Lipovina Brut
Méthode Traditionnelle — ELESKO TOKAY

Quality sparkling wine
VRoT, Malá Tŕňa, Makovisko Vineyard

This wine features sparkling bubbles, rich foam and golden-yellow shades mixed with straw-yellow hues. Its bouquet of meadow flowers with tones of acacia and pome fruits is accompanied by an extremely fresh fruity taste with biscuit and citrus tones. A full and mature bouquet with a nice final note of apricots and tropical fruit. A clarified sparkling wine, it was adjusted by 7.5 grams of residual sugar.

[6,500 l] • 0.75 l • € € € • L-6/12 • 11.5 % vol. • 🍷 • ① • ● {9} • ❄ • 🖌 • ★★★★1/2

Sekt Pálffy Rosé
Méthode Classique, extra dry — VÍNO NITRA

Sparkling wine from the Slovak Republic

This wine features persistent sparkling of small bubbles of carbon dioxide, and an attractive raspberry-red color with salmon-pink edges. It is a clear, sparkling wine made from a rosé Cabernet Sauvignon variety. Its creamy aroma reminiscent of ripe forest raspberries and strawberries with whipped cream will surprise you. The taste shows a balanced content of fruit acids and a dosage of 14 grams of residual sugar per liter after fermentation.

CS [2,250 l] • 0.75 l • € € • L656/10 • 12.0 % vol. • 🍷 • ❄ • ① • 🖌 • ★★★★1/2

SPARKLING WINES

Sekt Matyšák Brut 2011
Méthode Traditionnelle — VÍNO MATYŠÁK
Quality sparkling wine

This bright, golden-yellow wine features long foam stability and a dense sparkling of carbon dioxide bubbles. Its biscuit-fruity smell bears tones of butter brioche, while the refreshing body with a dosage of 8 grams of sugar offers a mixture of citrus fruit with traces of grapefruit, vanilla and roasted almonds. The long, pure aftertaste with a swift finish provides a nice overall impression worthy of a great party.

PB, CH, PN • [3,000 l] • 0.75 l • €€ • L-85 • 13.0 % vol. • 🍷 • ① • ● {9} • ❄ • 🔪
• ★★★★1/2

Rizling rýnsky Brut 2011
Méthode Classique — HACAJ
Quality sparkling wine, VRoSC, Svätý Jur

The light yellow-green shade and crystal clarity appear after the thick creamy foam of this unique varietal sparkling wine dissipates. This winery's excellently mastered classical method of secondary fermentation is one of its great assets. The smell of linden blossom and butter pears carries traces of acacia honey drops. The passionate and fresh taste with a piquantly fruity character is emphasized by the precise bonding of carbon dioxide in the wine structure, while the long biscuit and citrus aftertaste is hard to resist. A charming sparkling wine with a longer horizon of maturing in the bottle.

[400 l] • 0.75 l • €€€ • L08/13 • 12.5 % vol. • 🍷 • ❄ • ① • ● {14} • ▭ • ★★★★1/2

Sekt Pavelka Blanc de Blancs Brut
Méthode Traditionnelle — VPS – PAVELKA A SYN
Sparkling Wine from the Slovak Republic

The greenish-yellow shade, rich density of foam and long and endless sparkling of small bubbles of carbon dioxide. This blend of Chardonnay, Rhein Riesling and Pinot Blanc stands out by its fine fruity aroma reminiscent of butter brioche with shredded lemon peels and fresh apples with linden honey. Thanks to 12 months of maturing on lees, its pleasant acids and low residual sugar content, the taste features tones of lime juice with the fresh pulp of gooseberries.

[1,000 l] • 0.75 l • €€€ • L • 12.0 % vol. • 🍷 • ① • ▭ • ● {12} • 🔪 • ★★★★

Hubert L´Original Brut
Méthode Transvals, dry — HUBERT J.E.
Quality white sparkling wine

Golden-yellow, stable foam and a persistent sparkling of small carbon dioxide bubbles. The elegantly fruity and floral aroma of this sparkling wine with modest citrus biscuit tones only confirms the longer secondary fermentation process with the use of original Méthode Transvals. The balanced and juicy taste with a refreshing acid and an adequate dosage of nine grams of sugar per liter creates a nice sensation of exotic pineapples, grapefruit and tangerines with a trace of roasted nuts, apples and cinnamonn in its after taste.

[15,000 l] • 0.75 l • €€ • L132701127 • 11.5 % vol. • 🍷 • ① • ▭ + ● {9} • ❄ • 🔪
• ★★★★

SLOVAK WINE AND CHEESE

The history of cheese production on the territory of present day Slovakia is closely connected with shepherding and mountain farming. It begins with the first settlements and the domestication of livestock. It is believed that the first cheese originated in the Middle East where milk was stored in earthen, amphora-like vessels. Since they were kept next to the fire, the milk quickly turned sour and became cheese. Shepherds, goatherds and cowherds deserve credit for creating the first cheese from sweet milk. They preserved milk in dried animal stomachs which contained the residue of digestive enzymes. Due to the warmth and the motion when carried, the milk curdled and the whey was eventually separated from the firm white curd of fresh cheese. Original cheese production in the territory of Slovakia was founded on the processing of sheep milk.

Walachian colonization in the 14th century significantly influenced the method of milk processing and cheese production in the mountain and sub-mountain regions.
The first shops for the production of bryndza (a soft and creamy processed sheep cheese) appeared in Central Slovakia in the 18th century and the processing of cow milk predominated over sheep and goat milk by the end of the 19th century thanks to the establishment of diary cooperatives.
The rich history of cheese and bryndza production enabled Slovakia to preserve the original formulas of several original cheeses, four of which have acquired certificates of protected geographical indication and designation of origin.

CHEESE DEGUSTATION

A sommelier's recommendations at a cheese degustation are similar to those when assessing the sensory qualities of wines. We analyze cheese visually according to its shape, surface and cut. The appearance and color of the rind is also a significant visual attribute if the rind is part of its surface. The color and texture of cheese after cutting concludes the complex of commentaries describing its appearance. The aroma is one of the important qualities in determining the method of production and ripening, as well as freshness and safety for consumption. Olfactory notes of cow, sheep and goat milk (primary aromas) are complemented by the tones which came about by the fermentation by the milk cultures of bacteria (secondary aromas). We know them in form of scents resembling almonds, hazelnuts, mushrooms (champignons, truffles) as well as flowers, grass, straw, garlic, cabbage and even onion. Similarly to wine aging in wooden barrels or bottles, richer aromas are achieved during the ripening of cheese that distantly resemble the aging bouquet of wine (tertiary aromas). This comparison of cheese and wine aromas is connected to notes of wood, smoke and cellars (where cheese was ripening instead of wine), stables or soil. The serving temperature at a cheese degustation is as important as that at a wine degustation. In order to bring out the best aroma and flavor it is recommended that the cheese be taken from the cellar, pantry, cooling box or refrigerator at least 1 hour prior to tasting. Acidity, sweetness, bitterness, acerbity and dry matter content (roughness, butteryness) are basic manifestations from gustative perceptions. The spectrum of flavors is full of shades where we can recognize herbal, spicy, creamy, wooden, chestnut, nutty and almond tones according to the butterfat content and method of ripening in cooperation with the original microflora. A buttery flavor can be enriched in the same cheese during ripening and further processing by traces of hay, rottenness, smoke, ashes and fat. Many wine lovers perceive cheese as a common component of gastronomy and thus they frequently deprive themselves of the unique experience of pairing. The flavor of cheese is best perceived as it gradually melts on the tongue. We cannot get to know the true qualities of cheese if it is quickly "chewed" and swallowed before the aromas reach the required concentration thanks to the temperature in the mouth. The sense of touch in the mouth is therefore important for discovering flavor structure. It enables you to define the creaminess, chalkiness, roughness, elasticity, softness, butteryness, compactness, firmness, granularity, dryness, rubberyness, flourness, sandiness and even stickiness of the cheese. The dry matter, protein and salt content significantly affect the manifestation of the flavor. The saltiness of cheese can be balanced, increased, excessive or missing. What do the most famous Slovak cheeses taste like and which Slovak wines best complement them?

Bryndza (Processed Sheep Cheese)

Natural cheese from farms produced in the mountainous regions of Slovakia. The first bryndza shop was founded by Ján Vagač in the town of Detva in 1787. Sheep and cow milk is used for the production of this white or slightly yellowish cheese with a smooth creamy and occasionally grainy texture. The secret of its production is based on cutting lumps of sheep cheese or a mixture of cow and sheep cheese and then kneading it while adding salt or a salt solution. The weight of genuine Slovak bryndza is at least 50 % of the weight of sheep cheese in dry matter. Thanks to natural microflora contained in raw sheep milk and in sheep cheese lumps, brydnza acquires its characteristic sensory qualities. Fresh bryndza has the flavor and aroma of sheep cheese. It is piquant and slightly salty with a maximum 3 % salt content. The butterfat in the dry matter is higher than 38 % of the weight and the dry matter is at least 44 % of the weight. Genuine non-pasteurized Slovak bryndza contains a wide spectrum of microorganisms from the Lactobacillus, Enterococcus, Lactococcus, Streptococcus, Kluyveromyces marxianus, and Geotrichum candidum genuses. However it may not contain any pathogenic microorganisms. Bryndza was originally packed in wooden, barrel-like vessels called geleta weighing 5 to 10 kg. Nowadays, our bryndza producers pack it in small wooden buckets or other retail packaging, most frequently rolled into a cylindrical shape with a thin wooden protective cover or like sticks of butter. Slovak bryndza is one of the food products with protected geographical indication and designation of origin.

- **Grüner Silvaner**, 2012, late harvest, dry
- **Furmint Brut**, quality sparkling wine, dry
- medium bodied dry white wines with a herbal and even floral-fruity character, fresh acidity and slight minerality or dry and extra dry sparkling wines traditionally of the Tokaj variety

Edam Cheese

This popular, semi-hard cheese produced in most dairy plants in Slovakia is characterized by several local names; usually it is connected with a typical form of spheres (brick, block, salami cheese). It is made by pressing the cheese curds of partially skimmed cow milk (with no vegetable fats added) that is heated to a low temperature. The minimum aging time for quality cheese is one month. Edam cheeses with shorter aging periods have a more sour milky flavor and neutral aroma. Their texture is hard and even elastic, and white up to white-yellowish in color. More aged cheeses whose butterfat content in dry matter ranges from 40 to 45 % of the weight have a straw-yellowish color, with a delicate, sweet milky and cheese aroma and a creamy and nutty flavor. The texture is soft and supple. This cheese leaves a buttery and milky impression on the tongue with well-balanced to neutral salinity. The weight of Edam-type cheeses from cow milk from the mountainous region of Liptov are from 45 to 53 % of the butterfat in dry matter, and the aging period in paraffin wax is up to 2 months. They have a golden-yellow natural rind after removing the paraffin wax coat.

- **Pinot Blanc**, 2013, late harvest, dry
- **Blanc de Blancs Brut**, quality sparkling wine, dry
- white wines with fresh acidity, adequate up to low alcohol content, medium bodied with a soft fruity bouquet or a fine bouquet of meadow flowers and ripe fruits or sparkling wines made of Chardonnay, Pinot Blanc or the brut category of Grüner Veltliner

Hiadlovec

Ripening, full-fat cheese made of fresh non-pasteurized milk from the Braunvieh breed of cattle. Depending on the aging/ripening period (3 to 24 months) it has a distinct aroma and flavor. According to the level of ripening, the rind is crimped, milky and even golden yellow with darker shades of amber and orange and brown. The rind can be up to 6 mm thick. The color of the cheese is straw yellow with smaller and eventually larger cracks, whose texture in the course of ripening resembles small granules or even small fragments. This cheese has a fine milky and even perfumed aroma; when aged for a longer period, it tastes like peanut butter, nuts and truffles. The flavor in "ripened" cheeses is affected by its high dry matter and butterfat content, which in this case exceeds 50 %. It also contains unsaturated fatty acids which are beneficial for reducing cholesterol, high blood pressure and healthy digestion. Two year old "archive" Hiadlovec shows a rare note of garlic (wasabi) in the aftertaste on the tongue, similar to the taste of Oriental cuisine.

- Milia, 2012, selection of grapes, semi-dry
- Hron, 2009, quality, varietal wine, dry
- Rosa, 2012, selection of berries, semi-sweet
- less ripe cheese / younger, semi-dry white wines of medium bodied flavor with predominant floral and fruity perfumed tones, low acidity and adequate alcohol content; more ripe cheese / mature red wines with a rich aroma of berries with notes of spices and flowers, medium long dry and semi-sweet flavor with adequate alcohol content, fresh body and delicate vtannin

Oravský korbáčik and Zázrivský korbáčik (Braided String Cheese)

Steamed, non-smoked and smoked string cheese braids are made in both regions according to preserved traditional formulas. Both types of korbáčik are made of string (originally known as vojky) with a firm and elastic texture. They are made of cow cheese curds steamed in water with temperatures ranging from 70 to 95 °C. Compact steamed cheese is hand kneaded, pulled and folded until smooth. It is easily pulled in the shape of strings (vojka). Immediately after pulling, the strings are placed in cold drinking water and wound on a niddy noddy. The skeins of cheese are tied up with cheese string and inserted in a salty bath; afterwards, they are dried and manually interwoven into fine braids. The braid is tied up with a single string one third of its length from the bottom to prevent it from coming loose. Korbáčiks designated for smoking are smoked directly with smoke up to 30 °C, until golden yellow. The elasticity of strings is reduced by aging. In spite of this, the strings maintain pulling firmness. The stringy structure makes it easy to enjoy. Korbáčiks have a delicate aroma and salty flavor. When fresh, it gives off a slightly acidic impression, while smoked varieties have a slightly smoky flavor. The dry matter content is at least 40 % of the weight, and the milkfat content is at least 25 % of the weight. The salt content can reach a maximum of 4.5 % of the weight in non-smoked varieties and 5.5 % of the weight in smoked korbáčiks. From a microbiological aspect, korbáčiks contain sour milk microflora of the Lactococcus, Streptococcus and Lactobacillus genuses.

- Pinot Gris, 2012, late harvest, dry
- Chardonnay barrique, 2009, selection of grapes, dry
- for non-smoked korbáčik – dry white wines with a more distinctive fruity structure, lower alcohol content and low acidity; for smoked varieties: dry white wines of barrique type with medium full flavor with an herbal and even balsamic character and adequate alcohol content.

SLOVAK WINE AND CHEESE

Oštiepok (Smoked Sheep Cheese)

This shepherd's cheese is made at mountain sheep farms in several regions of Slovakia. Its production has been known since the beginning of the 18th century. Similar to parenica, the basis for its production is semi-fat sheep cheese curds or cheese curds made of sheep and cow milk or only cow milk. A piece of fresh cheese curd is pressed into a carved wooden form (ring) and the whey is pressed off. The Oštiepok in the ring is repeatedly dipped into whey at a temperature of 55-60 °C. Thus the characteristic shape of this cheese is created in the form of a large egg and decorated by imprints of ornaments from the wooden form. When the cheese is taken out of the wooden form, the last decorations which are characteristic for its origin and producer are manually impressed at both ends. The cooled oštiepok is dipped in a salty bath for 12 to 24 hours depending on its size. After drying out, the oštiepok is smoked for 6 – 10 days with cold smoke from hard wood. After smoking, the rind attains a golden yellow or golden brown color. This firm, slightly brittle cheese, which is butter yellow in color, shows small cracks. It bears a distinctive, slightly spicy up to delicately sour aroma and an adequately salty flavor. The smokiness of the hue depends on the method and intensity of smoking. The dry matter content is 48 % of the weight, and the fat content is 38 % of the weight; it is one of the Slovak cheeses with protected geographical indication and designation of origin.

- Petit Merle, 2011, quality, varietal wine, dry
- Pinot Noir, 2011, late harvest, dry
- younger red wines with a medium full fruity flavor with lower alcohol content, well balanced tannin and adequate however not distinctive acidity and aged in wooden barrels for a short period of time

Parenica (Steamed Sheep Cheese)

This unique semi-firm, non-ripening, semi-fat sheep cheese that is cream yellow in color stands out among all cheeses due to its appearance. Parenica looks like a coiled ribbon with an elastic juicy texture due to steaming. It is made of freshly fermented sheep cheese curds. The content of dry matter is 53 % of the weight, the fat content in dry matter is 20-25 % of the weight and the protein content is 22-25 % of the weight. It dates back to the 18th century when a new method of processing was discovered while making cheese curds. The cheese curds are cut into pieces and manually kneaded in a bowl with water at a temperature of 65 °C. The cheese is then pulled by hand and folded twice or three times before it is formed in a wooden riffle. The strip of cheese is briefly dipped in a salty bath and coiled into the shape of a large S. After being tied up with cheese string, its surface is quickly dried out and lightly smoked in cold smoke from oak or beech chips. Non-smoked parenica has a fine and delicate salty, milky flavor. The color of smoked parenica is golden yellow to brown yellow. Its aroma and flavor are saltier and spicier. Slovak parenica in Europe has protected geographical indication and designation of origin.

- Saint Laurent, 2011, late harvest, dry
- Zweigeltrebe, 2012, quality, varietal wine, dry
- younger red wines of medium full and soft flavor with lower alcohol content, light tannin underlined by fine fruity acid

Cheeses with White Fungus on the Rind

The formula for popular soft cheese made of pasteurized or non-pasteurized cow milk was created in 1791 in Normandy, France. Thanks to its pure, fruity milky aroma and pleasant tone of mushrooms and creamy herbal flavor, it found its way to several cheese-making regions, including Slovakia. The white fungus on its rind, more specifically, the white bloomy cover of fungus Penicillium camemberti, is the distinctive feature of this cheese. A cylindrical cake 10.5 to 12 cm in diameter has a traditional weight of 250 grams up to 1 kilogram. However, several dairy plants adjust the size of their forms for simpler recognition. The rind is bloomy white up to white yellow due to the fungus. The cheese itself is yellow or creamy yellow depending on the fat content in dry matter and has a slightly creamy texture. The fat content of fair cheeses of this type from Slovak farms and dairy plants in dry matter ranges from 40 – 45 % of the weight. In the best stage of its ripening, a cheese with white fungus ripens all the way to the middle. Its aroma is rich and fruity with traces of mildew, however it must not show sharp traces of ammonia. The optimum maturity for the more distinctive and full flavor of cheeses with white fungus on the rind and their charming fruity and slightly sour note is three to five weeks of ripening.

- Cabernet Sauvignon, 2011, selection of grapes, dry
- Merlot OAK WOOD, 2009, selection of grapes, dry
- dry red vintages of wine with pleasant acid content, tasty sweet tannin structure aged in older wooden barrels with the flavor of ripe fruit and dry flowers

Blue Cheeses

The group of blue, semi-soft crumbly cow cheeses which ripens with Penicillium roqueforti mold cultures. It is added when the cheese is made and in the course of ripening, and spiked with rods to create small veins to let oxygen circulate in the core. It also helps the mold to grow thanks to which green, blue or black veins or spots of mold are created throughout the body. The best quality blue cheeses have a fat content in dry matter of at least 50 % of the weight. Their shape is like a cylindrical oval of 10.5 up to 20 cm in diameter, 6 – 10 cm in height and 350 up to 1,500 grams in weight. In the course of ripening, the cheese acquires a creamier up to a spreadable texture with an intensive aroma. Its color remains white up to creamy with blue veins. The flavor is pleasant and spicy, slightly sweet and sour with a more distinctive salty flavor. The cheese matures for three to four months while wrapped in aluminum foil.

- Botris late harvest, 2011, quality, branded wine, sweet
- Tokaj cuvée Saturnia, 2011, straw wine, sweet
- ISTER, 2011, quality, branded wine, dry
- reductive naturally sweet wines made from the Tokaj variety of grapes with a high percentage of grapes with Botrytis cinerea (raisins), straw wine with higher acidity or robust red wines made of new red clones with a bouquet of marmalade fruits and exotic spices

Volovec

This cheese from Eastern Prussia is made of pasteurized cow milk with cheese curds heated at low temperatures according to the original formula. It is one of the group of semi-hard, ripening cheeses of the Tilsiter variety with a washed rind of golden yellow and with a 45 % fat content in dry matter. A solution with a bacterial culture of Brevibacterium linens is regularly spread over the cheese rind in the process of its production. The cheese body ripens gradually from the surface towards the core. Ripened Volovec has a rind of amber red and a strong aroma of milky cream with a hint of walnuts. Younger cheese has a slightly sour to sweet and sour flavor, but after ripening it takes on an intensive spiciness with a well-balanced saltiness. The cut of the cheese reveals many small holes created by the decomposing of lactacid and glutamic acid. Carbon oxide is one of the products of this decomposition which then creates the holes. The optimal ripening period is 3 to 5 months.

- Pinot Noir, 2011, selection of grapes, dry
- Blauer Portugieser, 2012, selection of grapes, semi-dry
- younger red wines of medium full taste with tones of ripe red fruits and flowers with lower alcohol content and smooth sweet tannin

This is by no means an exhaustive survey of Slovak cheese specialties. The assortment of our farmers and dairy plants includes fresh sheep curd cheeses, sheep korbáčiky, summer and winter bryndza, Liptov sheep bryndza, cow milk cheeses of various stages of ripening, soft ripening cheeses with white fungus on the rind or blue cheeses, goat ripening cheeses starting with fresh ones up to those with washed rinds. The topic of pairing Slovak cheeses and wines inspires me to write another separate book. At the end of this gourmet column, allow me one more recommendation. Regardless of the selection of cheese at a wine tasting, first taste the wine and only then the cheese. Otherwise your taste buds will lose their sensitivity (according to the fat and dry matter in the cheese) as cheese blocks your taste buds by the residues left on the surface of the tongue.

SLOVAK WINERIES FROM A TO Z

This chapter contains profiles of 50 Slovak winemakers which are significant in terms of the volume and quality of their production. Along with information on yearly production, vineyard area and winemaking methods, you will find contact details which will surely be appreciated by wine-tourists. In SOMMELIER'S TIP, I present my opinions on the best wines that are currently on offer. The profiles also mention significant awards from prominent competitions: CH – Champion of the category, GGM – grand gold medal, GM – gold medal, SM – silver medal, BM – bronze medal.

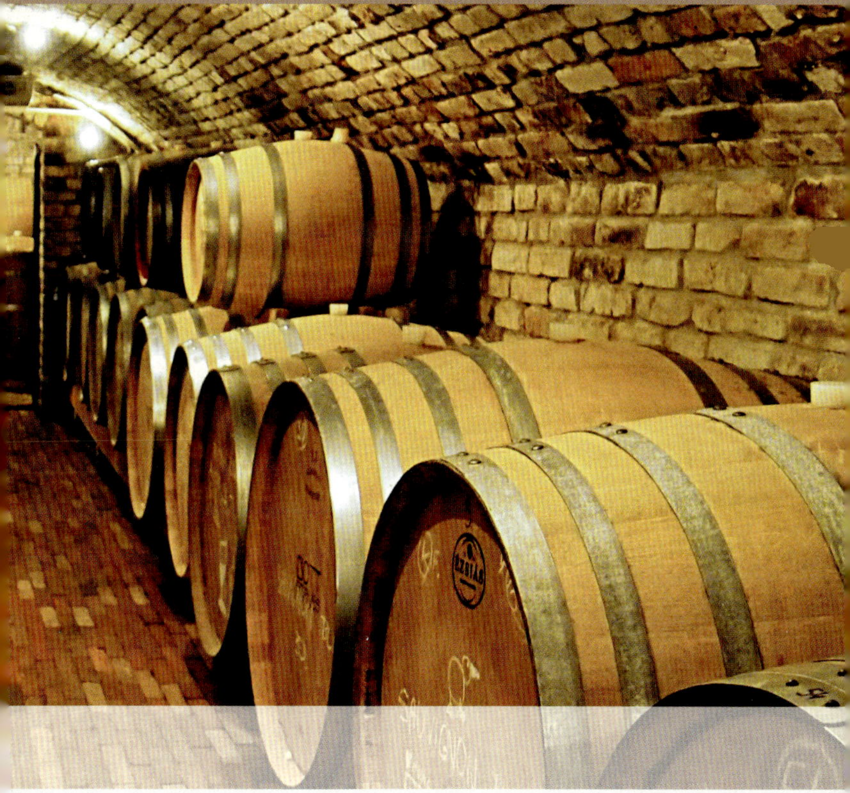

BOTT FRIGYES

Euro-Agro, spol. s r. o.
Obchodná 3, 945 04 Komárno-Nová Stráž
M: +421 905 222 995, +421 905 296 595
www.bottfrigyes.sk, info@bottfrigyes.sk

VRoSS • 2005 • 9 ha • 30,000 l •

The Frigyes Bott family winery currently farms on 9 ha of vineyards above the village of Mužla at an elevation of 230 meters above sea level. The village is situated at the foot of the southern part of the Mužla hills within the geographical triangle formed by the Hron and Danube rivers and the town of Štúrovo. Its clay-loam soil of volcanic origin with a high calcium content is rich in minerals. As a result, the wines of this region have a higher acid and extract content which distinguishes them from other wines and makes them unique from an analytical and sensory point of view. The varietal composition of this winery's vineyards is diverse. Italian Riesling occupies an area of 1.2 ha, Rhein Riesling - 1.5 ha, Lipovina - 0.5 ha, Grüner Veltliner - 1.2 ha, Lemberger (Blaufränkisch) - 0.7 ha, Feteasca Regala - 0.8 ha, Kadarka - 0.6 ha, Pinot Noir - 0.5 ha, Pinot Blanc - 0.5 ha, Sauvignon Blanc - 0.5 ha, Traminer - 0.5 ha and Juhfark - 0.5 ha. In terms of agro-technology, they strive to preserve the special character of the location.

The training of plants is low (trunk height of 50 cm) with a low bud load. They make wines the traditional way, in wooden barrels with spontaneous alcoholic fermentation and subsequent maturing on fine lees. As Frigyes Bott says, his wines reflect not only the place of birth and cultivating conditions of the grapevine, but also the God-given beauty of the surroundings.

SOMMELIER'S TIP

Riesling 2013 quality varietal wine, dry,
Rhein Riesling ⊢ p. 81

Super Granum 2013 quality varietal wine, dry,
Cuvée ⊢ p. 125

Frankovka modrá 2013 quality varietal wine, dry,
Lemberger (Blaufränkisch) ⊢ p. 90

Pinot Noir 2013 quality varietal wine, dry,
Pinot Noir ⊢ p. 94

SLOVAK WINERIES FROM A TO Z

Furmint 2013
quality varietal wine, dry

Wine with protected indication of origin VRoSS, Mužla

This attractive, green-yellow wine features a smell of green fruits with pits and yellow grapefruit complemented by a honey note spiced up by oak wood. The taste is more intensive than the smell. It contains a fresh mineral component of acids enriched by fruity up to herbal aromas consisting of pear pulp, honey wax and straw. The alcohol in the aftertaste is not burning; its medium-full up to full sensation is accompanied by a pinch of grated lemon zest with a piquant, fruity bitterness.

[750 l] • 0.75 l • €€€ • L09/0714 • 13.0 % vol. • ▪ • ① • ▪ • ✦ • ★★★1/2

Lipovina 2013
quality varietal wine, dry

Wine with protected indication of origin VRoSS, Mužla

A yellowish wine with brilliant clarity and an intoxicating flower-herbal up to balsamic smell with licorice undertones. Tones of ripe mango, hibiscus and meadow flowers can also be detected. The long and pleasantly mineral taste of this wine is markedly enriched by fruit acid. A mild bitterness along with a juicy citrus sensation in the aftertaste develops on the palate after swallowing.

[1,500 l] • 0.75 l • €€€ • L08/0714 • 13 % vol. • ▪ • ① • ▪ • ✦ • ★★★

ČAJKOVIČ WINERY

Marián Čajkovič - WINERY
Hurbanova 900/38, 952 01 Vráble
M: +421 944 461 342
www.almazia.sk, almazia@almazia.sk

VRoN • 2011 • 5 ha • 30,000 l •

This family boutique winery was founded by Marián Čajkovič and his wife Dagmar after 20 years of winegrowing and winemaking experience that Marián acquired as a viticultural technologist in several successful wineries in Slovakia and the Czech Republic, and which is reflected in their own wines. Thus, the realization of his lifelong dream has also brought success. The winery specializes in the production of varietal wines and wines with attributes from classical regional varieties and with the use of grapes grown in vineyards in the viticultural region of Nitra. Their target customers are private clients, wine shops and gastronomic facilities. They also sell their wines in their own shop - ALMAZIA on Kollárová Street in the town of Vráble, which is the site of regular wine tasting events for up to 30 guests. In addition to their own production, they stock wines from premium wineries from all over the world.

SIGNIFICANT WINE AWARDS

Chardonnay 2012 grape selection, dry
SM Víno Hlohovec 2014
SM Vínne trhy Pezinok 2013

Sauvignon Blanc 2014 Exclusive,
late harvest, medium sweet
GM Vínne trhy Pezinok 2015

SOMMELIER'S TIP

Sauvignon 2014 Exclusive,
late harvest, medium sweet,
Sauvignon ⊢ p. 87

SLOVAK WINERIES FROM A TO Z

Veltlínske zelené 2014
Classic, quality varietal wine, dry
VRoN

A light yellow-green Grüner Veltliner, this wine has a pure, fruity smell of freshly picked apples and acacia flowers. The taste, which is similar to the aromatic profile, is dominated by proper fresh acids. This light summer drink with a shorter finish leaves a tender almond bitterness with an exotic undertone of pink grapefruit juice on the root of the tongue.

[1,000 l] • 0.75 l • € • L 42 • 12.0 % vol. • ♀ • ① • ◯ • ✎ • ★

Chardonnay 2012
grape selection, dry
VRoN

The yellowish shade with golden hues and the pleasant fruity smell of ripe grapes and peaches are evidence of the processing of quality material. The center of the medium-full and pure taste shows pieces of yellow melon with an admixture of nuts. On the palate we will feel the presence of beeswax. The mature aftertaste of this wine is in harmony with the smell and confirms that the 2012 vintage is culminating.

[1,000 l] • 0.75 l • € € • L 16 • 13.0 % vol. • ♀ • ① • ◯ • ▮ • ★★★1/2

Dunaj 2014
Exclusive, late harvest, dry
VRoN

A dark red wine with purple edges. The aroma of ripe juniper and elderberries is in nice harmony with tones of cloves. The delicate and smooth taste with soft tannins indicates the careful processing of grapes from young plantings and features the tones of plums, while the aftertaste leaves a light overall impression on the tongue. This is a pleasant alternative for various gastronomical combinations and is suitable for enjoying in the summer months.

[2,000 l] • 0.75 l • € € • L 37 • 11.5 % vol. • ♀ • ① • ◯ • ✎ • ★★★1/2

ELESKO TOKAY

ELESKO TOKAY, a. s.
Elesko wine park
Partizánska 2275, 900 01 Modra
T: +421 2 209 226 40, M: +421 911 668 017
+421 911 110 382
www.elesko.sk
info@elesko.sk, obchod@elesko.sk

VRoT • 2009 • ☐ 15 ha • 70,000 l •

The ELESKO TOKAY vineyards are part of the Makovisko vineyard, the most famous Slovak Tokaj vineyard situated above the village of Malá Tŕňa. The stone skeletal soils, so called metamorphic cambisols with a considerable fraction content, are deposited on volcanic bedrock. In connection with the traditions of cultivating Tokaj varieties in the southeastern Zemplín region, the company renewed the original planting of vineyards at the foot of Lastovičie Mount in the center of the Slovak Tokaj viticultural region. The western section of the Makovisko vineyard was revived by the Furmint, Lipovina and Yellow Muscat varieties. Oremus, originally a Hungarian new clone which has a high yield of raisins and is also known as Zeta, is a complementary variety. The vineyard has a total area of 15 ha and produced first fruit in 2009. The annual production of its 70, 000 l of wine does not take place in the company cellar (simply because it doesn't have one). Instead, the grapes are processed by a contractual partner which has a valid production registration and is also a member of the Tokaj Regnum association. The company owns another 10 ha of land on the boundary of the villages of Malá and Veľká Tŕňa in the Tokaj vineyards of Keska and Fazekaš, where it intends to plant new vineyards and build a winery with a classical tuff cellar.

SIGNIFICANT WINE AWARDS

Lipovina Brut Méthode Traditionnelle
SM International Wine Challenge AWC, Vienna 2012
CH Vínne trhy, Pezinok 2012
Národný salón vín SR 2012-2013
GM Košické slávnosti vína 2012

Furmint Brut Méthode Traditionnelle
BM Vínne trhy, Pezinok 2013

Muškát žltý Demi Sec Méthode Traditionelle,
SM Vínne trhy, Pezinok 2013

Lipovina 2011 grape selection, medium dry
SM Tokaj, Viničky 2012

Lipovina 2011 straw wine, sweet
2nd place in category TESCO slovenský vinár roka 2013
BM Vínne trhy, Pezinok 2013
GM Vitis Aurea, Modra 2012
SM Vínne trhy, Pezinok 2012

Zeta 2011 quality branded wine, medium sweet
CH Vinum Superbum, Nitra 2012

SOMMELIER'S TIP

Lipovina Brut Méthode Traditionnelle
Sparkling Wines ← p. 132

Furmint 2011 grape selection, medium dry,
Furmint ← p. 98

Lipovina 2011 straw wine, sweet, Wines made of Tokaj varieties ← p. 99

SLOVAK WINERIES FROM A TO Z

Furmint Brut
Méthode Traditionnelle

Quality sparkling wine, VRoT, Malá Tŕňa, Makovisko Vineyard

Furmint grapes grown in its own Tokaj vineyard were used for the production of this quality sparkling wine, which after its secondary fermentation matured for 9 months on yeast. Its thick foam is accompanied by an ongoing sparkling and small bubbles of CO_2, which is the result of fermentation. Its sparkly, golden-yellow color and rich honeycomb aroma with an herbal note is in nice harmony with the fresh mineral taste with a hint of walnuts and lemon grass.

[6,500 l] • 0.75 l • €€€ • L-6/11 • 13.0 % vol. • 🍷 • ① • ⦿ {9} • ✾ • ⚒ •
★★★★

Muškát žltý Demi Sec
Méthode Traditionelle

Quality sparkling wine, VRoT, Malá Tŕňa, Makovisko Vineyard

An attractive sparkling wine, yellow-green in color with golden hues on the edges. The powdery aromatic smell shows traces of sweet grape must, vineyard peaches and intoxicating honey-muscatel flowers with a light, spicy finish. The taste is juicy, fruity and spicy with a pleasant muscatel and almond aftertaste. After dosage, this sparkling wine contains 39 grams of residual sugar per liter.

[8,300 l] • 0.75 l • €€€ • L-5/11 • 13.5 % vol. • 🍷 • ③ • ⦿ {9} • ✾ • ⚒ •
★★★1/2

Lipovina 2011
grape selection dry

Wine with protected indication of origin D.S.C.
VRoT, Malá Tŕňa, Makovisko Vineyard

This is a golden-yellow wine with beautiful viscosity. The aroma is mature, spicy up to fruity with tones of candied grapefruit and gooseberries with a piquant trace of white pepper. The harmonious taste is culminated by an elegant fruit acid of a mixture of apples and citrus fruit. The palate registers traces of lime peels with bitter notes of hazelnuts and an attractive herbal undertone.

[9,200 l] • 0.75 l • €€ • L-2/11 • 13.0 % vol. • 🍷 • ① • ◓ {3} • ⬭ • 🍾 • ★★★1/2

Zeta 2011
quality branded wine, medium sweet

Wine with protected indication of origin D.S.C.
VRoT, Malá Tŕňa, Makovisko Vineyard

This golden-yellow wine with light greenish edges has a pleasant smell that is discreet and carries a more distinct note of ripe pears and cloves in an admixture of pineapple. Thanks to 44 g/l of natural residual sugar in combination with an extract, its unobtrusive fruity taste gradually develops into an opulent dessert wine. Its aftertaste carries traces of overripe grapes and ripe peaches.

[4,000 l] • 0.50 l • €€€ • L-7/11 • 12.0 % vol. • 🍷 • ③ • ⬭ • 🍾 • ★★★

ELESKO

ELESKO a. s.
Partizánska 2275, 900 01 Modra
T: +421 2 209 226 40
M: +421 911 668 017, +421 911 110 382
www.elesko.sk
info@elesko.sk, obchod@elesko.sk

VRoSC • 2008 • ☐ 108 ha • 500,000l •

ELESKO entered the Slovak wine market in 2009 and has vineyards in the VRoSC and the VRoT. It is also the proud owner of the most modern wine park in Central Europe. It is characterized by quality, the exceptional taste of traditional Slovak gastronomy presented in a new style and an interest in Postmodern art. The ELESKO WINE PARK winery and agro-tourist complex sensitively blends in with the landscape and is connected to the existing road system. Visitors can enjoy a tour of the winery and lunch or dinner in the restaurant, stay in luxury suites with a fully equipped relaxation center or take a walk along the ampelographic path. Art lovers will be enchanted by the largest collection of the original works of Andy Warhol in Slovakia, thematic vernissages, concerts and dramatic productions in the Zoya Gallery.

ELESKO, one of the most progressive wineries today, has preserved its local character and is naturally assimilated into the picturesque surroundings of the Small Carpathians. The Elesko Monolith, situated in the middle of the vineyards and bearing the name of the medieval Ostrý Kameň castle, is proof of this. Wine production and the provision of complete gastronomical services are subordinated to the quality of the final product according to their motto: We do ordinary things extraordinarily well. ELESKO's grapevine wines, wines with low-alcohol content and varietal grapevine juices are attractive not only because of their diversity but because of the micro-climate of the Modra area. Since its establishment, this winery has enjoyed considerable success at international exhibitions and competitions. ELESKO and ELESKO TOKAY wines are served to international visitors at the government level and at Slovak embassies where the best possible products from Slovakia are served. They have been enjoyed by Dutch and Swedish royalty, and appeared as official wines at the Olympic Games in London and Sochi. They have successfully expanded to Hong Kong, Malaysia, Taiwan, China, Russia, France, Netherlands, Finland and Poland. The current annual capacity of this winery is 500,000 bottles with a production potential of one million bottles of wine made exclusively from the grapes from their own vineyards. Thanks to this, the company will be able to significantly increase its exports in the future.

SIGNIFICANT WINE AWARDS

Pinot noir rosé Brut Méthode Traditionelle,
SM Vínne trhy Pezinok 2014
CH Vínne trhy Pezinok 2013
SM International Wine Challenge AWC, Vienna 2013

Pinot Gris 2013 "1" late harvest, dry
GM Vínne trhy Pezinok 2015
SM Vitis Aurea, Modra 2015
GM Les Grands Concours du Monde 2014
GM International Wine Challenge AWC, Vienna 2014

Gewürztraminer 2013 late harvest, medium dry
GM Vitis Aurea, Modra 2014
SM Agrovíno, Nitra 2014
SM Víno Tirnavia 2014

Pálava 2013 "2" grape selection, medium sweet
GM Grand Prix Vinex, Brno 2014
CH Muvina Prešov 2014
SM International Wine Challenge AWC, Vienna 2014
GM Víno Tirnavia 2014
GM Vinfest Vinica 2014
GM Vínne trhy Pezinok 2014
SM Agrovíno Nitra 2014

SLOVAK WINERIES FROM A TO Z

Pálava 2011 straw wine, sweet
GM Vínne trhy Pezinok 2015
GM Grand Prix Vinex, Brno 2014
SM Vinalies Internationales, Paris 2013
GM Bakchus, Madrid 2013
GM Terravino Israel 2012
CH Vitis Aurea, Modra 2012
GM International Wine Challenge AWC, Vienna 2012
CH Muvina, Prešov 2012

Traja jazdci 2012 quality branded wine, white, dry
SM Concours Mondial du Bruxelles, Brussels 2014

Frankovka modrá rosé 2013 late harvest, medium sweet
GM Agrovíno Nitra 2015
GM Košické slávnosti vína 2015
2nd place Metro víno roka 2015
SM Vitis Aurea Modra 2014
BM Vínne trhy Pezinok 2015, 2014
SM Agrovíno Nitra 2014
SM Víno Tirnavia 2014

Dunaj 2012 grape selection, dry
GM Vinfest Vinica 2014
SM Muvina Prešov 2014
SM International Wine Challenge AWC, Vienna 2014
GM Košické slávnosti vína 2014

Rosa 2012 selection of berries, medium sweet
BM Vinfest Vinica 2014

Petit Merle 2011 quality branded wine, dry
SM Vínne trhy Pezinok 2015
SM Grand Prix Vinex, Brno 2013
SM International Wine Challenge AWC, Vienna 2013
GM Košické slávnosti vína 2013
VGM Sauvignon forum, Brno 2013

Veterlín 2011 quality branded wine, red, dry
SM Vitis Aurea, Modra 2015
SM Vínne trhy Pezinok 2015
CH Cuvée Ostrava 2013
SM International Wine Challenge AWC, Vienna 2013
GM Sauvignon forum, Brno 2013
SM Muvina Prešov 2013

SOMMELIER'S TIP

Pinot Gris 2013 "1" late harvest, dry,
Pinot Gris ← p. 77

Pálava 2013 "2" grape selection, medium sweet,
Pálava ← p. 103

Pálava 2011 straw wine, sweet,
Pálava ← p. 103

Dunaj 2012 grape selection, dry,
Dunaj ← p. 108

Rosa 2012 selection of berries, medium sweet,
Rosa ← p. 110

Veterlín 2011 quality branded wine, red, dry,
Cuvée ← p. 122

SLOVAK WINERIES FROM A TO Z

Gewürztraminer 2013
late harvest, medium dry

Wine with protected indication of origin D.S.C.
VRoSC, Vištuk, Zoya Vineyard

This bright green and yellow wine has slightly viscous edges. Its piquant spicy smell displays tones of white pepper, curry, cloves and a trace of white carnations with a hint of dried fruit. The taste is fresh up to juicy with a pleasant medium-long aftertaste of peaches and pineapples which is complemented in the finish by tender tones of cinnamon.

[9,750 l] • 0.75 l • €€€ • L-5/13 • 12.0 % vol. • 🍷 • ② • ◯ • ⚒ • ★★★1/2

Traja jazdci 2012
quality branded wine, dry

Wine with protected indication of origin D.S.C.
VRoSC, Vištuk, Zoya and Iveta Vineyard

A yellow-green cuvée with golden hints in viscous edges, its intensive smell is reminiscent of a combination of overripe fruit with a distinctive trace of vanilla, nutmeg and mowed meadow herbs. The taste is complex and fruity with a delicate hint of wood. The higher alcohol content and honey-nutty aftertaste indicate an interesting development in the bottle.

SH, P, T • [5,250 l] • 0.75 l • €€€ • L-21/12 • 13.5 % vol. • 🍷 • ① - ② • 75 % ◯ + 25 % 🛢 {6} • ⚒ • ★★★★

Frankovka modrá rosé 2013
late harvest, medium sweet

Wine with protected indication of origin D.S.C.
VRoSC, Vištuk, Zoya and Iveta Vineyard

The light, cherry-pink shade of this Lemberger (Blaufränkisch) rosé is accompanied by a delicate smell of forest raspberries and compote strawberries, and a light fruity taste with just the right amount of residual sugar. The wine was made of free run must after a short maceration of berries in press; the yogurt aftertaste with pieces of sweet cherries and raspberries is pleasantly finished by a well-balanced acid in a fuller citrus sensation. This rosé is at its peak phase and should not be stored away for long because another successful year is coming.

[15,000 l] • 0.75 l • €€ • L-14/13 • 11.5 % vol. • 🍷 • ③ • ◯ • 🍾 • ★★★

Petit Merle 2011
quality branded wine, dry

Wine with protected indication of origin D.S.C.
VRoSC, Vištuk, Zoya Vineyard

This dark ruby-red wine with violet sparkles has an attractive viscosity on the edges. Its fuller, fruity and balsamic smell features tones of ripe berries and plums complemented by tones of vanilla with fresh toast acquired by long maturing in new oak barrique-type casks. The taste is complex and supported by a higher alcohol content and velvety tannin accompanied by sour cherries in liquor on the root of the tongue.

ME • [6,300 l] • 0.75 l • €€€ • L-28/11 • 14.5 % vol. • 🍷 • ① • 🛢 {13} • ⚒ • ★★★★

FEDOR MALÍK & SYN.

Fedor Malík a syn., s. r. o.
Kalinčiakova 21, 900 01 Modra
M: +421 903 587 447
www.fedormalik.sk, vino@fedormalik.sk

VRoSC • 2006 • 10 ha • 20,000 l •

The Fedor Malík & syn. family winery offers wine from the royal viticultural town of Modra in the heart of the Small Carpathians. It focuses on the production of premium still and sparkling wines for demanding customers who are looking for wine with character. The taste of Malík's wines are due to the healthy and ripe grapes from their own vineyards, honest winegrowing and winemaking and the town of Modra. The vineyards have an average age of 25 years. Thanks to the reduction of yields, an emphasis on demanding green work and a sustainable approach free of herbicides, the family succeeds in making wines with a complex expression. The currently cultivated white varieties of Pinot Blanc, Chardonnay, Grüner Silvaner, Grüner Veltliner, Feteasca Regala, Sauvignon, Muscat Ottonel and Moravian Muscat compete with the red varieties of Hron, Cabernet Sauvignon, Neronet and Dornfelder. The ratio of white to red wines in the total annual production is 80 : 20. The winery sells its products from its own home and distributes them by courier and mail. The wines of this famous Modra winegrowing and winemaking family of intellectuals, teachers and the only professor of wine, who by his unbiased and eternally timeless attitude blazed the trail abroad for Slovak wine, deserve not only sincere and selfless attention but the ambition to follow them on the difficult path to premium wine cabinets and shops.

SOMMELIER'S TIP

Pesecká leánka 2014 quality varietal wine, medium dry, Feteasca Regala ← p. 84

Veltlínske zelené 2013 quality varietal wine, dry, Grüner Veltliner ← p. 74

Silvánske zelené 2013 quality varietal wine, dry, Terroir-respecting Wines ← p. 114

Chardonnay 2013
quality varietal wine, dry

Wine with protected indication of origin D.S.C.
VRoSC, Modra, Mittelberg Vineyard

The green-yellow shade and full fruity smell with a hint of Modra viticultural peach from Mittelberg will encourage even serious introverts. The pure taste of this wine with herbal and floral tones supported by fresh acid leaves a distinctive note of lemon balm and hazelnut on the tongue. The gooseberry, lime and bitter almond aftertaste says that the party may begin.

[1,000 l] • 0.75 l • €€ • L-104/0614 • 13.0 % vol. • ① • {6} • •
★★★★

GEORGINA – RODINNÉ VINÁRSTVO

Georgina s.r.o.
Mierová 1842/63, 946 03 Kolárovo
M: +421 944 461 342
www.georginafarma.sk

VRoSS • 2000 • 5 ha • 12,000 l •

This small family winery of Gejza Nagy and his wife Veronika focuses on processing grapes from the viticultural areas of Strekov and Štúrovo while using manual winemaking methods. The base for their traditional varietal structure is comprised of 2 ha of vineyards in the village of Mužla and 3 ha in the village of Strekov. From the very beginning, the winemaking has been oriented on preserving the natural qualities of wine which, thanks to the careful reduction of yields, the gravitational processing of grapes, musts and wine without filtration and conventional methods of clarification and stabilization, gives the character of the wine a new dimension. A local farmer's cheeses and cheese products prepared since 2012 from the milk of his own goat breeding are promoted as a specialty to be served with the wine. High quality cheeses made of goat and cow milk in combination with the wine of a single brand are therefore a reason for the development of rural tourism. The farm and winery offer tasting for smaller groups of guests with children and accommodations in a picturesque lakeside area near the river Váh.

SOMMELIER'S TIP

Chardonnay 2013 Slovak regional wine, dry, Innovative Wines ⊢ p. 120

Cuvée Cabernet 2012 quality wine, red, dry, Cuvée ⊢ p. 125

Veltlínske zelené 2013
Slovak regional wine, dry
Wine with protected indication of origin, VRoSS, Mužla

The rich, golden-yellow shade of this Grüner Veltliner has higher viscosity on the edges and its rich herbal bouquet indicates the excellent ripeness of the grapes and their longer maceration on skins. The aromatic profile features grapes, apricots and linden tree tones. The lighter, medium-full and pure taste is reminiscent of apple and clementine mash. A refreshing, drinkable wine with a smooth aftertaste that will make you wonder how it disappeared from the glass.

[1,200 l] • 0.75 l • €€ • L-3 • 12.0 % vol. •

SLOVAK WINERIES FROM A TO Z

Pinot Gris 2013
Slovak regional wine, dry

Wine with protected indication of origin, VRoSS, Mužla

Amber yellow in color with a slightly opalescent appearance. This natural, pleasantly drinkable wine was made according to the sur lie method, thanks to which the bouquet shows tones of pear, bread crust and white pepper. Maturing in oak barrels left a fine note of vanilla pudding, while the aftertaste contains pieces of apricots and leaves traces of candied fruit on the tongue.

[900 l] • 0.75 l • €€ • L-2 • 14.0 % vol. • ♀ • ① - ② • ◯ • 🛢 {6} • ⚔ • ★★★1/2

Cuvée Tradícia 2012
quality wine, dry

Wine with protected indication of origin, VRoSS, Mužla

This golden-yellow wine with higher viscosity has a smell that speaks of a mixture of fruity and herbal tones. It inspires notes of yellow plums, licorice and a tender but impressive hint of nutmeg. The taste suits the smell, and shows tones of ripe grapes and artichokes with an appropriate bitterness in the finish.

IR, GV • [2,100 l] • 0.75 l • €€ • L-12 • 13.5 % vol. • ♀ • ① • ◎ • 🛢 • 🍾 • ★★★

Cuvée Sírius 2013
Slovak regional wine, dry

Wine with protected indication of origin, VRoSS, Strekov

This purple wine with violet hints on the edges has a rich and aromatic character, which is a reflection of the maceration of the grapes on skins. After racking from lees and resting in casks, the wine was bottled with the use of gravitation without filtration. Its smell shows tones of cassis, juniper and tobacco. The robust taste is full of tannins and fruit acid and has a long finish.

OR, CS, DU • [1,200 l] • 0.75 l • €€ • L-1 • 13.0 % vol. • ♀ • ① • ◎ • 🛢 + 🛢 • ⚔ • ★★★1/2

SLOVAK WINERIES FROM A TO Z

HACAJ

HACAJ, s. r. o.
Cajlanska 66, 902 01 Pezinok
M: +421 907 792 087
www.hacaj.sk, hacaj@hacaj.sk

VRoSC · 1994 · ☐ 4.5 ha · 25,000 l ·

The roots of the HACAJ family winery go back to the first half of the 19th century. This wine manufacturer currently produces varietal wines with attribute and sparkling wines. The production of sparkling wines through the use of traditional Champagne technology of secondary fermentation directly in bottles is a specialty of this brand. The basic wine for sparkling wines is made by carefully pressing entire bunches of grapes. After fermentation, the sparkling wine matures together with yeasts in bottles for a minimum of 9 months, thanks to which it acquires a typical yeast-biscuit flavor and fine thick and long sparkling. As a result, the consumer gets it in the bottle in which the secondary fermentation took place. Since all of the operations of this difficult technological process are done manually, HACAJ sparkling wine can be designated as a handmade product. Fans of sparkling wines look for the category of a winemaker's sparkling wine (pestovateľský sekt) made from the grapes from a winery's own vineyards. HACAJ winery uses grapes farmed exclusively in the Viticultural region of the Small Carpathians. They supply their products only to selected wine shops and gastro facilities. They also invite visitors to taste their wine and tour the three hundred year old cellar in their house on M. R. Štefánik Street in Pezinok.

SIGNIIFICANT WINE AWARDS

Sauvignon Brut 2012 Méthode Classique
GM Vinoforum, Trenčín 2014

Feteasca regala Dry 2011 Méthode Classique
GM Muvina, Prešov 2013

SOMMELIER'S TIP

Rizling rýnsky Brut 2011, Méthode Classique, Sparkling Wines ⊢ p. 133

Rulandské modré Brut 2011, Méthode Classique, Sparkling Wines ⊢ p. 132

Svätovavrinecké Rosé Extra Dry 2011

Méthode Classique, quality varietal sparkling wine
VRoSC, Svätý Jur

The persistent sparkling of small bubbles of carbon dioxide and the comprehensively balanced aroma and taste indicate secondary fermentation and the longer contact of the wine with yeasts in bottles. The basic blend of salmon-pink comes from a free-run must. The fruity up to creamy smell is dominated by an impressive combination of forest raspberries and strawberries. The juicy taste with lime tones has the gift of a pleasant harmony of acids and 15 g/l of residual sugar. An elegantly pink varietal sparkling wine bearing the clear style of the winemaker.

[450 l] · 0.75 l · €€€ · L07/13 · 12.5 % vol. · ♢ · ⚛ · ② · ● · {14} · ✦ ·
★★★★

HUBERT J.E.

Hubert J. E., s. r. o.
Vinarska 137, 926 01 Sereď
T: +421 31 788 10 12
www.hubertsekt.sk, info@hubertsekt.sk

VRoN • 1825 • 10,500,000 l •

The history of the Hubert J.E. company began in Bratislava in 1825, when it became one of the first companies outside of France to make sparkling wine according to the traditional method. This brand enjoyed significant success and development, especially under the management of Johann E. Hubert and his wife Paulina. At the opening exhibition of the Millennium Celebrations in Budapest in 1896, Emperor Franz Josef I said, "This champagne is excellent!" In 1952, the operation was transferred to Sereď. In 2000, the company became part of the Henkell&Co group. By the end of 2008, Hubert J. E. added the production of still wines and spirits of the Vitis Pezinok brand to its portfolio, making it the largest winemaking company in Slovakia. The fundamental heraldic element of this brand is the coat of arms granted to the Hubert family by the emperor and which first appeared on the J. E. Hubert labels at the beginning of the 19th century. Johann E. Hubert sparkling wine made according to the traditional method of fermentation in bottles stands out from the abundant collection. Hubert L'Original is the successor of great brands. Hubert Club and Hubert de Luxe sects are also extremely popular. Sparkling wines made in Sereď are popular not only with the general public. Experts also appreciate their quality, which has been proven by several domestic and foreign awards. Hubert de Luxe won the silver medal at AWC Vienna 2012, Johann E. Hubert has won several gold medals (Muvina 2012, AGROVINO 2012). Pauline Hubert Extra Brut, named after the wife of Johann E. Hubert and made according to the traditional method, is the newest member of the family of premium brands. Still wines and spirits produced under the Vitis Pezinok brand are other important products of this company. The most famous include Chateau Pezinok, Vitis Galeria, Kláštorné and others. Karpatské Brandy Špeciál is among the top spirits in Slovakia, while Karpatské Brandy Original is a new addition.

SIGNIFICANT WINE AWARDS

Hubert L´Original Rosé Brut, Méthode Transvals
Národný salón vín SR (Slovak National Wine Salon) 2015

Johann E. Hubert Extra Dry 2009,
Méthode Traditionelle
SM Effervescents du Monde, Dijon 2014

Hubert de Luxe Doux
GM Košické slávnosti vína, Košice 2015
SM International Wine Challenge AWC, Vienna 2015, 2014
SM Cuvée Ostrava 2015
SM Bacchus, Madrid 2015
SM Mundus Vini, 2014

SOMMELIER'S TIP

Johann E. Hubert Extra Dry 2009
Méthode Traditionnelle
Sparkling Wines ⊢ p. 131

Hubert L´Original Brut Méthode Transvals
Sparkling Wines ⊢ p. 133

SLOVAK WINERIES FROM A TO Z

Hubert Club Brut
Méthode Charmat
Quality white sparkling wine

This green and yellow sparkling wine with golden hues is made according to the Charmat method. It shows a lively persistence of foam and a thick, long sparkling of carbon dioxide upon pouring, and a pure fruity smell with citrus tones which overlaps with the fresh medium full taste with nuances of dried apples, lime peels and gooseberries. The aftertaste is of fragile vanilla biscuits sprinkled with linden honey.

[60,000 l] • 0.75 l • € • L124401317 • 12.0 % vol. • ♀ • ⚘ • ① • ◯ {6} • ⚲ • ★

Hubert L´Original Rosé Brut
Méthode Transvals
Quality rosé sparkling wine

The salmon-pink shade, fine sparkling of carbon dioxide and sweet compote smell with tones of red garden fruit are complemented by fresh notes of citrus peels. The taste is more intensive than its smell thanks to the piquant fruit acid. The light creamy and fruity bouquet features traces of strawberries, raspberries and cherries.

[15,000 l] • 0.75 l • €€ • L123431355 • 12.0 % vol. • ♀ • ⚘ • ① • ◯ + ⦿ {9} • ⚲ • ★★★

Hubert Grand Rosé Medium Dry
Méthode Charmat
Quality rosé sparkling wine

A sparkling wine with a rich creamy foam combined with the dense release of carbon dioxide bubbles which appears immediately after pouring. Its light, ash-rose color with golden amber hues immediately sparks attention. The pleasantly harmonized fruity smell and taste of this sparkling wine are refreshed by juicy tones of strawberries, raspberries and apples. The taste is ensured by a well-balanced ratio of acid content and 35 g/l of residual sugar after dosage.

[40,000 l] • 0.75 l • €€ • L122034310 • 12.0 % vol. • ♀ • ⚘ • ③ • ◯ {6} • ⚲ • ★★★1/2

Hubert Club

Méthode Charmat, demi-sec

Quality white sparkling wine

This yellowish sparkling wine with hints of green has a decent persistence of foam with a finer sparkling of carbon dioxide bubbles in the goblet and a light, fruity smell with a proper harmonious taste. It made according to the Charmat method and will be interesting for fans of finer and fruitier sparkling wines with a higher dosage. Notes of ripe apples and peaches with a hint of walnut appear in the aftertaste.

[60,000 l] • 0.75 l • € • L130811133 • 11.5 % vol. • ♀ • ⚘ • ③ • ◯ {6} • 🍾 • ★

Hubert de Luxe Doux

Quality aromatic white sparkling wine

The intensive production of foam after pouring is accompanied by a fine sparkling of larger bubbles of carbon dioxide. The perfumed honey and floral smell is reminiscent of acacia honeycomb, nutmeg and candied exotic fruit. The sweet taste of the freshly pressed grape must is smooth and delicious and leaves traces of overripe grapes and dried apricots. Thanks to its primary fermentation of musts of aromatic varieties, it keeps its intensive floral and fruity, up to honey esprit.

MM, IO, MT • [120,000 l] • 0.75 l • €€ • L138094120 • 7.0 % vol. • ♀ • ⚘ • ④ • ◯ • 🍾 • ★

CHÂTEAU BELÁ

Château Belá, s. r. o.
943 53 Belá
M: +421 903 201 780
www.chateau-bela.com
admin@chateau-bela.com

VRoSS • 2001 • 40,000 l •

Those who have not tasted the Rhein Riesling from Belá cannot claim to know the genuine taste of Slovak Riesling. The winery is situated in a reconstructed chateau in the village of Belá, in the Štúrovo viticultural area. The late Baroque chateau with church, which was built from 1732 to 1735, was later rebuilt in Louis style, and saw the addition of Classicistic elements in 1834. In 2000, the ruins of the chateau were purchased from the state by Countess Ilona von Krockow, the granddaughter of the last owner. She had the complex reconstructed and today the chateau offers the services of a five-star luxury hotel.

The winery was created in the chateau thanks to the Countess's cooperation with Egon Müller, a prominent winemaker from Mosel, Germany. Miroslav Petrech, an experienced enologist, has been the chief technologist of this chateau since the founding of this brand. His premier 2001 vintage won an impressive 94 points from Robert Parker. Grapes for the production of the brand's quality varietal wines are supplied by the RIVEL Company of Mužla. Their mineral composition and extract of local wine is the result of sandy and clay up to clay soil with a high calcium carbonate content (8 – 10 %). The gradient of the vineyards is 9 up to 10 % with a gorgeous southern orientation towards the Danube river, which can be classified as excellent conditions for winegrowing in first class vineyards. The Rhein Riesling of Mužla in reduced harvests creates a substantial volume of this winery's wines with attributes. It also processes the grapes of white varieties such as Grüner Veltliner and Italian Riesling and red varieties, especially Cabernet Sauvignon, Pinot Noir and Alibernet. The elegant taste of Breslava is the Slovak new clone that is worth tasting.

SOMMELIER'S TIP

Rizling rýnsky 2012 selection of berries,
medium sweet, Rhein Riesling ⟻ p. 79

Rizling rýnsky 2011 grape selection,
medium sweet, Rhein Riesling ⟻ p. 79

Rizling rýnsky 2013 nobly rotten raisin selection,
sweet, Rhein Riesling ⟻ p. 78

Rizling rýnsky 2011, ice wine, sweet,
Rhien Riesling ⟻ p. 78

Cabernet Sauvignon Barrique 2012
grape selection, dry,
Cabernet Sauvignon ⟻ p. 91

Cabernet Sauvignon Barrique 2011
grape selection, dry, Innovative Wines ⟻ p. 118

Rulandské modré Barrique 2011
grape selection, dry, Pinot Noir ⟻ p. 94

Alibernet Barrique 2011 grape selection, dry,
Odessa Red ⟻ p. 106

Cabernet Sauvignon 2013 straw wine, sweet,
Cabernet Sauvignon ⟻ p. 93

Cabernet Sauvignon 2011 ice wine, sweet,
Cabernet Sauvignon ⟻ p. 92

Alibernet 2012 ice wine, sweet,
Odessa Red ⟻ p. 108

SLOVAK WINERIES FROM A TO Z

Rizling rýnsky 2014

dry

Slovak varietal wine, VRoSS, Štúrovo viticultural area, Mužla

This yellow Rhein Riesling with a greenish shade features a combination of fruity smells with traces of Sicilian grapefruit and a hint of linden blossom honey and small bubbles in the background. The fresh reductive taste is a reflection of this vintage. It has a dry taste with a distinctively fruity hint of acids with pieces of quince and dried apples. The mineral character of the wine is manifested by a fuller, spicy aftertaste and a distinctive note of citrus fruit with a predominance of limes.

[2,000 l] • 0.75 l • €€ • L 08 • 12.0 % vol. • ♀ • ① • ◎ • ▢ • ✤ • ★★★1/2

Rizling rýnsky 2013

grape selection, medium dry

Quality varietal wine with attribute, D.S.C. VRoSS, Štúrovo viticultural area, Mužla

The crystal clear, golden-yellow color of this Rhein Riesling is accompanied by a bouquet of floral and fruity smells with a trace of mountain herbs and honey drops and a complex rich taste with a piquant body. The long, medium-dry taste with traces of gooseberries, peaches and pomelo feature a grape-honey up to basil-herbal note. The rich extract of the wine shows a full aftertaste with a distinctive note of dried fruit and omnipresent dry honey drops.

[1,500 l] • 0.75 l • €€€ • L 06 • 14.0 % vol. • ♀ • ② • ◎ • ▢ • ✤ • ★★★★

Rizling rýnsky 2008

late harvest, dry

Quality varietal wine with attribute VRoSS, Štúrovo viticultural area, Mužla

This is a mature, golden-yellow Rhein Riesling with yellow-green hues. The rich multilayered smell of summer tangerines and apricots is complemented by linden blossoms. A full and intensive wine, its long extractive taste is well balanced with its smell. The piquant content of acids is wrapped in a firm fruity body structure with tones of tropical lime, mango and lemon grass. The longer potential for maturing supports the comprehensive overall impression of this firm vintage refined by an aromatic note of acacia blossoms.

[5,000 l] • 0.75 l • €€€ • L 06 • 13.0 % vol. • ♀ • ① • ◎ • ▢ • ✤ • ★★★★

Rulandské modré Barrique 2012

late harvest, dry

Quality varietal wine with attribute, D.S.C. VRoSS, Štúrovo viticultural area, Mužla

This Pinot Noir is raspberry-red with a light, garnet-red shade and a pleasant aroma of licorice interwoven with a fine hint of stone fruit and a predominance of sour cherries. Airing in the carafe will release its secret nuances hidden under velvet tannins which leave a lively, fruity structure on the palate in harmony with the delicious acids and alcohol. The earthy aftertaste is unique due to the combination with notes of oak wood. Its beauty needs time to fully develop while tasting.

[1,200 l] • 0.75 l • €€€ • L 08 • 13.0 % vol. • ♀ • ① • ▤ • {16} • ✤ • ★★★★

CHATEAU MODRA

Chateau Modra, a.s.
Dolná 120, 900 01 Modra
M: +421 903 776 146
www.chateaumodra.sk,
office@chateaumodra.sk

VRoSC • 1998 • 780 ha • 150,000 l •

PhDr. Eduard Šebo began to write the story of this winery in the 1990s when he continued in the winegrowing and winemaking tradition of his predecessor. He started his business as an independent farmer, which led to the opening of the Chateau Modra winery in 1998. Nowadays, the winery specializes in the production of premium wines with an emphasis on the quality of grapes grown exclusively in his own vineyards. The vineyards are situated in three viticultural regions of Slovakia, the Small Carpathians (Modra, Pezinok, Šenkvice), Nitra (Malanta) and Southern Slovakia (Galanta, Hubice, Strekov). In addition to traditional varieties, such as Grüner Veltliner, Lemberger (Blaufränkisch) and the legendary Grüner Silvaner from the Modra site of Stará hora, the winery can be proud of its production of exclusive Slovak new clones such as Dunaj, Nitria, Hron, Milia and Noria. Chateau Modra wines are proud holders of hundreds of domestic and international awards. In the first half of 2015 alone, wines born in the cellars of this winery won two dozen awards at significant Slovak and international wine competitions.

SIGNIFICANT WINE AWARDS

Milia 2013, Premium, quality varietal wine, dry
GM Agrovíno, Nitra 2014
SM Danube Wine 2014

Chardonnay 2013, Premium,
grape selection, medium dry
GM Vinalies Internationales, Paris 2014
SM Vínne trhy Pezinok 2014
SM Víno Bojnice 2014

Alibernet 2012, Premium, grape selection, dry
GM Valtické vínne trhy, Valtice 2014
GM Muvina, Prešov 2014
SM Vínne trhy Pezinok 2014
SM Linčanský džbánek, Zeleneč 2014

SOMMELIER'S TIP

Milia 2013, Premium, quality varietal wine, dry, Milia ⟻ p. 105

Chardonnay 2013, Premium, grape selection, medium dry, Chardonnay ⟻ p. 85

Rizling rýnsky 2012, Premium, grape selection, medium dry, Rhein Riesling ⟻ p. 78

Tramín červený 2012, Premium, grape selection, medium sweet, Traminer ⟻ p. 82

SLOVAK WINERIES FROM A TO Z

Silvánske zelené 2012
Premium, quality varietal wine, dry

Wine with protected indication of origin D.S.C.
VRoSC, Stará hora Vineyard

This Grüner Silvaner with a brilliant green and yellow shade and nice viscosity shows straw-yellow hues on the edges. The smell of a summer cocktail of apricots is impressive. It leaves a slightly spicy note with a pinch of nutmeg on the palate. The fuller, fruity taste of ripening pears and citrus develops in a pleasant grapefruit and citrus finish after swallowing. A swift and refreshing vintage with a complex overall impression.

[3,700 l] • 0.75 l • € € • L11 • 12.0 % vol. • ★★★★

Alibernet 2012
Premium, grape selection

Wine with protected indication of origin D.S.C.
VRoSS, Galanta, Za Bibicou I Vineyard

The ink-red shade with violet hues and intensive, fruity-balsamic smell indicate a rich wine. The bouquet of dark berries and ripe poppy heads is based on the beneficial impact of micro oxidation in wooden casks and confirms a note of the toasted crust of nut bread with coffee beans in the background. The longer and more mature aftertaste of this impressive vintage is spiced up by a dry tannin and pleasant juniper-bitter finish.

[10,000 l] • 0.75 l • € € • L51 • 12.5 % vol. • {14} • ★★★★

CHÂTEAU RÚBAŇ

Vienna DC, a.s.
Rúbaň 1, 941 36 Rúbaň
T: +421 35 64 99 102, M: +421 905 692 298
www.vinoruban.sk, info@vinoruban.sk

VRoSS • 2013 • ☐ 126 ha • 8,600 l •

The Château Rúbaň winery is located in a historical park in the village of Rúbaň near the town of Nové Zámky. The summer seat of the Zichy House was built in the second half of the 18th century on the older foundations of a classicistic aristocratic manor house that recently underwent reconstruction. The current owner also repaired and restored the original cellar with barrel ceiling. The sensitively buried modern cellar with technology for processing grapes and wine making is situated near the chateau. Although operations at the new winery space were officially launched in September 2015, the first vintages were available for the general public two years earlier and were well received. Château Rúbaň also caught the attention of the international general public when it became the first winery from Slovakia to win the expert jury award for the most beautiful wine labels at the prestigious Red Dot Design Award ceremony at an international symposium in Berlin. The holders of the "design Oscar" make wine directly at the site of origin and process grapes grown in local vineyards. The winery's activities benefit from cooperation with Ing. Ondrej Korpás and his son, internationally acknowledged grapevine cultivators.

SOMMELIER'S TIP

Veltlínske zelené 2013, quality varietal wine, dry, Grüner Veltliner ← p. 73

Noria 2013, quality varietal wine, medium sweet, Noria ← p. 104

Devín 2013, quality varietal wine, medium sweet, Devín ← p. 101

Svoj sen 2013

quality branded wine, medium dry

Wine with protected indication of origin
VRoSS, Strekov, Pod vinohradmi Vineyard

A light, green-yellow wine, with the smell of almond marzipan mixed with tones of butter pears. Its medium full taste carries dominant traces of alcohol manifested by a tingling on the tongue. Its fruity up to honey character with a hint of linden blossom will especially attract Feteasca Regala and Riesling connoisseurs. At the end of his life, professor Vilém Kraus donated part of his breeding material (the last of the working new clones) to Ing. Ondrej Korpás in Rúbaň. Perhaps the professor's dream will come true in the form of a new variety.

[500 l] • 0.75 l • €€€ • L04 • 15.0 % vol. • ★★★1/2

Mília 2013

quality varietal wine, medium sweet

Wine with protected indication of origin
VRoSS, Strekov, Pod vinohradmi Vineyard

This golden-yellow wine with yellow hues has an interesting and intensive muscatel and spicy smell. The taste, which is milder than the smell, contains decent acids with harmonious residual sugar. The character of the wine is close to a Müller Thurgau, however its smell is reminiscent of Traminer. The body is more subtle and finer than the smell. The elegant aftertaste is evocative of green tea with jasmine and hibiscus petals.

[500 l] • 0.75 l • €€€ • L02 • 13.0 % vol. • 🍷 • ③ • ▢ • 🍾 • ★★★1/2

Rizling rýnsky 2013

quality varietal wine, medium sweet

Wine with protected indication of origin
VRoSS, Strekov, Ormok Vineyard

A bright, golden-yellow Rhein Riesling, whose piquant spicy and fruity smell shows pieces of quince, petals of linden blossom and carnations along with a trace of white pepper. The taste has more bouquet in comparison with the smell; it is long and full with higher residual sugar, adequate acids and a more massive extract. Citrusy notes in the aftertaste are enhanced by tones of grapefruits and vineyard peaches. This lively vintage is approaching the culmination of its maturity.

[1,500 l] • 0.75 l • €€€ • L07 • 12.5 % vol. • 🍷 • ③ • ▢ • 🍾 • ★★★★

Svätovavrinecké 2013

quality varietal wine, dry

Wine with protected indication of origin
VRoSS, Strekov, Góré Vineyard

This garnet-red Saint Laurent with ruby-red edges has a fresh smell featuring cherries and ripe plums. The taste requires sensitive cooling since it shows a delicate fresh acid. The overall impression is thin and fine, with a red beet and stone fruit finish of the aftertaste.

[2,000 l] • 0.75 l • €€ • L05 • 13.0 % vol. • 🍷 • ① • ▢ • 🍾 • ★★★1/2

CHÂTEAU TOPOĽČIANKY

Vinárske závody Topoľčianky, s.r.o.
Cintorínska 31, 951 93 Topoľčianky
T: +421 37 630 11 31
www.vinotop.sk, info@vinotop.sk

VRoN / VRoSS • 1933 • □ 520 ha • 6,000,000 l •

This Topoľčianky winemaker is one of the prominent wine producers in the Nitra wine region with a long tradition and many years of experience. The company, which was founded in 1993, continues in its successful tradition and markets its products under the trademark Château Topoľčianky. The quality of a wine starts with the vineyard; therefore the company heavily invests in its own vineyards. It manages a total of 520 ha of vineyards in the Nitra and Southern Slovakia wine regions. Many of the vineyards underwent revitalizing by the planting of young grapevines situated in top locations. The careful processing of grapes through the use of modern technologies under the supervision of experienced experts results in light, fresh wines typical for their variety. Its portfolio includes a wide spectrum of white and blue varieties in the categories of quality wines and quality wines with attributes. The winery offers wines affordable for the general public as well as wines designated for gastronomical facilities, wines suitable for archiving and the top categories of wines with attributes. The combination of the unique, more northern climate and the variability of soil conditions under the supervision of skilled winegrowers and winemakers contributes to the creation of interesting wines in Topoľčianky which have convinced expert juries at domestic and foreign competitions of their quality. The company has won the highest awards in the Czech Republic, Moldavia, Italy and France.

SIGNIFICANT WINE AWARDS

Sekt 1933 Grand Rosé Dry
GGM Finger Lakes Wine Competition, New York 2014

Sauvignon 2014, late harvest, dry
GM Bacchus Madrid 2015

Devín 2013, straw wine, sweet
GM Austrian Wine Challenge, Vienna 2014

Frankovka modrá 2013, straw wine, sweet
GGM Finger Lakes International Wine Competition, New York 2015
GM Vinalies Internationales, Paris 2015
GM Bacchus Madrid 2015

SOMMELIER'S TIP

Sekt 1933 Brut, Méthode Traditionelle, dry, Sparkling Wines ↤ p. 132

Veltlínske zelené 2012 Retro, late harvest, dry, Grüner Veltliner ↤ p. 74

Modrý Portugal barrique 2011 Retro, quality varietal wine, dry, Blauer Portugieser ↤ p. 97

Dunaj barrique 2011 Retro, grape selection, dry, Dunaj ↤ p. 109

Rizling vlašský 2011 straw wine, sweet, Italian Riesling ↤ p. 75

Frankovka modrá 2011 straw wine, sweet, Lemberger (Blaufränkisch) ↤ p. 90

SLOVAK WINERIES FROM A TO Z

Sekt 1933 Extra Dry
Méthode Traditionelle

Sparkling wine, VRoN

The distinctive yellow-green shade of this sparkling wine with amber sparks, the thick sparkling of carbon oxide and well-matured, creamy bouquet confirm its longer maturing on lees in bottles after fermentation. The smell evokes tones of biscuit and dry linden blossom. Its well-balanced taste with an adequate dose of sugar is dominated by a fresh apricot mash with lime with traces of walnut in the finish.

RR • [3,500 l] • 0.75 l • €€ • L-612 • 12.5 % vol. • 🍷 • ② • ⦿ {9} • ❋ • 🗝 •
★★★1/2

Rizling vlašský 2013
HoReCa Selection, late harvest, dry

Wine with protected indication of origin D.S.C.
VRoSS, Sikenička

This light yellow-greenish Italian Riesling, with brilliant clarity, and a medium fruity and herbal aroma will please with tones of orange zest, linden blossom and apples. The taste is underlined by a sufficient acid content. It is a reductive, pleasantly drinkable and piquant fresh wine with a well-balanced intensity of smell and taste that will attract attention thanks to its exotic fruity nature empowered by a trace of yellow grapefruit in the finish.

[20,000 l] • 0.75 l • € • L464 • 13.0 % vol. • 🍷 • ① • ◯ • 🗝 • ★★1/2

Chardonnay 2012
Retro, grape selection, dry

Wine with protected indication of origin
VRoN, Veľké Zálužie, Kezidomby Vineyard

It has a bright yellow color with a hint of straw-green; in the nose of the wine there is an intensive smell of toast and vanilla complemented by tones of dried oranges. The taste is more distinctive, thanks to its piquant acidity and higher alcohol content. We can recognize bits of licorice, cinnamon, hazelnuts, as well as a drop of honey on the root of the tongue refreshed by pear skin.

[1,500 l] • 0.75 l • €€€ • L360 • 13.5 % vol. • 🍷 • ① • ◯ • 🛢 {3} • 🗝 •
★★★1/2

J. & J. OSTROŽOVIČ

J. & J. Ostrožovič
Nižná 233, 076 82 Veľká Tŕňa
T: +421 56 679 33 22, M: +421 908 996 042
www.ostrozovic.sk, marketing@ostrozovic.sk,
odbyt@ostrozovic.sk

VRoT • 1990 • ☐ 55 ha • 110,000 l •

Ostrožovič is the oldest private company operating in the Slovak Tokaj region. After twenty years of hard work and its first modest production of three small barrels, the family succeeded in building a greenfield winery of global quality. In 2012, the wines of this brand placed highly at global wine competitions such as Vinalies Paris, Bacchus Madrid, the Finger Lakes International Wine Competition and the Austrian Wine Challenge. The gold medal from the Vinhos do Brasil competition for its Tokajský výber 5-putňový (five tubs selection) vintage 2004, is the most precious award to date. The company's greatest asset is its 55 ha of vineyards situated above the village of Malá Tŕňa. The highest quality Tokaj vineyards of Makovisko, Vlčina, Domik and Chotár feature carefully farmed Furmint, Lipovina and Yellow Muscat bearing plantings. The varietal composition is complemented by the new Zeta clone (synonym Oemus) and Tučné hrozno (Kövérszőlő – Fat Grapes), another forgotten variety from the southern part of the Zemplín region. All of the vineyards are farmed in a system of integrated production. The company makes quality Tokaj wines according to original formulas by using oxidative technology and oxygen in individual stages of the production and maturing of Tokaj samorodni wines and Tokaj selections. The nobly rotten raisins are harvested manually in the best vintages. Tokaj wines mature for several years in tuff cellars 13 m underground in original 136 l goncs casks. The winery also began the production of their own grape seed oil cold pressed from the grape seeds.

SIGNIFICANT WINE AWARDS

Furmint 2013 Anniversary Edition, nobly rotten raisin selection, sweet
GM Bakchus Madrid 2015
GM Terravino Israel 2015
GM Chisinau Wines 2015
GM Vinoforum Trenčín 2014
GM Víno Bojnice 2014

Hankove Special Collection 2012
grape selection, medium dry
SM Danube Wine, Bratislava 2015

Tokaj cuvée Saturnia 2011 straw wine, sweet
GM Vinalies Paris 2014
GM Terravino Israel 2013
GM Finger Lakes International, New York 2013
CH Vinagora, Budapest 2013
GM International Wine Challenge AWC, Vienna 2013
GM Národný salón vín SR (Slovak National Wine Salon) 2013-2014
VGM Wine Snow Donovaly 2012

Muškát žltý Saturnia 2010 straw wine, sweet
BM Finger Lakes International, New York 2013
GM Bakchus Madrid 2013
GM International Wine Challenge AWC, Vienna 2013

Tokajský výber 5 putňový 2004, sweet
GM Národný salón vín SR (Slovak National Wine Salon) 2013-2014
VGM Wine Snow Donovaly 2013
GM Víno Bojnice 2012

Tokajský výber 6 putňový 2003
GM Selections Mondiales des Vins Canada 2015
SM Bakchus Madrid 2014
CH Víno mesta Košice 2013
SM Monde Selection Brussels 2013
SM Finger Lakes International, New York 2013
SM International Wine Challenge AWC, Vienna 2012
GM Vinoforum Maribor 2012
GM Agrovíno Nitra 2012
GM Muvina Prešov 2012

SLOVAK WINERIES FROM A TO Z

SOMMELIER'S TIP

Hankove Special Collection 2012 grape selection, medium dry, Terroir-respecting wines ⟵ p. 115

Lipovina NATUR Special Collection 2011 grape selection, medium dry, Lipovina ⟵ p. 98

Tokaj cuvée Saturnia 2011 straw wine, sweet, Cuvée ⟵ p. 123

Muškát žltý Saturnia 2010 straw wine, sweet, Yellow Muscat ⟵ p. 99

Furmint 2013 Anniversary Edition, nobly rotten raisins selection, sweet, Furmint ⟵ p. 98

Tokajský výber 5 putňový 2004, Classical Tokaj wines ⟵ p. 127

Lipovina 2014 Abbrevio Collection
medium dry

Wine with protected indication of origin, VRoT

A golden-yellow wine with a fuller fruity smell and hints of walnuts, grapes and honey. The fresh tones of taste are emphasized by the aroma of the skins of grapefruit and summer pome fruits. The well balanced acid content leaves a pleasant, bitter, citrus-spicy up to tenderly mineral finish in the aftertaste. This medium-full harmonious wine reflects its unique origin and noble processing while using state of the art methods.

[9,000 l] • 0.75 l • €€ • L16 • 11.0 % vol. • ♇ • ② • ▢ • ✦ • ★

Furmint Solaris 2014
kabinett, dry

Wine with protected indication of origin, VRoT

Green-yellow sparkly hues, the smell of sliced butter pears topped with acacia honey and sprinkled by citrus zest. The concentrated mineral bouquet of this wine will open after the first sip. However it surely won't be your last. The introverted nature of this wine hides fiery passion! Its taste is extractive, with a fruity taste of apricots and a rich mixture of linden blossoms with a pinch of white pepper up to ginger.

[9,000 l] • 0.75 l • €€ • L20 • 11.0 % vol. • ♇ • ① • ▢ • ✦ • ★★★1/2

SLOVAK WINERIES FROM A TO Z

Muškát žltý Solaris 2014
late harvest, medium sweet
Wine with protected indication of origin, VRoT

The smell of this Yellow Muscat carries wonderful tones of muscatel blossoms, baked butter biscuits and tropical fruit. The lively fruity taste in the embrace of fresh acids and nutmeg is accompanied by a swift note of lytchee, Marjory and ripe loquats. The full perfumed aftertaste of this wine confirms the optimal ripeness of its grapes and pure reductive processing.

[14,000 l] • 0.75 l • € € • L8 • 11.5 % vol. • ♀ • ③ • ❄ • ◯ • ✍ • ★★★1/2

Tokajské samorodné sladké 2003
Slovak Tokaj Wine, VRoT, Malá Tŕňa, Makovisko Vineyard

This elegant, golden-yellow Tokaj samorodni has a typical Tokaj bready character in its smell with tones of sweet raisins and dried summer fruit. The full extractive taste reveals its Tokaj vineyard origin ennobled by 15 hours of maceration on skins, spontaneous fermentation by original yeasts and slow maturing in oak casks in a classical Tokaj cellar. You definitively won't forget the rich aftertaste of honey drops on fallen leaves with a hazelnut note combined with citrus peels.

F, L, YM • [4,290 l] • 0.375 l • € € • L28 • 13.0 % vol. • ♀ • ④ • 🗄 {36} • ⌫ • ★★★★

Tokajský výber 6 putňový 2003
Slovak Tokaj Wine, VRoT, Malá Tŕňa, Makovisko Vineyard

This six-tubs selection has an aristocratic, brick-orange color with ruby-red veins in shades of black gold and is made only in extremely favorable vintages from manually picked nobly rotten raisins. The intensive botrytis smell with notes of dried dates, linden honey and roast hazelnuts weds with an abundant extractive (overall extract of 40 g/l) and sweet (residual sugar of 152 g/l) taste of raisins, orange jam and licorice. A very long aftertaste in each drop with an excellent potential for maturing.

[7,500 l] • 0.375 l • € € € € • L27 • 11.5 % vol. • ♀ • ④ • 🗄 {48} • 🍇 • ⌫ • ★★★★1/2

KARPATSKÁ PERLA

KARPATSKÁ PERLA, s.r.o.
Nádražná 57, 902 01 Šenkvice
T: +421 33 649 68 55
www.karpatskaperla.sk, vino@karpatskaperla.sk

VRoSC • 1991 • ☐ 50 ha • 400,000 l •

The KARPATSKÁ PERLA winery of Šenkvice was founded in 1991 by Margita and Ladislav Šebo who are continuing in the several hundred years of winemaking of the Záruba and Šebo families. In 2011 and 2012, the winery won the prestigious Winery of the Year award, as a result of numerous awards at international competitions and the winery's progressive orientation in all areas, starting with its care for vineyards, through modern technologies up to its cozy presentation spaces. KARPATSKÁ PERLA farms on 50 hectares of its own vineyards in the VRoSC. The 28 hectares in Suchý vrch, situated in the middle of the protected territory of Martinský les, is its most significant vineyard. The majority of wines with protected indication of origin from the collections of JAGNET, VARIETO, DÍLEMÚRE and 4ŽIVLY cuvée come from this vineyard. Every wine made by KARPATSKÁ PERLA respects individual varietal characteristics and uniqueness. 4ŽIVLY cuvee are made by assembling the 4 best varieties of the vintage which come from their own vineyards. In addition, the company produces mass wine for Spolok sv. Vojtecha (St. Adalbert's Association) and wines in limited editions. All of the wines from this winery can be sampled on the tasting premises with a capacity of 50 in the village of Šenkvice. At the beginning of 2015, they opened new tasting and representative premises suitable for social events and with a capacity of 60. I also recommend visiting the KARPATSKÁ PERLA cellars and production spaces and climbing the 21 meter tower to feast on the panorama of the Small Carpathians.

SIGNIFICANT WINE AWARDS

Muškát Moravský 2014 Jagnet, dry
GM Prague Wine Trophy, Prague 2015
GM Výstava vín Šenkvice 2015
Národný salón vín (Slovak National Wine Salon) 2015-2016

Veltlínske zelené 2013 Varieto, grape selection, dry
GM Sélections mondiales des Vins, Canada 2014
GM Oenoforum 2014
GM Víno Tirnavia 2014
GM Vienále Topoľčianky 2014
SM Vinalies Internationales, Paris 2015

Rizling rýnsky 2013 Varieto, late harvest, dry
SM Selezione del Sindaco, Roma 2014
SM International Wine Challenge AWC, Vienna 2014
GM Muvina Prešov 2014
GM Vínne trhy Pezinok 2015
Národný salón vín (Slovak National Wine Salon) 2015-2016

Pinot Gris 2013 Varieto, late harvest, dry
GM International Wine Challenge AWC, Vienna 2014
GM Muvina Prešov 2014
SM Bakchus Madrid 2015
CH Prague Wine Trophy, Prague 2015

Devín 2013 Varieto, grape selection, dry
SM International Wine Challenge AWC, Vienna 2014
SM Mundus Vini 2014

4 ŽIVLY 2013 late harvest, white, dry
GM Cuvée Ostrava 2014
CH Prague Wine Trophy, Prague 2015

SIGNIFICANT WINE AWARDS

Frankovka modrá 2012 Varieto,
grape selection, dry
GGM Sakura Awards, Japan 2015
GM Vínne thry Valtice 2014
GM Oenoforum 2014
Národný salón vín (Slovak National
Wine Salon) 2014-2015
GM Agrovíno, Nitra 2014
GM Medzinárodný festival Frankovky modrej,
Rača 2014
CH Prague Wine Trophy, Prague 2015

Alibernet 2011 Varieto, grape selection, dry
CH Prague Wine Trophy, Prague 2014
SM International Wine Challenge AWC,
Vienna 2014
GM Vínne trhy Pezinok 2014
Národný salón vín (Slovak National
Wine Salon) 2015-2016

4 ŽIVLY 2009, late harvest, red, dry
GM Muvina, Prešov 2013
SM International Wine Challenge AWC,
Vienna 2014

Aurelius 2013 Dílemúre, raisin selection, sweet
Národný salón vín (Slovak National
Wine Salon) 2014-2015
GM Agrovíno, Nitra 2014

Pálava 2011 Dílemúre, straw wine, sweet
GM Vinalies Internationales, Paris 2014
GM International Wine Challenge AWC,
Vienna 2013
SM Vínne trhy Pezinok 2014
CH Vítis Aurea, Modra 2015
GM Vínne trhy Pezinok 2015

SOMMELIER'S TIP

Muškát Moravský 2014 Jagnet, dry,
Moravian Muscat ← p. 100

Veltlínske zelené 2013 Varieto, grape selection, dry,
Grüner Veltliner ← p. 73

Rizling rýnsky 2013 Varieto, late harvest, dry,
Rhein Riesling ← p. 79

Pinot Gris 2013 Varieto, late harvest, dry,
Pinot Gris ← p. 76

4 ŽIVLY 2013 late harvest, white, dry,
Cuvée ← p. 123

Frankovka modrá 2012 Varieto, grape selection, dry,
Innovative Wines ← p. 118

Alibernet 2011 Varieto, grape selection, dry,
Alibernet ← p. 107

4 ŽIVLY 2009, late harvest, red, dry,
Cuvée ← p. 122

Aurelius 2013 Dílemúre, raisin selection, sweet,
Terroir-respecting Wines ← p. 115

Pálava 2011 Dílemúre, straw wine, sweet,
Pálava ← p. 103

Müller Thurgau 2014

Jagnet, dry

Wine with protected indication of origin
VRoSC, Šenkvice, Nad Polankou Vineyard

This brilliantly clear, yellow-green wine smells of apples and hazelnuts with a lovely note of ripe citrus fruit in the background. The taste is light and juicy with an appropriate acid content and a well-balanced fruity finish. It features a mixture of gooseberries, passion fruit and roses in blossom which in the taste aromatics of this vintage creates an imposing overall impression. The 2014 vintage will provide a sufficient amount of freshness and fruitiness even after a year or two of maturing in bottles.

[18,000 l] • 0.75 l • € • LR 0614 • 12.0 % vol. • ⌥ • ① • ◯ {6} • 🍾 • ★★★1/2

Devín 2013

Varieto, grape selection, dry

Wine with protected indication of origin
VRoSC, Šenkvice, Suchý vrch Vineyard

This straw-yellow wine has a bouquet with a spicy-floral smell, the center of which is filled with elderberry flowers and petals of wild roses with a pinch of anise in distinctive fruitiness. The medium-full taste is reminiscent of pieces of tangerines and pomelo. The medium-full impression is supported by a juicy extract of fruit acids and rounded out by 7.3 g/l of residual sugar. Spicy notes of cloves and hazelnuts are also present in the aftertaste of this brilliant grape selection which is medium dry on the tongue.

[8,000 l] • 0.75 l • €€ • LR 0813 • 13.5 % vol. • ⌥ • ② • ◯ • 🛢 {2} • ✒ • ★★★★

KASNYIK RODINNÉ VINÁRSTVO

Kasnyik rodinné vinárstvo, s. r. o.
Strekov 1117, 941 37 Strekov
M: +421 903 251 950, +421 907 252 473
www.kasnyikwine.sk, winery@kasnyikwine.sk

VRoSS • 2006 • ☐ 5 ha • 18,000 l •

Altough brothers Tomáš and Gabriel Kasnyik first toyed with the idea of making their own wine at the end of 2004 and the beginning of 2005, pinpointing the exact beginning of their actual relationship with grapes and wine and the moment of the founding of their winery is quite difficult because they worked in the family vineyard and cellar during their childhood. Their first wine is related to the vintage of 2006. However, the true change of view of winegrowing and winemaking occurred in 2008, when they decided to take the authentic path based on the natural conditions of Strekov, winegrowing close to nature and winemaking based on traditional methods. Today, they operate their own winery with the active cooperation of the family. The company farms on approximately 5 ha of vineyards nestled in the Strekov hills in the center of the Strekov viticultural area. They make their wines from ripe and healthy grapes after the strict reduction of the yield and spontaneous fermentation in predominantly wooden casks. They do not use any additional substances such as active genera of wine yeasts, macerating and clarifying enzymes or other clarifying substances, which in their opinion, makes the life of the winemaker easier; on the other hand, it results in strange tones and disfigures the genuine character of the origin. The uniqueness of wines from the Kasnyik family winery comes from the vineyards and soil in Strekov.

SOMMELIER'S TIP

Rizling rýnsky 2013 Selection, quality varietal wine, sweet, Rhein Riesling ⊢ p. 80

Frankovka modrá 2013 Selection, quality varietal wine, dry, Lemberger (Blaufränkisch) ⊢ p. 89

Rizling vlašský 2013

Selection, quality varietal wine, dry

Wine with protected indication of origin
VRoSS, Strekov, Členské Vineyard

A bright yellow Italian Riesling with golden sparkles on the edges. The smell of green tea and burnt wood leaves a sharp empyreumatic impression. An oak cask flavor combined with yeast lysate enriched the wine with a balsamic sensation from under which a bitter grapefruit aftertaste timidly peeks. This is a long wine with higher alcohol content and green bitterness with a dry finish.

[845 l] • 0.75 l • €€€ • L-11 • 14.0 % vol. • ♀ • ① • ◎ • 🛢 {10} • ◯ • ✒ •
★★★

Veltlínske zelené 2012

Selection, quality varietal wine, dry

Wine with protected indication of origin
VRoSS, Strekov, Farkas Vineyard

This yellow-green Grüner Veltliner features traces of oak wood, beeswax and acacia at the base of its herbal up to floral smell. The taste of ripening apples and nuts along with a higher alcohol content makes a massive first impression which gradually gives way to fruity tones of quince and bitter almond. The finish of the aftertaste offers refreshing notes of vanilla, citrus peels and ferns.

[1,330 l] • 0.75 l • €€ • L-4 • 14.0 % vol. • ♀ • ① • ◎ • 🛢 {5} • ◯ • ✒ •
★★★1/2

MARTIN POMFY - MAVÍN

Martin Pomfy - MAVÍN
Rázusova 30/A, 902 01 Pezinok
M: +421 918 532 798, +421 908 777 066
www.mavinvino.sk, mavin@mavinvino.sk

VRoSC / VRoSS • 2001 • 400,000 l •

The Martin Pomfy – MAVÍN Winery is situated in the picturesque winegrowing and winemaking village of Vinosady. It was founded in 2001 by Martin Pomfy, an ambitious winemaker with the intention of producing quality bulk wine. A few years later, after achieving this goal, he changed to the production of quality wines with attribute and completed the construction of new cellars. The grapes used in his wine come from his own vineyards in the Region of the Small Carpathians where he cultivates typical white varieties such as Grüner Veltliner, Italian Riesling and Rhien Riesling. He also buys grapes from tried and tested winegrowers from the region of Southern Slovakia. The Region of the Small Carpathians gives wines mineralization, freshness, piquancy and higher fruitiness. In the Region of Southern Slovakia, Burgundy (Pinot) varieties and red varieties with rich extract and varietal characteristics are particularly interesting. Modern technologies proceed from the careful processing of healthy grapes, through fermentation and the creation and maturing of wines in stainless steel tanks which bring out the unique aromatics of white and rosé wines. Red wines and a smaller portion of white wines mature in barrique casks according to the French model, which inspires the creation of more complex vintages of premium quality. Pomfy's wines have been highly awarded at international competitions. As he says, he is fanatical about winemaking. Currently the winery strives to produce modern wines with minimum intervention. The assortment of products features quality with potential and volume to significantly complement the Slovak market.

SIGNIFICANT WINE AWARDS

Rulandské šedé 2014 late harvest, dry
SM Concours Mondial de Bruxelles, Brussels 2015

Sauvignon 2014 grape selection, dry
Concours Mondial de Bruxelles, Brussels 2015

Chardonnay 2014 late harvest, medium dry
Národný salón vín SR (Slovak National Wine Salon) 2015-2016

Rizling rýnsky 2013 late harvest, dry
SM Vínne trhy Pezinok 2014

Cabernet Sauvignon Special Selection 2012
selection of berries, dry
Národný salón vín SR (Slovak National Wine Salon) 2015-2016

SOMMELIER'S TIP

Veltlínske zelené 2014 late harvest, dry, Grüner Veltliner ← p. 74

Sauvignon Blanc 2014 kabinet, dry, Sauvignon ← p. 86

Chardonnay 2014 grape selection, medium dry, Chardonnay ← p. 85

Rizling rýnsky 2013 late harvest, dry, Rhein Riesling ← p. 80

Cabernet Sauvignon blanc 2014 late harvest, dry, Cabernet Sauvignon ← p. 92

Cabernet Sauvignon rosé 2014 late harvest, dry, Rosé Wines ← p. 112

Devín 2014 grape selection, medium dry, Devín ← p. 101

Pinot noir Special Selection 2012 grape selection, dry, Pinot noir ← p. 93

Pinot noir Special Selection 2011 grape selection, dry, Pinot noir ← p. 94

SLOVAK WINERIES FROM A TO Z

Sauvignon 2014
grape selection, dry

Wine with protected indication of origin, VRoSS, Jasová

A lively, yellow-green wine with golden hues on the edge of the goblet. Its aromatic profile is more mature and intensive. It confirms the processing of ripened grapes and features tones of peaches and a hint of pines, red currents and honey. The taste is medium full, and its intensity is well balanced with the smell. It leaves traces of overripe forest raspberries and banana peel on the palate, and is emphasized in the finish by a drop of elderberry syrup.

[2,625 l] • 0.75 l • €€€ • L2 • 14.0 % vol. • ▼ • ① • ▭ • ⬧ • ★★★★

Rulandské šedé 2014
late harvest, dry

Wine with protected indication of origin, VRoSS, Jasová

An onion-yellow Pinot Gris with golden hues. The fruity and relatively developed primary smell is dominated by tones of mashed pears and butter biscuits. The taste is fuller than the smell, and in addition to traces of the omnipresent pears it also features a hint of vineyard peaches, gooseberries and lime, especially in the finish. Ideal for fast consumption when its aromatic nuances will be on full display without unnecessary maturing.

[6,000 l] • 0.75 l • €€ • L8 • 12.5 % vol. • ▼ • ① • ▭ • ⬧ • ★★★1/2

Chardonnay 2014
late harvest, medium dry

Wine with protected indication of origin, VRoSS, Belá

This summer Chardonnay is yellow-green with green hues and has a tender smell of overripe tropical fruit. The bouquet of mango and yellow melon with a drop of acacia honey also dominates the taste. The medium dry note suits its smell, while the soft, fruity finish with tones of beeswax and hazelnuts makes it hard to resist. Do not put this wine in the archive, enjoy it now.

[2,250 l] • 0.75 l • €€€ • L5 • 13.0 % vol. • ▼ • ② • ▭ • ⬧ • ★★★1/2

SLOVAK WINERIES FROM A TO Z

Cabernet Sauvignon Special Selection 2012
selection of berries, dry

Wine with protected indication of origin, VRoSS, Jasová

This attractive, ruby-red wine has dark violet hues. It has a full, distinctive smell with notes of overripe cassis berries complemented by cocoa beans and a pinch of black pepper. The taste sensation is also wide, intensive and persistent. In addition to dried cranberries, it shows tones of vanilla, tobacco leaves and coffee.

[6,000 l] • 0.75 l • €€€ • L-14 • 14.5 % vol. • 🍷 • ① • 🛢 • ⊶ • ★★★★

Cabernet Sauvignon Special Selection 2011
selection of berries, dry

Wine with protected indication of origin, VRoSS, Strekov

This dark, almost opaque garnet-red wine with brick-red hues has a rich, concentrated smell of candied red currents and elderberries, while decanting brings notes of roasted coffee, gingerbread spices and chocolate. Forest viola appears in hints. Its deep structured taste with a long overall impression promises a longer life of this wine in the bottle.

[6,750 l] • 0.75 l • €€€ • L-21 • 15.0 % vol. • 🍷 • ① • 🛢 • ⊶ • ★★★★1/2

MÁTYÁS – RODINNÉ VINÁRSTVO

Mátyás – Rodinné vinárstvo
Nová Vieska 154, 943 41 Nová Vieska
M: +421 905 329 887
www.matyaspince.sk, vinomatyas@gmail.com

VRoSS • 2005 • ☐ 12 ha • 18,000 l •

The philosophy of this winery is a return to traditional methods in wine growing and wine making. In terms of winegrowing agro-technology, they switched to ecological methods, i.e., they do not use any herbicides, system pesticides or industrial fertilizers which would cover the mineral substances penetrating the grapes and future wine from the soil. They use only traditional contact (copper, sulfur) and biological remedies (herbal extracts) for fungal diseases, and even then only to a limited extent. In an effort to achieve the highest grape quality, they reduce the yield to 0.5 – 1.5 kg for each plant. They also prefer traditional methods of vinification before reductive technology and alcoholic fermentation and maturing in wooden casks. Except for sulphur, they do not use any auxiliary preparations for stabilizing the wine, not even selected yeast cultures, which on one hand make the life of winemakers easier, but also brings strange tones to the wine. The effort of this winery is to make wines that reflect the terroir of their own vineyards as much as possible. This is also confirmed by the fact that starting with its 2013 vintage the company produces and sales bio wine with a certificate of ecological agriculture and is a founding member of the Autentista Slovakia association of winemakers.

SOMMELIER'S TIP

Rizling rýnsky 2013 Bio, quality varietal wine, dry, Bio Wines ⊢ p. 129

Pinot Blanc 2013
Bio, quality varietal wine, dry
Wine with protected indication of origin
VRoSS, Strekov viticultural area, Nová Vieska

This clear, yellow-green wine has a golden shade. Its rougher balsamic smell with tones of wooden cask distinctively overlays the fruity structure of its volatile components. The taste is medium long up to long and is reminiscent of a mixture of early picked apples with a relatively piquant fruity acid and more distinctive tannins coming from the wood.

[1,500 l] • 0.75 l • € € • L 80 • 13.0 % vol. • 🍷 • ① • 🛢 {9} • ◯ • ↓SO₂ • ✦ •
★★1/2

Frankovka modrá 2013
Bio, quality varietal wine, dry
Wine with protected indication of origin
VRoSS, Strekov viticultural area, Nová Vieska

This Lemberger (Blaufränkisch) has a dark, ruby-red color with purple hues. The smell makes a fresh impression with its piquant spiciness and reveals the distinctive impact of a wooden cask to its character. The feeling of fullness is completed by an extract in addition to a higher alcohol content with distinctive tannins. This fiery wine, bottled without filtration, is full of life. However, it needs to slowly mature in bottles in order to achieve full harmony.

[1,000 l] • 0.75 l • € € • L 84 • 14.0 % vol. • 🍷 • ① • 🌀 • 🛢 {12} • ✦ • ★★★1/2

MILOŠ MÁŤUŠ

**Vinohradníctvo a vinárstvo
Miloš Máťuš, s.r.o.**
Detvianska 33, 831 06 Bratislava - Rača
M: +421 905 202 818
www.vinomatus.sk, matus@vinomatus.sk

VRoSC • 2007 • 12 ha • 35,000 l •

Miloš Máťuš and his wife continue in the Máťuš family winegrowing and winemaking tradition which is firmly rooted in Rača. They farm on an area of 12 ha of older vineyards with a relatively diverse representation of varieties. Their white wines include Rhein Riesling, Grüner Veltliner, Müller Thurgau and Traminer, and to a lesser extent Pinot Blanc, Pinot Gris, Chardonnay and Italian Riesling. Their red varieties are comprised of Lemberger (Blaufränkisch), followed by Dornfelder, Odessa Red and André. They grow their own grapes and their care and maintenance of their own vineyards is excellent. They reach the highest hectare yields after reductions to 3 to 9 tons per hectare according to the variety, vintage and age of the vineyard. This allows them to process the best quality harvest in the form of structured and complex wines with distinctive qualities confirming their origin.

SOMMELIER'S TIP

Rizling rýnsky 2013 Terroir Rača "E", medium sweet, Terroir-respecting wines ⟼ p. 113

Frankovka modrá 2012 "S" Terroir Rača, dry, Lemberger (Blaufränkish) ⟼ p. 88

Frank André cuvée 2012

quality branded wine, dry
Wine with protected indication of origin
VRoSC, Bratislava – Rača

A darker purple shade with ruby sparkles, the intensive aroma of baked plums, black pepper, burnt wood and calf skin. The animal nature of the taste is complemented by lively fruit aci and an impressive tone of smoke. The spicy aftertaste carries enchanting notes of blackberries emphasized by tannins and a bitter almond character.

BF, AN • [900 l] • 0.75 l • € € • L-9/014 • 12.5 % vol. • ① • {15} •
• ★★★★

MOVINO

MOVINO, spol. s r.o.
Osloboditeľov 66, 990 01 Veľký Krtíš
T: +421 47 483 05 87
www.movino.sk, agro-movino@agro-movino.sk

VRoCS · 1993 · ☐ 220 ha · 1,600,000 l ·

The MOVINO winery in Veľký Krtíš is a dominant and experienced producer of wines in the VR of Central Slovakia. Thanks to the soil and climatic qualities of the viticultural region, it offers a wide spectrum of wines with typical character. Annual production has recently stabilized at 12,000 to 16,000 hl, of which approximately 22 % are quality wines with attribute. MOVINO is also a winegrower. It farms on 220 ha which are situated in one of the most ecological regions of Slovakia. The favorable climatic conditions allow the cultivation of such grape varieties as Rhein Riesling, Pinot Blanc, Chardonnay, Grüner Veltliner, Müller-Thurgau and Traminer. Red varieties include Saint Laurent and Cabernet Sauvignon. The Lemberger (Blaufränkisch) has an excellent taste, while the Devín and Dornfelder varieties are novelties. The MOVINO winery classifies its production of wines in several collections. Privat Exclusive quality varietal wines with attribute and collections entitled Exclusive, Sweet and Castle are the company flagships. It also introduced quality varietal wines to the market under the brands Premium, Special and Traditional. Currently, MOVINO sells 60 types of bottled wines. The most successful come from the viticultural villages of Čebovce, Príbelce and Bušince.

SIGNIFICANT WINE AWARDS

Chardonnay 2014 Exclusive, grape selection, dry
SM Víno Bojnice 2015
SM Vinfest Vinica 2015

Devín 2014 Exclusive, grape selection, dry
GM Bacchus, Madrid 2015
SM Vinfest Vinica 2015

Tramín červený 2014 Privat Exclusive, grape selection, medium sweet
GM Les Grands Concours du Monde, Strasbourg 2015
GM Concours Mondial Bruxelles, Brussels 2015
GM Oklevél 2015
GM Vinfest Vinica 2015
SM Muvina, Prešov 2015
SM Vitis Aurea, Modra 2015

Frankovka modrá 2014 Castle, late harvest, dry
SM Vienále Topoľčianky 2015
SM Vinfest Vinica 2015

Svätovavrinecké 2013 Privat Exclusive, late harvest, dry
SM International Wine Competition AWC, Vienna 2014
CH Vienále Topoľčianky 2014

Cabernet Sauvignon 2013 Privat Exclusive, grape selection, dry
SM International Wine Competition AWC, Vienna 2014
CH Výstava vín Plachtince 2014
GM Hontiansky súdok, Dudince 2015
GM Valtické vínne trhy 2014
GM Víno Hlohovec 2014
GM Vinoforum, Trenčín 2014
Národný salón vín SR (Slovak National Wine Salon) 2015

SOMMELIER'S TIP

Devín 2014 Exclusive, grape selection, dry,
Devín ← p. 102

Tramín červený 2014 Privat Exclusive, grape selection, medium sweet,
Traminer ← p. 83

Cabernet Sauvignon 2013 Privat Exclusive, grape selection, dry,
Cabernet Sauvignon ← p. 93

SLOVAK WINERIES FROM A TO Z

Chardonnay 2014
Exclusive, grape selection, dry

Wine with protected indication of origin, VRoCS, Čebovce

This yellow and green wine with golden-yellow hues has an intensive aromatic tone of a basket of summer fruit dominated by ripe oranges, nectarines and peaches. The appropriate acid content in its fresh and medium-long taste nicely complements the traces of citrus pits and yellow melon. A well-balanced, fruity Chardonnay with a pleasant, pure and more mature overall impression.

[22,500 l] • 0.75 l • € • L-21 • 11.5 % vol. • ⚐ • ① • ◯ • ✦ • ★★★1/2

Frankovka modrá 2014
Castle, late harvest, dry

Wine with protected indication of origin, VRoCS, Čebovce

A dark, ruby-red Lemberger (Blaufränkisch) with violet shades. The fruity and spicy smell is delicate and reminiscent of tones of cinnamon and stone fruit. Notes of bitter almonds and plums are present in the richer, medium-long and relatively distinctive tannin taste with a fresh bouquet, while the harmonious content of acids, tannins and alcohol leaves traces of cherry pits and nuts on the palate after swallowing.

[27,000 l] • 0.75 l • € • L-27 • 13.0 % vol. • ⚐ • ① • ◯ • ✦ • ★★★★

Svätovavrinecké 2013
Privat Exclusive, late harvest, dry

Wine with protected indication of origin
VRoCS, Príbelce, Nad kanál Vineyard

A dark ruby Saint Laurent with violet hues on the edges. The smell of dark berries and blackberries is distinctively affected by maturing in new oak casks. The bouquet features traces of roasted coffee, dried paprika and cocoa. Distinctive tannins in the aftertaste leave a dark chocolate flavor on the palate.

[15,000 l] • 0.75 l • €€ • L-23 • 13.5 % vol. • ⚐ • ① • 🛢 {4} • ✦ • ★★★1/2

NATURAL DOMIN & KUŠICKÝ

Víno Natural Domin & Kušický, s. r. o.
Poľná 5, 990 01 Veľký Krtíš
M: +421 907 808 720
www.naturalvino.sk, natural@naturalvino.sk

VRoCS • 2001 • ☐ 40 ha • 100,000 l •

The Natural Domin & Kušický winery owns 40 ha of vineyards which, in terms of Slovakia, makes it a medium-large winegrowing and winemaking company. The first Slovak family winery oriented on the production of bio wine made its first bio wine from the harvest of the 2001 vintage. Since 2006, after the reconstruction and three-year conversions, all of the vineyards, including winemaking, are certified as ecological. The assortment was planted according to the soil and climatic conditions, the suitability of the varieties and partially also according to the requests of the market. The white varieties include two clones of Traminer, two clones of Pinot Gris, four clones of Sauvignon, and two clones of Chardonnay, Pinot Blanc, Italian and Rhein Riesling, which represent 68 % of the planting. Red varieties include Cabernet Sauvignon, and 2 clones of Pinot Noir, Hron and Merlot, each with a total area of 32 % of planting. The Pinot varieties, which have the largest representation (42 %). Their growing requirements are best suited to the regional conditions. The red varieties comprise 32 % in terms of area, but only 28 to 30 % of regulated yields. The yields of white and red varieties are regulated from 50 to 60 q/ha, and 45 to 55 q/ha respectively. 95 % of the portfolio of wines is comprised of dry varietal wines and wines with attributes. The selection of red wines was enlarged in 2014 by interesting cuvée (blends). Wines of this brand are available in higher category restaurants, wine shops and through direct sale. For a long time, the company has complied with the strict conditions for the production, control and labeling of ecological products that are similar to the conditions for all EU Member States.

SIGNIFICANT WINE AWARDS

Chardonnay 2012 late harvest, semidry
SM Challenge International du Vin, Paris 2015
GM Vinfest, Vinica 2015

Rulandské šedé 2011 grape selection, dry
BM Challenge International du Vin, Paris 2015

Cabernet Sauvignon 2009 grape selection, dry
GM Tucet netuctových vín, Bratislava 2013

SOMMELIER'S TIP

Chardonnay 2011, late harvest, dry,
Bio Wines ← p. 130

Tramín červený 2011, grape selection, dry,
Bio Wines ← p. 130

Cabernet Sauvignon 2009, grape selection, dry,
Bio Wines ← p. 129

Rulandské modré 2009, grape selection, dry,
Bio Wines ← p. 129

Sauvignon 2012
grape selection, dry

Wine of Central Slovakia, Veľký Krtíš, Viničky Vineyard

The intoxicating smell of honeycomb joins with the fruity up to herbal tone of overripe peaches and rhubarb in this light, yellow-greenish wine with straw-yellow hues. The intensity of the medium-full and pure taste is well balanced with the smell. It features pieces of tropical fruit with traces of pineapple and yellow melon. However, the sweetish aftertaste is not the result of residual sugar. The pleasant overall impression is affected by the higher mineral character, glycerol, and alcohol content in particular. A bio wine with a beautiful primary aroma.

[7,50 l] • 0.75 l • € € • L 1 • 13.5 % vol. • ★★★★

PIVNICA CSERNUS

Csernus Karol
Nová Osada 302/3, 991 11 Balog nad Ipľom
Pivnica: Pod Strážom 1471, 991 28 Vinica
M: +421 903 178 632
www.pivnicacsernus.sk
karol.csernus@gmail.com

VRoCS • 2012 • 1.2 ha • 3,700 l •

The Family of Karol Csernus has been involved in winegrowing and winemaking since 1969. Their winery is situated near the village of Vinica on the picturesque southern slope of the volcanic Mount Stráž. The soil contains volcanic andesite and firm loam layers. Through the use of oxidation technology they observe traditional winemaking methods. They make quality wines with great care, free of preservatives and with a minimum carbon dioxide content. After fermentation, their wines mature in the cellar for one or two years, and some even longer on yeast lees (Chardonnay) before being bottled. The main white varieties include Italian Riesling, Grüner Veltliner, Rhein Riesling, Feteasca Regala, Chardonnay, Irsai Oliver and Mädchentraube. From the red varieties of André, Zweigeltrebe and Alibernet, they make schiller rosé with a preserved fruity smell and the taste of red grapes.

SOMMELIER'S TIP

Schiller Cuvée 2014 quality wine, dry,
Cuvée ← p. 126

Cabernet Sauvignon 2011 quality wine, dry,
Terroir-respecting wines ← p. 116

Batonnage Chardonnay 2013

quality wine, dry

VRoCS, Vinica

Golden-yellow color, drops of glycerol and a distinctive bouquet of lysates with a hint of hazelnuts up to beeswax confirm higher grape ripeness on one hand and longer contact on fine lees after fermentation. Wooden barrels have left their signature on the distinctive sensory profile of this wine and in its taste. The higher acid content overlays butter-grapefruit notes with woody bitterness which multiplies its distinctive mineral character. The marked influence of the environment and the voyage to a different face of Chardonnay can begin.

[410 l] • 0.75 l • €€ • L-05 • 12.5 % vol. • ① • {8} • ★★★

PIVNICA ORECHOVÁ

REGIA TT, spol. s r. o.
Orechová 89, 07251 Orechová
T: +421 56 698 11 80, +421 56 698 11 81
www.pivnicaorechova.sk
michalek@pivnicaorechova.sk

VRoES • 1994 • 54 ha • 300,000 l •

The winegrowing and winemaking production of Pivnica Orechová are closely connected. The history of the Regia TT s. r. o. – Pivnica Orechová brand dates back to 1994, when its operations replaced the original Orechová vine selection and hybridization center. The institution was in the administration of the Research Institute for Viticulture and Winemaking in Bratislava and the Orechová center was opened in 1966. Its role of was to breed new hybrids and grapevine clones suitable for the Viticultural Region of Eastern Slovakia and the cultivation of seedlings necessary for the dynamically developing winegrowing business in this part of the country. The building of the arched underground cellar represented the foundation for the later development of viticulture. After Regia TT, s. r. o. – Pivnica Orechová took over the premises, they gradually revitalized a larger portion of the original vineyards on an area of 25 ha, while in terms of the cultivation and treatment of grapevines they introduced a system of integrated production. In 2010, they essentially modernized the technology of grape processing and extended the capacity of the cellar. The operation includes a wooden barrel cellar designated for the maturing of red wines and an air-conditioned storage space. As part of the renewal of the plantings at the Sekerová vineyard, they added Dunaj and Neronet clones to the classical assortment of varieties. The most recent planting in the Filipová vineyard site of 2011 was expanded by Müller-Thurgau and Chardonnay. In 2013, the winery added wine-tasting to its program, and the premises are fully equipped for the provision of services related to wine tasting and wine gastronomy, which are also oriented on knowledge-based tourism.

SIGNIFICANT WINE AWARDS

Sauvignon 2013 grape selection, dry
SM Tokaj International Wine Competition,
Viničky 2014

Rulandské šedé 2013 grape selection, dry
(Pinot Gris)
GM International Wine Competition,
Dni vína, Vinné 2014

Dunaj 2013 grape selection, medium dry
GM Tokaj International Wine Competition,
Viničky 2014

SOMMELIER'S TIP

Müller Thurgau 2013 quality varietal wine, dry,
Müller Thurgau ├─ p. 76

Veltlínske zelené 2012 quality varietal wine, dry,
Grüner Veltliner ├─ p. 73

Muškát moravský 2013 quality varietal wine,
medium dry, Moravian Muscat ├─ p. 100

Rizling rýnsky 2013 grape selection, dry,
Rhein Riesling ├─ p. 81

Rulandské šedé 2013 grape selection, dry,
Pinot Gris ├─ p. 77

Svätovavrinecké 2012 quality varietal wine,
medium dry, Saint Laurent ├─ p. 91

Dunaj 2013 grape selection, medium dry,
Dunaj ├─ p. 109

SLOVAK WINERIES FROM A TO Z

Trayvel 2013
quality varietal wine, medium dry

Wine with protected indication of origin D.S.C.
VRoES, Orechová, Sekerová Vineyard

This gorgeous, golden-yellow wine with the smell of lime blossoms has a well-balanced, medium full structured taste of yellow butter pears, apricots and dried tropical fruit. After resting in the bottle, the taste is shorter, and less intensive than the smell, which is complemented by tones of rose petals with tender honey drops. It is reminiscent of selected grapes of the best ripeness. This vintage with the proper acid and residual sugar content is harmoniously summed up by an overall herbal impression.

T, GV • [6,000 l] • 0.75 l • € • L114 • 12.0 % vol. • ♀ • ② – ③ • ◎ • ○ • ♦ • ★

Sauvignon 2013
grape selection, dry

Wine with protected indication of origin D.S.C.
VRoES, Orechová, Sekerová Vineyard

This yellow-green wine with golden shades is full of the sun. It has an attractive, fruity and even herbal smell that features tones of overripe peaches and lemon balm. The taste of this vintage is in balance with its smell, pleasantly refreshed by its acid content and rounded off by a tender residual sugar. Its medium long finish is affected by traces of candied fruit with an impressively spicy note of nettle flowers.

[6,300 l] • 0.75 l • € € • L714 • 13.0 % vol. • ♀ • ① – ② • ◎ • ○ • ♦ • ★★★1/2

Tramín červený 2013
grape selection, medium dry

Wine with protected indication of origin D.S.C.
VRoES, Orechová, Sekerová Vineyard

The dark, yellow-green shade of this Traminer is accompanied by the smell of overripe raisins, candied pineapple, oranges and honey combs with a hint of a bouquet of carnations and even lilies of the valley complemented by notes of meadow herbs and exotic spices. Traces of roasted walnuts and caramel appear in the opulent spicy taste of this wine.

[4,000 l] • 0.75 l • € € • L1214 • 14.0 % vol. • ♀ • ② • ◎ • ○ • ♦ • ★★★1/2

Frankovka modrá rosé 2013
quality varietal wine, medium dry

Wine with protected indication of origin D.S.C.
VRoES, Orechová, Sekerová Vineyard

The Orange-pink spectrum of colors will capture us by its garnet-red shade, while the pleasant sweet smell of overripe plums and raspberries is complemented by a more mature, fruity taste. Seventeen grams of residual sugar is perhaps too much for rosé wine, but combined with its acid content and fine tannin, it creates an interesting equilibrium of perceptions.

[2,900 l] • 0.75 l • € • L 2113 • 11.5 % vol. • ♀ • ② • ◎ • ○ • ♦ • ★

Cabernet Sauvignon 2013

grape selection, dry

Wine with protected indication of origin D.S.C.
VRoES, Orechová, Sekerová Vineyard

It bears a claret-red hint with a bright garnet-red shade. The smell features tones of juniper, black currants and poppy heads. Despite the maturity of this vintage, the taste is refreshed by a proper acid content and fuller fruity tannin. It leaves traces of plums with a hint of green pepper on the tongue and in comparison with the smell, a note of red currents. Its brief maturing in oak casks brings up the presence of wood in the smell and taste.

[10,500 l] • 0.75 l • €€ • L1914 • 12.5 % vol. • ♀ • ① • ◎ • 🛢 {18} • ✦ • ★★★1/2

PIVNICA RADOŠINA

Pivnica Radošina s.r.o.
Office: Bratislavská 45, 917 01 Trnava
Prevádzka: Piešťanská 14, 956 05 Radošina
T: +421 38 53 98 113, M: +421 902 929 800
www.pivnicaradosina.sk,
pivnica@pivnicaradosina.sk

VRoN • 2004 • ☐ 33 ha • 200,000 l •

Pivnica Radošina continues in its long tradition of winegrowing and winemaking in the village of Radošina. This village was mentioned for the first time in 1156 as the property of Zobor Abbey, and later the Episcopate of Nitra. The first written reference to Radošina wine from the episcopate wineries is from 1400. It is said that the first Pinot varieties were planted on the southern slopes of the Považský Inovec mountains by Cistercians who also named the legendary wine of Radošina – Klevner. In addition to other occasions, it was served at the wedding of Queen Elizabeth II, and during her visit to Slovakia in 2008. Matej Bel also mentioned the significance of the Radošina vineyards in the 18th century. The breeding station was founded in Radošina at the end of the 19th century. In those days, wines such as Klevner, Sauvignon and Traminer won several awards at international wine competitions. Currently, the company farms on 33 ha of vineyards where they grow Pinot Gris, Pinot Blanc, Pinot Noir, Sauvignon, Traminer, Grüner Veltliner, Zweigeltrebe, Saint Laurent, Dunaj and Alibernet within an integrated production system. Grapes are processed with modern equipment, and the fermentation of musts with regulated temperatures and the biological elimination of malic acid are a matter of course. White musts and wines ferment and mature in stainless steel tanks, and the reds in 3,000 liter oak and barrique casks. Grapes from their own vineyards comprise 80 % of production; the other varieties of Devín and Riesling are purchased from the area of Šintava in particular. The winery offers a wide assortment of white, rosé and red wines with attribute. In favorable years, they produce such specialties as selection of berries, ice and straw wines.

SIGNIFICANT WINE AWARDS

Pinot Blanc 2013 late harvest, dry
GM Víno Hlohovec 2014

Radošinský Klevner 2013 late harvest, dry
SM Víno Bojnice 2014
SM Víno Hlohovec 2014

Rizling rýnsky 2013 late harvest, dry
SM Víno Bojnice 2014

Sauvignon Blanc 2013 late harvest, dry
SM Víno Hlohovec 2014

Tramín červený 2012 grape selection, medium dry
SM Dni vína, Nemčiňany 2013

Alibernet 2013, ice wine, red, sweet
GM Muvina Prešov 2014
GM Trunk fest, Bratislava 2014

Červený Klevner 2012 Terroir, late harvest, dry
GM Víno Hlohovec 2014
SM Dni vína, Nemčiňany 2014

Alibernet 2012 late harvest, dry
GM Muvina Prešov 2014
SM Trunk fest, Bratislava 2014
SM Concours Mondial Bruxelles, Brussels 2013

Rulandské modré 2009 grape selection, dry
SM Bacchus, Madrid 2014
SM Muvina Prešov 2011
BM Vínne trhy Pezinok 2011
BM Vinoforum, Ostrava 2010

SOMMELIER'S TIP

Radošinský Klevner 2013 Terroir, late harvest, medium dry,
Terroir-respecting wines ⊢ p. 115

Červený Klevner 2012 Terroir, late harvest, dry,
Terroir-respecting wines ⊢ p. 117

Rulandské modré 2009 grape selection, dry,
Pinot Noir ⊢ p. 95

Alibernet 2013, ice wine, red, sweet,
Alibernet ⊢ p. 107

SLOVAK WINERIES FROM A TO Z

Pinot Blanc 2013
late harvest, dry

Wine with protected indication of origin D.S.C.
VRoN, Vinohrady nad Váhom

This yellow-green wine with a fruity and spicy smell is particularly interesting because of its lively citrus tones and decent notes of linden blossoms and white pepper. The taste of the wine copies its aroma in intensity and character. It is medium-long and distinctively fresh thanks to the higher acid content. The aftertaste is accompanied by pieces of pome fruits, predominantly quince, emphasized by a trace of pepper.

[3,000 l] • 0.75 l • €€ • L 304 • 12.0 % vol. • ♀ • ① • ◯ • ✦ • ★★★

Rizling rýnsky 2013
late harvest, dry

Wine with protected indication of origin D.S.C.
VRoSS, Dvory nad Žitavou

The bright, yellow-green intensity of this Rhein Riesling, along with its fluid surface and rich herbal-kerosene bouquet will especially interest classical Riesling fans. The impressive aromatic profile shows traces of peaches, gooseberries and rose petals which will fully develop after the airing of the wine in a goblet. The piquant acid and appropriate extract against a background of dry honey drops finish the medium-full overall impression.

[7,000 l] • 0.75 l • €€ • L 307 • 13.0 % vol. • ♀ • ① • ◯ • ✦ • ★★★1/2

Sauvignon Blanc 2013
late harvest, dry

Wine with protected indication of origin D.S.C., VRoN, Radošina

This greenish-yellow wine with an attractive smell of elderberry blossoms and freshly sliced vineyard peaches immediately creates a feeling of refreshment. Its lighter, fruity taste is well balanced with its smell. It does not confirm the general cliché related to Sauvignon that these wines must be consumed at a young age. On the contrary, this juicy vintage with a fine almond aftertaste and delicious residual sugar has perspective for maturing in bottles for another two years.

[1,300 l] • 0.75 l • €€ • L 306 • 12.0 % vol. • ♀ • ①-② • ◯ • ✦ • ★★★1/2

Tramín červený 2012
grape selection, medium dry

Wine with protected indication of origin D.S.C., VRoN, Radošina

A Traminer from a young vineyard, it is interesting because of its full, golden-yellow color and crystal clarity. After two years of maturing in bottles, the aroma features a smooth combination of ripe grape berries, dried pineapples and carnations, with a taste that is enhanced by tones of peaches and lavender soap. The medium-long, medium dry aftertaste is in nice harmony with the precisely appropriate acid content and piquant alcohol in the bottle bouquet.

[1,000 l] • 0.75 l • €€ • L 209 • 13.0 % vol. • ♀ • ② • ◯ • ♠ • ★★★1/2

SLOVAK WINERIES FROM A TO Z

Dunaj 2013
late harvest, dry

Wine with protected indication of origin D.S.C., VRoN, Radošina

This dark, ink-red wine with the smell of juniper and cassis has a more distinct full taste which contains a relatively large amount of tannins and fruit acids. However, it leaves a less complex overall impression in comparison with its smell. A product of young planting in Radošina, it has tones of bitter sour cherry, dark chocolate and elderberry leaves on the palate.

[2,800 l] • 0.75 l • €€ • L 315 • 12.0 % vol. • ⓘ • ◯ • ✦ • ★★★

Pinot Noir 2013
grape selection, dry

Wine with protected indication of origin D.S.C., VRoN, Radošina

A brick-red wine with pink shades on the edges and the smell of plums, forest strawberries and wood. Its spicy taste with a distinctive note of tannins reminiscent of the seeds of pome fruit, ripening hips and skins of walnuts creates an impressive bitter aftertaste after swallowing. The fruit acid along with the rougher wooden finish need time to achieve harmony with the bouquet and come close to the 2009 vintage.

[2,900 l] • 0.75 l • €€ • L 317 • 13.0 % vol. • ⓘ • 🛢 {24} • ⟶ • ★★★

Alibernet 2012
late harvest, dry

Wine with protected indication of origin D.S.C. VRoN, Vinohrady nad Váhom

This dark violet wine smells like blueberries, open poppy heads and roasted coffee. Its intensive tannin taste is long, and contains notes of juniper, plums and dark sour cherries. The fresh acid emphasizes the bitter nature of tannins. The finish again features forest berries.

[1,100 l] • 0.75 l • €€ • L 216 • 12.5 % vol. • ⓘ • ◯ • ✦ • ★★★1/2

PIVNICA TIBAVA

Pivnica Tibava s. r. o.
073 01 Tibava 210
T: +421 56 652 22 81
www.tibava.sk, obchod@tibava.sk

VRoES • 1999 • 180 ha • 1,000,000 l

Tibava Cellar is one of the renowned winegrowers and winemakers in Slovakia and a true leader in the viticultural region of Eastern Slovakia. They only process grapes cultivated in their own vineyards at the foot of the Vihorlat Mountains in the cadastral territory of the villages of Tibava and Vyšné Nemecké. In 2004, the company began to reconstruct the vineyards; by 2013 they had planted approximately 60 hectares of new vineyards and they continue to expand. All of the new vineyards are included in an integrated grape production system which guarantees their quality. Grape processing, wine production, storage and distribution are concentrated in their plant in the town of Sobrance. The company stresses the comprehensive use of modern technology in grape processing and winemaking to ensure that the qualitative potential of the input material is used to its fullest. This fact markedly affected the decision of the owner to embark on the extensive reconstruction of the processing and production capacities which was completed in 2010. The winery has two shops, one on the Sobrance premises and the other in Bratislava. Kamil Červenka, the owner of Pivnica Tibava, s. r. o., is the holder of the Decree for the Production of Mass and Liturgical Wine issued by Mons. Ján Babjak S.J., Archbishop and Metropolitan of Prešov. The quality of wines from Tibava was also acknowledged by the Ministry of Agriculture of the Slovak Republic which awarded it the SK quality brand for outstanding domestic products. The current assortment includes 12 wines that bear such award. Pivnica Tibava is also the holder of the ISO 9001:2008 certificate for winegrowing, winemaking and wine sales.

SIGNIFICANT WINE AWARDS

Pinot Noir Rosé 2013 grape selection, medium sweet
SM Biel Vinalia, Veľký Biel 2014

Devín 2013 grape selection, dry
BM Celoslovenská výstava vín, Skalica 2014

Pálava 2013 grape selection, dry
BM Celoslovenská výstava vín, Skalica 2014

Alibernet 2012 late harvest, dry
GM Celoslovenská výstava vín, Skalica 2014
SM Gustus Juvenilis, Nitra 2014

SOMMELIER'S TIP

Devín 2013 grape selection, dry,
Devín ← p. 102

Tramín červený 2012 straw wine, sweet,
Traminer ← p. 82

Alibernet 2012 late harvest, dry,
Alibernet ← p. 107

SLOVAK WINERIES FROM A TO Z

Pálava 2013

grape selection, dry

Wine with protected indication of origin D.S.C.
VRoES, Tibava, Nad pivnicou Vineyard

Another of the new clones from the last planting in the Nad pivnicou Vineyard offers this dark, golden-yellow wine with a bouquet of white pepper, cloves and dried tropical fruit. Notes of grapes and hazelnuts are present in the perfumed spicy taste. The finish of this wine has a shorter aftertaste, however it offers an elegant view of the careful processing of overripe grapes with pure varietal character.

[150 l] • 0.75 l • €€ • L-9/14 • 13.0 % vol. • ♀ • ① • ◯ • ╪ • ★★★1/2

Tramín červený 2012

raisin selection, medium sweet

Wine with protected indication of origin D.S.C.
VRoES, Tibava, Nad pivnicou Vineyard

This Traminer features shades of yellow with golden hues on the edges. Its lovely smell with jasmine blossoms, St. John's wort and honey is harmoniously complemented by a delicious, slightly spicy medium long taste with sufficient mineral acids. Herbal and fruity notes appear in its aftertaste and are supported by piquant alcohol which emphasizes a trace of rare cloves on the base of the tongue.

[2,000 l] • 0.50 l • €€€ • L-9/12 • 13.0 % vol. • ♀ • ③ • ◯ • ╱ • ★★★★

Pinot Noir Rosé 2013

grape selection, medium sweet

Wine with protected indication of origin D.S.C.
VRoES, Tibava, Hrun Vineyard

This lively, garnet-red and pink wine with pretty orange sparkles smells of overripe red fruit, mainly cherries and strawberries, sprinkled with crystal sugar. Its fruity taste is mature and appropriate for its smell. A higher residual sugar and alcohol content, along with an aftertaste of concentrated dried stone fruit and sweet grapes, round out its character.

[600 l] • 0.75 l • €€ • L-10/14 • 13.5 % vol. • ♀ • ③ • ◯ • ╪ • ★★★1/2

PIVNICA ZSIGMOND

SHR Gabriel Zsigmond
Hontianska 100/48, 991 28 Vinica
M: +421 907 133 759
www.zsigmond.sk, vino@zsigmond.sk

VRoCS • 1996 • 22 ha • 70 ha of rented wineyards • 44,000 l

This family vineyard and winery was created on its own farm in the 1990s. They make wines exclusively from the grapes from their own vineyard planted in 2001 on 20 ha of heavy clay soils. According to regionalization, the vineyard of Gabriel Zsigmond is situated in the Vinica viticultural area, on the southern slopes of the hills of Krupinská vrchovina, 220 meters above sea level. Their assortment of white wine grape varieties includes Rhein Riesling, Pinot Blanc, Pinot Gris and Chardonnay, and aromatic varieties such as Traminer, Pálava, Yellow Muscat and Moravian Muscat. The new Hungarian clone Zenit is also an interesting variety. Pinot Noir, Cabernet Sauvignon, Saint Laurent, Lemberger (Blaufränkisch) and Alibernet comprise the basis for their production of red wines. Part of the harvest of red grapes is used for the production of rosé wine. Their production methods and processing of grapes are connected with traditional and modern knowledge of both generations of the Zsigmond family of winegrowers and winemakers. The grapes are harvested manually and placed in crates with a maximum of 20 kg of grapes per crate. Basic enological procedures are based on the reductive processing of musts and pure fermentation into a form of young wine. Maturing and treatment take place in stainless steel tanks and wooden barrels. Wines from the Zsigmond Cellar reflect the style of the winegrower and winemaker connected with the vineyard refined over the course of time in exemplary balance.

SOMMELIER'S TIP

Rizling rýnsky 2013 late harvest, dry,
Rhein Riesling ⊢ p. 81

Rulandské šedé 2013 grape election, dry,
Pinot Gris ⊢ p. 77

Cabernet Sauvignon 2013 grape selection, dry,
Cabernet Sauvignon ⊢ p. 93

SLOVAK WINERIES FROM A TO Z

Zenit – cuvée 2014
quality branded wine with attribute, kabinett, dry

VRoCS, Vinica area, Vinica

This light golden wine with shades of yellow was made from the Zenit variety, which was bred in Hungary from the Ezerjó and Bouvier varieties, but is not registered in the List of Registered Varieties in Slovakia. Its spicy smell is reminiscent of citrus fruit and ripe wine grapes before pressing. This pleasant and fresh wine has sufficient acid content and is easy to drink. A refreshing summer wine.

[750 l] • 0.75 l • €€ • L-11 • 12.5 % vol. • ♀ • ① • ◯ • 🍾 • ★★★

Tramín červený 2012
berry selection, medium dry

Wine with protected indication of origin
VRoCS, Vinica area, Vinica

The golden-yellow shades, spicy floral smell and rich varietal taste of this Traminer immediately reveal quality grapes and processing. The development of the bouquet in the bottle leaves traces of enchanting tones of lily and lily-of-the-valley; one can feel the pulp of tropical pineapple and acacia honey in the mouth. Spicy tones also present in the aftertaste are reduced by tender residual sugar. This wine is already past the peak of maturing, however it still has something to offer, especially to fans of this precious aromatic variety.

[1,500 l] • 0.75 l • €€ • L-07 • 13.5 % vol. • ♀ • ② • ◯ • 🍾 • ★★★1/2

REPA WINERY

Ing. Jozef Repa – repa winery
Vištucka 1265/5, 900 81 Šenkvice
M: +421 911 126 922
www.repawinery.sk, repawinery@gmail.com

VRoSC • 2009 • ☐ 50 ha • 50,000 l

The official seat of the Repa Winery is located on the premises of the former Research Winegrowing and Winemaking Station in Šenkvice, where famous Slovak breeder Dorota Pospíšilova also used to work. The main portion of the wine of this brand is made from grapes from older bearing vineyards in the Small Carpathians. Some varieties whose representation is not sufficient for the requirements of the VRoSC are purchased in the VRoSS and VRoN. Jozef Repa focuses on the production of the best quality wines with protected indication of origin and emphasizes the varietal character in combination with his own unmistakable winemaking style. In addition to wine production, he produces grape must. He was the first in Slovakia to introduce them on the market in the form of a law-pasteurized natural product with sediments from direct pressing. This is one of the healthiest fruit drinks available, with a beneficial impact on the human organism.

SIGNIFICANT WINE AWARDS

Chardonnay 2012 grape selection, medium sweet
SM Concours Mondial de Bruxelles
2013 Brussels

Pinot blanc 2012 Oaked, late harvest, dry
SM Concours Mondial de Bruxelles
2013 Brussels
Národný salón vín SR (Slovak National Wine Salon) 2013

SOMIELLER'S TIP

Rizling cuvée 2012, quality wine, dry,
Cuvee ↦ p. 124

Pinot Noir – Blanc 2012, late harvest, dry,
Innovative Wines ↦ p. 119

Pinot Blanc 2012, Oaked, late harvest, dry,
Innovative Wines ↦ p. 120

Frankovka modrá 2011, Oaked, grape selection, dry, Lemberger (Blaufränkisch) ↦ p. 90

Chardonnay 2012
grape selection, medium sweet

Wine with protected indication of origin D.S.C.
VRoN, Drženice, Baričky Vineyard

The smell of this straw-yellow wine features intoxicating fruity-honey tones of yellow tropical fruit with an admixture of white flowers and beeswax. Traces of hazelnut appear in its aromatic profile after opening. Its full-bodied taste features a fruit concentrate of a combination of citrus fruit, ripe grapes and freshly picked nectarines.

[2,090 l] • 0.75 l • €€ • L07 • 12.0 % vol. • 🍷 • ③ • ☐ • ✄ • ★★★★

RODINNÉ VINÁRSTVO ĎURÍK

Jana Ďuríková VITIS
Opatovská Nová Ves 222
991 07 Opatovská Nová Ves
M: +421 905 535 287
www.vinohradnictvo.sk, vitis@vinohradnictvo.sk

VRoCS • 1997 • ☐ 16 ha • 50,000 l •

Jana Ďuríková VITIS was founded in 1995. The business activities of this family company are oriented on winegrowing and fruit growing, predominantly the production and sale of grapevine plants which are subject to regular health and seedling checks by the inspectors of the Central Institute for Supervising and Testing in Agriculture. In 1999, the company planted 6 ha of stock plantations in the highest level of multiplying from where it supplies virus-free seedlings to winegrowers. Winemaking from their own vineyard is also a significant activity. The company cultivates Rhein and Italian Riesling, Chardonnay, Devín, Traminer, Pinot Gris, Blanc and Noir, Lemberger (Blaufränkisch) and Cabernet Sauvignon. In addition, it has become active in the field of agro tourism connected with fishing and accommodations.

SIGNIFICANT WINE AWARDS

Rizling rýnsky 2012 grape selection, sweet
CH Vinum Superbum 2013
GM Mun-dus, Dunajská Streda 2013

Pinot Noir 2012 grape selection, dry
GM Zlaté víno z Hontu 2014

SOMMELIER'S TIP

Rizling rýnsky 2012 grape selection, sweet,
Rhein Riesling ← p. 80

Rizling vlašský 2012 grape selection,
medium sweet, Italian Riesling ← p. 75

Pinot Noir 2012 grape selection, dry,
Pinot Noir ← p. 95

Sv. Juraj 2009 barrique, medium dry,
Cuvée ← p. 126

Tramín červený 2013
grape selection, dry
Quality wine with attribute, VRoCS, Želovce

This is a clear, light yellow-green Traminer with higher viscosity and a distinctively spicy and fruity bouquet of nutmeg with a note of rose hips and honey. After opening the bottle, you can smell an attractive mixture of soap and candied tropical fruit. The taste is dry, medium-full, spicy and slightly milder than the smell. It is underlined by lively acids and an extract with a higher alcohol content.

[800 l] • 0.75 l • €€ • L-3 • 14.5 % vol. • ★★★1/2

RODINNÉ VINÁRSTVO MAGULA

VINO MAGULA, s.r.o.
Suchá nad Parnou 586,
919 01 Suchá nad Parnou
M: +421 905 645 520
www.vinomagula.sk, vlado@vinomagula.sk

VRoSC • 2009 • ☐ 5 ha • 6,000 l •

The MAGULA family winery tradition dates back to 1931. They make their wines with love and thoroughness from grapes cultivated in their own vineyards. Processing is done traditionally in a beautiful stone cellar on a romantic hill in the middle of the vineyards. All production methods are governed by the rule "less is more." Thanks to this approach, they reflect the natural varietal character and unique terroir of Ružová and Vlčia dolina. Vineyards in the villages of Suchá nad Parnou, which for centuries have borne excellent wines, were described by František Hečko in his famous novel Červené víno (Red Wine). This terroir is characterized by deep loess with a skeleton content of 8 to 10 %, a gradient of 10 to 20 % and a high energy balance with many sunny days and low precipitation. The MAGULA cellar features Lemberger (Blaufränkisch), Blauer Portugieser, Grüner Veltliner and Italian Riesling. They will soon be complemented by Dunaj, Hron, Rosa and Pinot Noir, and the white wine varieties of Traminer and Devín from newly planted vineyards. The aim of the new investment is to gradually plant 12 ha of vineyards and increase production from their own grapes to 50,000 bottles. The recent history of this winery begins from 2007 when they planted a new vineyard of Lemberger (Blaufränkisch) on the restituted vineyards of their grandfathers. The excellent 2011 vintage from this young site won its first important award, the gold medal at Concours Mondial de Bruxelles, followed by the gold medal at the International Lemberger Festival and the title of champion of red wines at the national Vinum Superbum competition.

SIGNIFICANT WINE AWARDS

Modrý Portugal 2012 Classique, quality wine, dry
SM Danube Wine, Bratislava 2015

Modrý Portugal barrique 2012 quality wine, dry
GM Danube Wine, Bratislava 2015

Frankovka modrá 2012 grape selection, dry
SM Festival Frankovky modrej a ružových vín, Rača 2015
CH Výstava vín, Suchá nad Parnou 2015

SOMMELIER'S TIP

Modrý Portugal barrique 2012 quality wine, dry, Blauer Portugieser ⭠ p. 96

Frankovka modrá 2012 grape selection, dry, Lemberger (Blaufränkisch) ⭠ p. 113

Frankovka modrá 2012 Unplugged, quality wine, dry, Terroir-respecting wines ⭠ p. 89

Modrý Portugal 2012
Classique, quality wine, dry
VRoSC, area of Orešany, Suchá nad Parnou

The clear, ruby-red Blauer Portugieser shows violet sparkles on the edge of the goblet. A Cuvée of Blauer Portugieser from old vineyards in the valley of Vlčia dolina, it matured in used oak caskets for 14 months and after bottling without filtration laid the foundation for the final product. It shows a lighter, fruity taste with fine tones of blackberries, a touch of cassis-plum and a refreshing fine acid in the finish.

[2,200 l] • 0.75 l • €€ • L 0137 • 12.0 % vol. • 🍷 • ① • 🗒 {14} • ④ • ↓SO₂ • ✒
★★★1/2

SLOBODNÉ VINÁRSTVO

SLOBODNÉ VINÁRSTVO, s.r.o.
Hlavná 56, 925 54 Zemianske Sady
M: +421 907 100 030
www.slobodnevinarstvo.sk
vinari@slobodnevinarstvo.sk

VRoSC • 2010 • 17 ha • 12,000 l •

The Zemianske sady farmstead is an independent family enterprise that was founded in 1912. During the period of the first Czechoslovak Republic, the wines from this farmstead were sold under the trade brand K trom boxerom (By the Three Boxers) and were popular among the art community in Prague. After the interruption of the family tradition during the post-war period of collectivization, the fourth and fifth generations now manage the operations. Renovating the winemaking heritage began in 1997 by revitalizing neglected vineyards. The first wine with the Slobodné vinárstvo brand was introduced to the market in 2010. The production places an emphasis on precision and an understanding of natural processes which they do not intend to change. All of the wines ferment naturally with their own wine yeasts. Creation and maturing take place free of permitted enological admixtures in order to preserve the structure of the natural smell and taste. From the very beginning of the renewed production, this company has made orange wines of white varieties which are fermented on skins. The return to traditional production methods resulted in the use of Georgian clay vessels called kvevri. In the fall of 2014, they placed them in the ground and began to use them in manual wine making.

SOMMELIER'S TIP

Pinoter 2013 white, dry,
Cuvée ⊢ p. 126

Interval 100 2012 white, medium sweet,
Terroir-respecting wines ⊢ p. 115

Partisan Cru 2011 red, dry,
Cuvée ⊢ p. 126

SLOVAK WINERIES FROM A TO Z

Deviner 2012
white, dry

Wine without geographical indication, VRoSC, Zemianske sady

This golden wine with orange tones was made by spontaneous fermentation after 16 hours of maceration on skins. The unfiltered medium will catch your olfactory interest with tones of fallen leaves, dried fruits, and meadow flowers with a trace of cloves and butter toast in the background. Its harmonious, fruity taste has an appropriate acid content.

DE, T, RR • [400 l] • 0.75 l • €€ • L43 • 13.0 % vol. • ♀ • ① • ◎ • ▤ {18} • ✦ •
★★★1/2

Cutis Pinot 2012
orange, dry

Wine without geographical indication, VRoSC, Zemianske sady

This wine features an orange shade in the goblet with onion-golden traces on the edges and the smell of caramelized strawberries with a hint of candied cherries and ferns. The taste is pure, medium-full and mature with a proper acid content and shows traces of grape pomace, rose hip marmalade and dry bread crust. It has an orange peel finish with bitter undertones of grapefruit and damp soil.

PG • [400 l] • 0.75 l • €€€ • L33 • 11.5 % vol. • ♀ • ① • ◎ • ▢ • ▮ • ★★★1/2

Alternativa 2012
red, dry

Wine without geographical indication, VRoSC, Zemianske sady

A ruby-red wine with purple hints on the edges, its earthy nature is a reflection of the wine processing involving the use of maceration, spontaneous fermentation and maturing in old oak casks. This is an unfiltered Lemberger with tones of plums, wood and bitter almonds, and contains relatively firm acids and tannins. Decant and let breathe before serving.

BF • [400 l] • 0.75 l • €€€ • L40 • 12.0 % vol. • ♀ • ① • ◎ • ▤ {18} • ✦ •
★★★

SOŠVO MODRA

Stredná odborná škola vinársko-ovocinárska Modra
Kostolná 3, 900 81 Modra
T: +421 33 647 25 80
www.svosmo.sk, info@svosmo.sk

VRoSC • 1884 • ☐ 3.5 ha • 12,000 l •

The Secondary Vocational School of Viticulture and Fruit Growing in Modra is one of the oldest vocational schools in Slovakia and Central Europe. The old distillery building was completely reconstructed from 2005 to 2007, and the conditions for the training of students in the Practical Training Center were improved with the support of the Bratislava self-governing region, thanks to which the original cellar on the school property received new equipment for ensuring proper fermentation and the regulation of the creation and maturing of grape wine and a semi-automated bottling line. The revitalization of 2 hectares of vineyards in the historical Emresovka vineyard in Modra was also part of the renovation project for the practical training of students, and with the support of the town of Modra, they leased another 1.5 hectares of bearing vineyards. While tending to the white varieties, students are constantly reminded that quality is born in the vineyard. They accommodate the agrotechnology of winegrowing and integrated protection in the selective production of wines with attributes. They purchase grapes for the production of red wines predominantly in the VRoSS and the VRoSC. Their own varietal composition is represented by Pinot Gris, Chardonnay, Traminer, Muscat Ottonel, Rhein Riesling, Grüner Veltliner and Muller-Thurgau.

The wine is made on modern equipment with a sensitive approach to de-stemming, pressing and must clarification. They ferment the must through the use of controlled alcoholic fermentation while closely monitoring the temperature and cooling. The quality of the school's wines is affected by the proximity of the vineyard and cellar and the related speed of processing of manually harvested grapes. The school sells the majority of its production in bottles. In addition to the professional training of students, the Practical Training Center strives to provide high quality wine at a reasonable price.

SIGNIFICANT WINE AWARDS

Veltlínske zelené 2013 quality varietal wine, dry
SM Vitis Aurea, Modra 2014

Rulandské šedé 2013 grape selection, dry
SM Vitis Aurea, Modra 2015

Muškát Ottonel 2013 quality varietal wine, medium dry
Wine of the Town of Modra 2014
SM Víno Bojnice 2014

SOMMELIER'S TIP

Muškát Ottonel 2013 quality varietal wine, medium dry, Muscat Ottonel ⊢ p. 87

SLOVAK WINERIES FROM A TO Z

Veltlínske zelené 2013
quality varietal wine, dry

Districtus Slovakia Controllatus, VRoSC, Modra

This green-yellow Grüner Veltliner has a more intensive fruit smell and a full spicy taste of green almonds and grapefruits against a background of a piquant herbal note reminiscent of rhubarb with a pinch of fresh celery top. The higher acidity in the taste is a lively complement to the medium-long, honey-citrus reductive finish.

[600 l] • 0.75 l • € • L 07 • 12.5 % vol. • ▼ • ① • ◯ • ✦ • ★★★1/2

Rulandské šedé 2013
grape selection, dry

VRoSC, Emresovka Vineyard

The opulent vintage of this Pinot Gris is yellow-green in color with a hint of white gold and a distinctive spicy-fruity bouquet of citrus fruits with a note of cloves and white pepper. The medium-long taste is affected by the wine's higher alcohol content in addition to acids. Tones of walnuts, apricots and pomegranate empower the full fiery finish of this sub-tropical vintage.

[500 l] • 0.75 l • 7.00 EUR • L 04 • 14.0 % vol. • ▼ • ① • ◯ • ✦ • ★★★1/2

Rizling rýnsky 2013
late harvest, dry

Districtus Slovakia Controllatus, VRoSC, Modra, Noviny Vineyard

This sparkly, golden-yellow Rhein Riesling features a distinct aroma of quince, gooseberries and citrus fruits mixed together and enriched by tones of exotic spices. The taste is also full and mineral with a trace of acids with a relatively long and piquant aftertaste. It bears the early tones of the tertiary aroma of dried herbs and hazelnuts with a drop of kerosene.

[700 l] • 0.75 l • € • L 08 • 12.0 % vol. • ▼ • ① • ◯ • ✦ • ★★★1/2

Svätovavrinecké 2012
quality varietal wine, dry

Districtus Slovakia Controllatus, VRoSC, Modra

This Fresh Saint Laurent, darker violet and ruby-red in color, has an intensive smell of fresh forest fruits. The lively, medium-full taste reflects piquant tones of stone fruits in good equilibrium with fruit acids and tannins. A hint of tones suggesting wild rose hips and cinnamon appears in the aftertaste finish.

[500 l] • 0,75 l • €€ • L 09 • 12,5 % vol. • ◯ • ▼ • ① • ◯ • ✦ • ★★★1/2

STREKOV 1075

Strekov 1075 s.r.o.
Strekov č. 1075, 941 37 Strekov
M: +421 905 649 615
www.strekov1075.sk, info@strekov1075.sk

VRoSS • 2002 • 12 ha • 30,000 l •

SOMMELIER'S TIP

Heion 2013 Special, dry, Innovative Wines ← p. 120

Frankovka modrá 2013 Classic, quality varietal wine, dry, Terroir-respecting wines ← p. 116

Svätovavrinecké 2012 Classic, quality varietal wine, dry, Saint Laurent ← p. 90

Modrý Portugal 2012 Classic, quality varietal wine, dry, Blauer Portugieser ← p. 96

Dunaj 2012 Selection II, quality varietal wine, medium dry, Terroir-respecting wines ← p. 116

Strekov 1075 focuses on the production of wine from their own 12 ha of vineyards which are farmed in accordance with strict standards of biological protection and related agro-technology. They prefer to plant traditional varieties such as Italian Riesling, Grüner Veltliner, Blauer Portugieser, Lemberger (Blaufränkisch) and Saint Laurent, but they are also cultivating two new Devín and Dunaj clones. All of their wines are made in compliance with the Charter of Autentists, i.e., through a careful technological approach, without using selected yeasts, enzymes or additives and the minimal use of sulfur.

Nigori 2013
Special, white, dry
Wine without geographical indication, VRoSS, Strekov

This bright, golden-yellow wine made by fermentation in new casks and subsequently bottled along with sediments is characterized by rich gross lees. The content of the cell wall is released in the wine after autolysis, and thus distinctively enriches the aromatic profile in smell and taste. Tones of acacia honey, pears, wood and dried citrus pleasantly harmonize with a fresh, tart taste.

IR • [150 l] • 0.75 l • € € € € • L-4-2 • 12.0 % vol. • ① • {9} • ↓SO₂ •
• ★★★1/2

Porta 2011 and 2012
Special, cuvée, white, dry
STREKOV 1075
Wine without geographical indication, VRoSS, Strekov

A clear, golden-yellow wine with a slightly opalescent appearance, a rich aroma of bread crust, butter pears with undertones of tobacco leaves and Artemisia reminiscent of noble sherry made by oxidative maturing under the flor (yellow wine). Its robust, full taste combines tones of wood, almonds, chestnut skins, citrus peels, cinnamon and dry honey drops, while the higher alcohol content underlines the style of spontaneous macro oxidation and creates a hot overall impression.

IR 2011, GV 2012 • [500 l] • 0.75 l • € € € € • L-12 • 14.0 % vol. • ① •
{20} • ↓SO₂ • ★★★★

SVV VINANZA

SVV a.s.
Levická 743, 952 01 Vráble
M: +421 918 327 916, T: +421 37 783 2037
www.vinanza.sk, vinanza@vinanza.sk

VRoN • 2008 • ☐ 65 ha • 700,000 l •

SVV VINANZA is the producer of quality varietal wines and quality wines with attribute from grapes cultivated almost exclusively in their own vineyards that were renovated on the site of the old Fermedza vineyard within the cadastral territory of the village of Veľké Lovce. In addition to the grapes from their own vineyards with diverse varietal composition, the company uses a smaller portion of grapes purchased from its partners from the sub-regions of Vráble, Žitava and Strekov. The viticultural regions of Nitra and Southern Slovakia feature a rare diversity; their micro climate and varied geological composition with excellent energy balance offer unique possibilities for the production of quality wines of varied styles which especially reflect their varietal nature. The winery divides them into four product collections according to structure, intensity and extract. The Silver and Red collections feature quality varietal wines and branded wines made from traditional varieties and are designated for daily consumption. Wines with a late harvest attribute and grape selection are the basis for the Patina collection, while the selection of the best wines can be found in the vintages with a gold label. The Gold collection is comprised of flagship wines such as limited volumes of naturally sweet vintages and the prestigious Predium and President blends, as well as the best grape selections of pure varieties from their own vineyards.

SIGNIFICANT WINE AWARDS

Rizling rýnsky 2013 late harvest, medium sweet
SM Dni vína, Nemčiňany 2015
SM Vinum Zoborensis, Nitra 2014

Pálava 2012 quality varietal wine, medium dry
GM Víno Hlohovec 2015

Svätovavrinecké rosé 2013 quality wine, dry
SM Vienále, Topoľčianky 2015

Cabernet Sauvignon 2012 late harvest, dry
SM Dni vína, Nemčiňany 2014

SOMMELIER'S TIP

Rulandské šedé 2014 quality varietal wine, dry,
Pinot Gris ← p. 78

Rizling rýnsky 2013 late harvest, medium sweet,
Rhein Riesling ← p. 82

Pálava 2012 quality varietal wine, medium dry,
Pálava ← p. 104

Tramín červený 2013

quality varietal wine, medium sweet
Wine with protected indication of origin, VRoN, Veľké Lovce

This light yellow Traminer with watery edges has the sweet aroma of orange peel and bergamot. Its mature oily taste copies the smell in its intensity. The perfumed tones in the mouth are refreshed by acid, while its aftertaste leaves a green, slightly spicy up to grassy tone on the root of the tongue. This impressively maturing vintage has a relatively complex aftertaste with residual sugar which is not offensive.

[1,600 l] • 0.75 l • € € • L-95 • 12.0 % vol. • ★★★1/2

SLOVAK WINERIES FROM A TO Z

Muškát Moravský 2013
quality wine, medium sweet

Wine with protected indication of origin D.S.C.
VRoN, Veľké Lovce

This Moravian Muscat is golden yellow and has sparkly purity. The exotic smell and taste of pineapple, banana, tangerine and marmalade pears in the background will please all fans of wine of this aromatic variety. Its taste is evenly mature with the smell, however its intensity is finer by a degree thanks to maturity. This is a drinkable, fruity-spicy Muscat with a pleasant alcohol content and perfumed impression.

[3,200 l] • 0.75 l • €€ • L-93 • 11.0 % vol. • ⑶ • ★

Svätovavrinecké rosé 2013
quality wine, dry

Wine with protected indication of origin D.S.C.
VRoN, Veľké Lovce

This intensive claret-red Saint Laurent rosé with garnet-red shades will please with the smell of marmalade cherries and strawberries. It leaves traces of stone fruit, citrus fruit and ripened garden fruit in a light fruity taste with adequate alcohol content. The overall impression is mature, which allows it to be served with various gastronomical specialties. Enjoy it while you can, because it won't last long.

[3,200 l] • 0.75 l • € • L-73 • 12.0 % vol. • ① • ★

Cabernet Sauvignon 2012
late harvest, dry

Wine with protected indication of origin D.S.C.
VRoN, Veľké Lovce

This dark crimson wine with brownish edges, tones of ripened black berries and a distinctive balsamic aroma dominate in a more massive smell. The late harvest taste is extractive and even earthy, and the wine contains a more distinctive tannin content whose bittersweet trace leaves a distinctive impression on the palate. The dry plum-cranberry aftertaste finishes with pepper on oak toast.

[2,800 l] • 0.75 l • €€ • L-33 • 12.0 % vol. • ① • {7} • ★★★

Alibernet 2012
quality varietal wine, dry

Wine with protected indication of origin D.S.C.
VRoN, Veľké Lovce

This claret-red wine with an aroma of juniper mash and tones of blueberries is lovely; along with its appearance, it documents a higher level of maturity. The taste impression is more intensive in comparison to its smell, while the joined equilibrium of acids, sweet tannins and residual sugar lacks a bit more alcohol. However this won't discourage fans of mature red wines with a smooth and finer aftertaste. A pleasant revelation for the 2012 Alibernet vintage.

[2,200 l] • 0.75 l • € • L-54 • 11.5 % vol. • ① • ★

TAJNA VINEYARDS AND WINERY

TAJNA s.r.o.
Tajná 163, 952 01 Tajná
M: +421 905 274 307
www.vinotajna.sk, info@vinotajna.sk

VRoN • 2012 • ☐ 16 ha • 30,000 l •

Tajná is the name of a new family winery oriented on the production of quality wines from their own cellars. The vision of this young brand is to achieve quality wine through the roots of their own vineyard and its matriculate farming and winemaking. The company history began in 2011 with the planting of a new vineyard with an area of 6.5 ha. The planting continued in 2013 on an area of 9.5 ha. Both vineyards are situated at the Sari site in the viticultural area of Vráble near the village of Tajná. The grapevines with a south-west exposure in the direction of predominating winds enjoy sufficient sun exposure and mineral soil. Approximately 40,000 bottles will be produced annually in the new underground premises. The first phase of building this winery was completed in 2012 with the construction of the premises for the viticultural technology and the staff. Building continued in 2013 with the reconstruction of the original building and cellar which was officially opened to the general public on June 12, 2015 and was accompanied by the introduction of a new collection of wine. The winery has beautiful tasting area with a large terrace situated directly in the vineyard and offering a panorama of the rural landscape. The premises for wine processing are equipped with modern economical technology, and include a warehouse and a cellar for maturing.

SIGNIFICANT WINE AWARDS

Chardonnay 2014 medium dry
GM Vínne hody, Vieska nad Žitavou 2015
GM Ročníkové víno 2015

Cabernet Sauvignon 2013 suché
GM Košické slávnosti vína 2015
GM Víno Vráble 2015
GM Vínne hody, Vieska nad Žitavou 2015

SOMMELIER'S TIP

Chardonnay 2014 medium dry,
Chardonnay ↤ p. 85

Rizling vlašský Tramín 2014 dry,
Cuvée ↤ p. 125

Semillon Sauvignon Blanc 2014 dry,
Sauvignon ↤ p. 86

Cabernet Sauvignon 2013 dry,
Cabernet Sauvignon ↤ p. 92

Pinot Noir 2013 dry,
Pinot Noir ↤ p. 95

Pinot Blanc 2014

medium dry

Wine with protected indication of origin, VRoN, Tajná

This wine with a light greenish shade and a golden sparkle has a fruity, tenderly spicy smell that is sincere, semi-aromatic and even assertive. Its fresh taste copies the smell in intensity and displays tones of freshly picked apples, ginger and pistachios. Its noble sufficiency in connection with a pure submissive body comprise a complex finish in balance with delicious residual sugar and decent acid content.

[1,980 l] • 0.75 l • €€ • L-03 • 13.5 % vol. • 🍷 • ◯ {3} • ② • ☐ • ✦ • ★★★1/2

SLOVAK WINERIES FROM A TO Z

Cabernet Sauvignon rosé 2014
medium dry

Wine with protected indication of origin, VRoN, Tajná

A sparkling rosé, light onion-pink in color, with a fruity and fresh smell reminiscent of freshly peeled pomelo sprinkled with white currants. Its taste impresses with a pleasant acid and an elegant touch of residual sugar. Its basis is created by a note of fresh summer fruit. In balance with the smell, the aftertaste is finished off with lemon grass tones.

[1,980 l] • 0.75 l • €€ • L-05 • 12.5 % vol. • ♀ • ② • ◯ • ♠ • ★★★1/2

Dunaj 2012
raisin selection, medium sweet

Wine with protected indication of origin, VRoN, Tajná

This wine is dark, claret-red with violet edges and has a higher viscosity. The rich spectrum of smells supported by a high alcohol content is accompanied by the taste and smell of stewed blueberries, blackberries and a pinch of exotic spices. The 30-day maceration on skins leaves a fiery aftertaste with a note of coffee beans and sour cherry chocolate.

[400 l] • 0.50 l • €€ • L02-2012 • 15.0 % vol. • ♀ • ◉ {1} • ③ • ◯ • ✒ • ★★★★

SLOVAK WINERIES FROM A TO Z

TERRA PARNA

Zenagro s. r. o.
Trstinská 10, 917 01 Trnava
M: +421 905 402 410
www.terraparna.sk, terraparna@terraparna.sk

VRoSC • 2007 • ☐ 6.6 ha • 17,000 l •

The TERRA PARNA family winery was built in 2008 on a "green field," better to say, close to the new vineyard in Suchá nad Parnou. However, the first fruit was harvested and processed in 2007. The goal of Jozef Zvolenský, the founder and owner of this boutique winery, is to make quality wines that reflect the historical terroir of the Orešany viticultural area. Therefore, Blauer Portugieser and Saint Laurent predominate in the young planting in the Trnavské vrchy vineyard before Alibernet and the Rhein Riesling and Sauvignon white varieties. TERRA PARNA is embodied by the resurrection of the famous Blauer Portugieser variety in a modern style which reflects the specific farming conditions of the southeast hills of the Small Carpathians sloping down to the Trnava plateau. Vineyards bathed in the sun are cooled by the night air streams from the northwest which prevent the development of fungal diseases, and in warm years preserves a sufficient amount of fresh acids in grapes. The poor soil on limestone bedrock combined with the micro climate creates conditions for the production of fresh white wines, bright rosé and intensive red wines made from healthy and ripe grapes. The secret behind the uniqueness of the wines from TERRA PARNA is the reduction of the yield by winter cuts, berry thinning in the vegetation period before their closing and the use of careful methods of ripe grape processing free of additives.

SIGNIFICANT WINE AWARDS

Rizling rýnsky 2013 quality varietal wine, dry
BM International Wine Challenge 2015

Alibernet 2009 quality varietal wine, dry
GM Vino Tirnavia, Trnava 2013

Alibernet 2012 ice harvest, sweet
GGM Ice Wine du Monde, Lednice 2014

SOMMELIER'S TIP

Modrý Portugal Barrique 2009 quality varietal wine, dry,
Blauer Portugieser ⟵ p. 96

Alibernet 2009 quality varietal wine, dry,
Alibernet ⟵ p. 106

Alibernet 2012 ice harvest, sweet,
Alibernet ⟵ p. 107

Rizling rýnsky 2013
quality varietal wine, dry
VRoSC, Suchá nad Parnou, Trnavské vrchy Vineyard

This Rhein Riesling with a greenish-yellow shade has an intensive smell of yellow grapefruit and tangerines with a linden blossom admixture. Its medium-full fruity taste is emphasized by fruit acids. This lively wine has an attractive aroma and taste and an adequate alcohol content. It leaves traces of citrus fruit in its aftertaste which are complemented by fresh basil leaves on the root of the tongue.

[1,500 l] • 0.75 l • €€ • L-3R • 13.0 % vol. • 🍷 • ① • ◯ • ✎ • ★★★1/2

TIBOR MELECSKY

Melecsky Strekov
Strekov č. 183, 941 37 Strekov
M: +421 905 723 924
www.rucnavyrobavina.sk,
melecsky@rucnavyrobavina.sk

VRoSS • 2012 • ☐ 1 ha • 4,000 l •

After more than twenty years of winegrowing and winemaking, Tibor Melecsky made his way from modern production trends through classical winemaking up to unusual solo winemaking in 2012. He employs methods that are long forgotten and shuns the use of modern machines, equipment and the impact of technology. Wines are created in his romantic stone cellar without the use of electricity and he processes the grapes manually – by stamping. The other production processes are also carried out by hand with the help of gravity. He adapts his independent winemaking techniques to an idea which is completely different from the convention of contemporary winemaking modernism, the uniform cliché and the global commercial understanding of wine culture.

SOMMELIER'S TIP

Rizling vlašský 2013 dry,
Terroir-respecting wines ⊢ p. 117

Veltlínske zelené 2013
dry
Wine without geographical indication, VRoSS, Strekov

This opalescent orange Grüner Veltliner with golden-yellow sparkles was created after fermentation by spontaneous microflora from grapes after 3 months of maceration on skins. The oxidative nature is manifested especially by the smell of candied lemons and roasted nuts. The taste is of bitter almonds and long with an intensive bread taste wrapped in the bark of acacia wood and supported by more distinctive acids.

[225 l] • 0.75 l • €€€ • L 2 • 13.0 % vol. • ⑴ • {3} • ↓SO₂ •
★★★

Frankovka modrá 2013
dry
Wine without geographical indication, VRoSS, Strekov

A ruby red Lemberger (Blaufränkisch) with violet edges and traces of glycerol. We can feel the use of oak caskets in the fiery smell with a hint of burnt wood. It is a rustic taste with a higher acid content and green maturing tannins that leaves a robust impression on the tongue. Juniper and dark chocolate with a pinch of thyme can also be detected.

[495 l] • 0.75 l • €€€ • L 4 • 12.0 % vol. • ⑴ • {2} • ↓SO₂ •
★★★1/2

TOKAJ & CO

TOKAJ & CO, s.r.o.
Medzipivničná 202, 076 82 Malá Tŕňa
t: +421 56 679 26 88
www.tokaj.sk, tokaj@tokaj.sk

VRoT • 1999 • ☐ 138 ha • 400,000 l •

TOKAJ & CO is a prominent winegrower and one of the largest makers of Tokaj wines in Slovakia. This company continues in its tradition of more than 60 years by tending 138 ha of vineyards. Current production is oriented on processing grapes from their own registered vineyards. The assortment is divided into Tokaj brand wines Svätý Urban (St. Urban), Omšové víno (Mass Wine), Tokaj quality varietal wines and Tokaj quality varietal wines with attribute, Tokaj selections and the specialties in the form of Tokaj forditás and Tokaj selection essence. Classical Tokaj wine matures in tuff cellars of up to 12 m of depth according to traditional production methods. Wine tasting for visitors is held in their 14th century cellar, which is a national cultural monument. In addition to winning many awards at competitions at home and abroad, wines from the TOKAJ & CO cellar represent the excellent quality of the Tokaj winery not only at the Slovak National Wine Salon, but through the prestigious Slovak Gold quality brand.

SIGNIFICANT WINE AWARDS

Tokajský forditáš 2005, sweet
GM Galicja Vitis, Lancut 2014
GM Agrovíno, Nitra 2014
GM Víno Bojnice 2014

Tokajské samorodné sladké 2006, sweet
SM Tokaj Viničky 2014
BM Vínne trhy Pezinok 2014
GM Vínne trhy Pezinok 2013

Tokajský výber 3 putňový 2009, sweet
SM Agrovíno Nitra 2015
GM Galicja Vitis, Lancut 2014

Tokajský výber 5 putňový 2003, sweet
National Winner of Grand Prix Vinex, Valtice 2015
GM Cuvée Ostrava 2014
GM Galicja Vitis, Lancut 2015, 2014
Národný salón vín SR (Slovak National Wine Salon) 2014

Tokajský výber 6 putňový 2006, sweet
GM Grand Prix Vinex, Valtice 2015
GM Cuvée Ostrava 2015, 2014
GM Galicja Vitis, Lancut 2015, 2014
GM Agrovíno Nitra 2014
GM Muvina Prešov 2014

Tokajská výberová esencia 2003, sweet
GM Tokaj Viničky 2015
CH Grand Prix Vinex, Valtice 2014
GM Cuvée Ostrava 2014
GM MUN-DUS, Dunajská Streda 2015, 2013
Národný salón vín SR (Slovak National Wine Salon) 2013-2014

SOMMELIER'S TIP

Tokajský výber 5 putňový 2003, sweet,
Classical Tokaj Wines ← p. 128

Tokajský výber 6 putňový 2006, sweet,
Classical Tokaj Wines ← p. 127

Tokajská výberová esencia 2003, sweet,
Classical Tokaj Wines ← p. 127

Tokajský forditáš 2005

Slovak Tokaj Wine, VRoT, Malá Tŕňa, Lastovičie Vineyard

This bright golden-yellow Tokaj fordítás with amber hues and a fine oily viscosity was created by the alcoholic fermentation of Tokaj samorodni wine poured over a raisin pomace. A specialty made according to the traditional formula, it has a smell of acacia honey, raisins and roasted hazelnuts. The pure well-balanced taste features dried figs in combination with residual sugar and mineral acid.

F 65 %, L 25 %, YM 10 % • [2,300 l] • 0.50 l • € € • L 03/11 • 11.0 % vol. • ♆ • ④ • ⚘ • ◐ • 🛢 {60} • ⚔ • ★★★★

Tokajské samorodné sladké 2006

Slovak Tokaj Wine, VRoT, Malá Tŕňa, Pahorok Vineyard

This Tokaj samorodné wine with a darker, golden yellow color has a honey, balsamic smell reminiscent of overripe raisins and candied pineapples sprinkled with grains of bee pollen. Its aromatic profile features traces of acacia wood and coffee with a pinch of tobacco leaves. The long and pleasantly earthy taste with refreshing acid contains tones of dried apples, cinnamon and nuts.

F 65 %, L 25 %, YM 10 % • [20,800 l] • 0.50 l • € € • L 03/13 • 12.0 % vol. • ♆ • ③ • ⚘ • ◐ • 🛢 {72} • ⚔ • ★★★1/2

Tokajský výber 3 putňový 2009

Slovak Tokaj Wine, VRoT, Malá Tŕňa

This three-tubs Tokaj selection shows a golden-brown color, higher density with visible glycerol content and bright clarity which confirms the perfect combination of ripe grapes and a higher share of raisins along with slow micro oxidation in wooden casks. The smell of Christmas ginger bread with plum marmalade sprinkled with cloves and cinnamon is attractive. The rich mineral taste with a sufficient amount of acids and residual sugars leaves a piquant trace on the tongue.

F 65 %, L 25 %, YM 10 % • [20,000 l] • 0.50 l • € € • L 14/14 • 10.5 % vol. • ♆ • ④ • ⚘ • ◐ • 🛢 {60} • ⚔ • ★★★★

TOKAJ MACIK WINERY

TOKAJ MACIK WINERY s.r.o.
Medzipivničná 174, 076 82 Malá Tŕňa
M: +421 905 313 352
www.tokajmacik.sk, info@tokajmacik.sk

VRoT • 1995 • ☐ 45 ha • 180,000 l •

The TOKAJ MACIK WINERY is a family winery in the heart of the Viticultural Region of Tokaj which produces unique, world known wines. This is the fourth generation of the Macik family who has dedicated their lives to winegrowing and winemaking. Thanks to the winemaking traditions, abundant experience and innovative practices, it is one of the prominent winemakers in Slovakia. Their selection includes trendy novelties and precious, classical Tokaj wines. Thanks to the high quality and unique nature of their wines, they won the Winery of the Year survey in 2009, 2010 and 2011. Wines of this brand were also successful in the following years of 2012, 2013 and 2014 in the Wine of the year survey. The Macik family has recently renovated old vineyards to ensure continuity for future generations. Their plan is to renovate over 25 ha of Tokaj vineyards. Along with its production and winegrowing activities, the family is involved in wine tourism. Visitors to this winery can spend a holiday in a local pension or organize a company event. Their restaurant for 120 guests offers goose and duck specialties. The facility also includes a small wellness center and a bike rental service. TOKAJ MACIK WINERY boasts of wines that have become famous not only in Slovakia, but also abroad. Wines are exported to 15 countries and have found their way into 17 world famous Michelin restaurants which has helped to spread the good name of Slovakia's Tokaj region. However, this winery also has a non-traditional specialty, the first Slovak Tokaj beer made in India Pale Ale style cooperation with the Rožňava Brewery. The formula, enriched by Tokaj nobly rotten raisins, is very popular with beer lovers and visitors to this winery.

SIGNIFICANT WINE AWARDS

TOKAJ SELECTION Tokajský výber
4 putňový 2006, sweet
GM Terravino Israel 2015

SOMMELIER'S TIP

BLANC FIZZ 2014 sparkling wine, medium dry, Innovative Wines ← p. 121

MONO Furmint 2014 quality varietal wine, dry, Terroir-respecting Wines ← p. 116

TOKAJ GRAND Macik cuvée 2013 grape selection, medium sweet, Cuvée ← p. 125

BOTRIS Late Harvest 2013 quality branded wine, sweet, Innovative Wines ← p. 119

TOKAJ SELECTION Tokajský výber 4 putňový 2006
sweet, Classical Tokaj Wines ← p. 128

TOKAJ SELECTION Tokajský výber 5 putňový 2006
sweet, Classical Tokaj Wines ← p. 128

TOKAJ CLASSIC Tokajský výber 5 putňový 2002
sweet, Classical Tokaj Wines ← p. 128

SLOVAK WINERIES FROM A TO Z

AXIS Furmint 2012
quality varietal wine, dry
Wine with protected indication of origin, VRoT

A bright golden wine with a medium-full, intensively fruity smell and tones of summer pome fruits indicating the presence of fresh grapefruit peels. The rich fruity taste with firm acid is complemented by nuances of limes and gooseberries, while the long finish on the root of the tongue leaves a feeling of dryness spiced up by basil leaves and quince juice.

[8,000 l] • 0.75 l • € • L6/12 • 13.0 % vol. • ⍮ • ① • ◯ • ⚔ • ★★★1/2

AXIS Lipovina 2011
quality varietal wine, medium dry
Wine with protected indication of origin, VRoT

This wine features a transparent straw-yellow up to greenish color with a herbarium of meadow herbs and flowers in the nose. The brisk fruity note of red plums with citrus appears in smell and taste. It has a pleasant floral and fruity taste with a medium-full intensity and a pure fresh finish. In comparison with the Furmint from the AXIS collection, the Lipovina is more harmonious and complex thanks to its higher natural sugar content and lower acid and alcohol concentration.

[8,000 l] • 0.75 l • € • L7/12 • 12.5 % vol. • ⍮ • ② • ◯ • ⚔ • ★★★★

TOKAJ GRAND Muškát žltý 2013
late harvest, medium dry
Wine with protected indication of origin, VRoT, Bara, Piliš Vineyard

This wine has a light green and yellow shade and an intensive floral and spicy smell reminiscent of hawthorn, blackberry with pomelo and cilantro traces. The perfumed smell followed by the delicious taste of brioche with citrus fruit and honey is supported by a more distinct acid content. The overall impression stays on the tongue for a long time after swallowing. It suits a rich table full of heavier specialties from the Southern Zemplín region. A direct and intensive suits wine.

[3,000 l] • 0.75 l • € € • L 5/14 • 13.0 % vol. • ⍮ • ② • ◉ • ◯ • ⚔ • ★★★1/2

VELKEER

VÍNO VELKEER 1113, s.r.o.
Sv. Kelemena 929, 941 07 Veľký Kýr
M: +421 905 177 901
www.velkeer.sk, info@velkeer.sk

VRoSS • 2011 • ☐ 10 ha • 35,000 l •

The Velkeer family has continued its tradition of wine growing and wine making for several generations. The location of its vineyards and winery on the boundary of two significant viticultural regions creates good conditions for the production of quality wines which reflect the unique microclimate and origin of the grapes. In 2014, the company decided to move its wine production from the family cellar to separate premises near the village of Veľký Kýr. The gradual building of their own vineyards in recent years has resulted in a successful expansion of the production area from less than 0.5 ha to 10 ha. New planting is dominated by traditional varieties such as Rhein and Italian Riesling, while blends of rosé, white and red wines with their own enological style are a new trend.

SIGNIFICANT WINE AWARDS

Tri ruže 2013 quality branded wine, rosé, dry
Diploma International Wine Challenge AWC, Vienna 2014

Devín 2013 grape selection, medium sweet
SM Concours Mondial Brussels 2014

Pálava 2013 grape selection, medium sweet
SM International Wine Challenge AWC, Vienna 2014
GM Výstava vín Šenkvice 2014
SM Výstava vín Budmerice 2014

Tramín červený 2013 selection of berries, sweet
SM International Wine Challenge AWC, Vienna 2014
GM Biel Vinalia 2014

Dunaj 2013 late harvest, dry
GM Víno Hlohovec 2014

SOMMELIER'S TIP

Müller Thurgau 2014 quality varietal wine, dry,
Müller Thurgau ← p. 76

Devín 2013 grape selection, medium sweet,
Devín ← p. 102

Pálava 2013 grape selection, medium sweet,
Pálava ← p. 103

Tramín červený 2013 selection of berries, sweet,
Traminer ← p. 83

SLOVAK WINERIES FROM A TO Z

Riesling - Pinot 2013
quality branded wine, white, dry
Wine with protected indication of origin, VRoN

The combination of two dominant yellow-green varieties confirms its maturing in new wood. The aroma of yellow fruits with a drop of acacia honey hides beneath the cleansing tones of vanillin, licorice and eucalypt. This wine's robust and long taste is supported by alcohol and distinct tannins. It resonates in the mouth in the form of baked bread crust with a trace of mashed bananas.

RR, PB • [420 l] • 0.75 l • €€€ • L1913 • 13.0 % vol. • ★★★1/2

Tri ruže 2013
quality branded wine, rosé, dry
Wine with protected indication of origin, VRoSS

This golden-pink rosé attracts by its sparkly, garnet-red shade and mature smell of cherries and plums. The taste sensation is slightly more intense than the smell, naturally with the proper fruit acid content. The extract combines a pleasant earthy character and the elegance of secondary smells of forest strawberries, butter pears and pomelo. This wine is at the peak of its maturity.

CS, ME, BF • [1,320 l] • 0.75 l • €€ • L1013 • 12.5 % vol. • ★★★1/2

Cabernet Sauvignon 2012
grape selection, dry
Wine with protected indication of origin, VRoN

A dark claret wine with higher viscosity in the goblet. The rich aroma of juniper, black pepper, balsamic wood and roasted coffee is influenced by the fiery alcohol, while the hot and long taste is borne by tones of incense and burnt wood. The massive tannins contrast with the sufficient acid content and are relatively astringent. They need ennobling and mellowing and nicely mature with a fiery aftertaste.

[700 l] • 0.75 l • €€€ • L0712 • 14.0 % vol. • ★★★

Dunaj 2013
late harvest, dry
Wine with protected indication of origin, VRoSS, Svodín

The intensive, carmine-red shade of this wine with dark violet sparkles and a full, fruity-spicy aroma make for a pleasant taste experience. Its slowly developing bouquet offers a range of tones of juniper, cassis and black pepper with a hint of coconut flesh. The harmonious alcohol and grape tannin content leaves sweet-bitter notes of sour cherries in chocolate with a dry aftertaste.

[1,275 l] • 0.75 l • €€€ • L0513 • 12.0 % vol. • ★★★1/2

… SLOVAK WINERIES FROM A TO Z

VILLA VINO RAČA

VILLA VINO RAČA, a. s.
Pri vinohradoch 2, 831 06 Bratislava
T: +421 2 492 02 435
www.villavinoraca.sk
sekretariat@villavinoraca.sk

VRoSC • 2004 (1949) • 27 ha
1,000,000 l

The viticultural village of Rača has been known by several names, such as Ratzersdorf and Recse, in the course of its long history. Thanks to its excellent location, beautiful vineyards and even better wine, it has prospered for centuries. In the past, Rača wine, the best and most expensive of the VR of Small Carpathians, made its way to the royal table of the Austro-Hungarian Monarchy, to Bohemia, Silesia, Poland and Russia. It was even served on the Titanic. Today, after hundreds of years, all of Europe is familiar with these local wines. Gold and silver medals from international competitions and exhibitions, such as Terravino, Mundus vini, Mondial du Rose, AWC Vienna, Vinoforum are proof of this. VILLA VINO RAČA was founded in May 2004 after the transformation of the legal form of the original agricultural co-op in Rača, the roots of which date back to 1949. The harmony of the soil composition of Rača's vineyards and specific features of individual varieties are reflected in the originality of red wines in particular, but also of white wines. The grape yields are limited by cutting and selection during harvesting, while the reliable elements of enological modernism are employed. The pneumatic pressing of grapes, the clarification of musts, and the physical and biological regulation of fermentation with their own genera of Saccharomyces cerevisiae are standard procedures here. VILLA VINO RAČA wines are authentic, original and unique. They are characterized by the five "E's". They are emotional, elegant, ethereal, emphatic and energetic. In addition, they are transparent and crystal clear. The production portfolio features traditional white varieties such as Italian and Rhein Riesling, Muller-Thurgau, Grüner Veltliner, Pinot Blanc, Traminer, while the selection of rosé and red wines is embodied by Lemberger (Blaufränkisch) followed by Cabernet Sauvignon. Rača Frankovka - Lemberger (Blaufränkisch) is the flagship brand and contains more antioxidants than the famous Vranac of Montenegro. However, the Lemberger (Blaufränkisch) from Rača is the true pride of this company, a great wine. Vinum pro corde, the wine of our heart. It will keep you at the table for a long time and with regular use it will also keep you alive and well.

SIGNIFICANT WINE AWARDS

Tramín červený 2013 Château Palugyay, ice wine, sweet
GM Terravino, Israel 2015
GM Muvina, Prešov 2014

Cisárske Svätovavrinecké 2013
grape selection, dry
Národný salón vín SR (Slovak National Wine Salon) 2014
GM Vienále, Topoľčianky 2014

SOMMELIER'S TIP

Cisárske Svätovavrinecké 2013 grape selection, dry, Saint Laurent ⊢ p. 191

Frankovka modrá 2012 Château Palugyay, grape selection, dry, Lemberger (Blaufränkisch) ⊢ p. 88

Račianska frankovka 2011 Exclusive Collection, quality branded wine, dry, Lemberger (Blaufränkisch) ⊢ p. 89

Tramín červený 2013 Château Palugyay, ice wine, sweet, Traminer ⊢ p. 83

SLOVAK WINERIES FROM A TO Z

Rizling vlašský 2013
Exclusive Collection, late harvest, dry
Wine with protected indication of origin, VRoSC

A Rhein Riesling with an elegant, greenish-yellow color and a distinctive smell of freshly picked greengages a tender honey bouquet. The herbal note is wrapped in pieces of artichoke with a piquant and more distinct acid. Its medium-full aftertaste leaves a refreshing impression and is especially inviting in warm months. The tender trace of residual sugar changes with the rest of the evaporated wine into the dew of meadow flowers after the fading intensity of taste.

[6,000 l] • 0.75 l • € • L-44 • 12.5 % vol. • ⚱ • ① • ◯ • 🗡 • ★★★1/2

Tereziánska frankovka 2011
Exclusive Collection, quality branded wine, dry
Wine with protected indication of origin, VRoSC, Rača, Rača Vineyard

This dark red Theresian Lemberger with purple edges has an opulent, balsamic, fruity bouquet which suggests baked plum pie with cinnamon and forest raspberries with a hint of oak barrel. The smooth, medium full taste with a velvet tannin is proof of the longer maturing of this wine in caskets. The noble aftertaste is affected by tones of hazelnuts and overripe marmalade cherries with a pinch of vanilla. This is a vintage with a well-balanced collection of individual aromatic and taste components.

[4,500 l] • 0.75 l • € € • L-85 • 12.0 % vol. • ⚱ • ① • ◎ • 🛢 {8} • 🗡 • ★★★★

VINÁRSTVO BERTA

Vinárstvo Berta, s. r. o.
Ružová 1017, 941 37 Strekov
M: +421 904 440 944
www.vinarstvoberta.sk, info@vinarstvoberta.sk

VRoSS • 2009 • 2 ha • 10,000 l •

The Berta Winery is a small, progressive family operation; every member of the family received viticultural education in Modra, Lednice na Morave or Nitra. This is an advantage that is not easily acquired; it is also the challenge and responsibility of the professional viticultural craft towards clients. At this company they respect traditional values and wisely use modern biotechnological methods. They try to provide their customers with wine that bears the distinct style of its place of birth and the winemaker who created it. It is said that the quality of a wine is born in the vineyard, and since the company's foundation, they strive to plant their own vineyards. This should ensure the filling of new cellars in the future. Their new production premises are equipped with the latest technological devices wich provide better possibilities for regulating the fermentation process. As a result, their wines will be more delicate to the nose and mouth and able to satisfy even the most demanding customers. The Berta family Winery is all about honest work and investment, and the wishes of the Berta family that its customers will relax and feel good while drinking their wines.

SIGNIFICANT WINE AWARDS

Rizling rýnsky 2013 grape selection, medium sweet
SM International Wine Challenge, Vienna 2015

SOMMELIER'S TIP

Rizling rýnsky 2013 grape selection,
medium sweet, Rhein Riesling ← p. 81

Petit Merlau 2013 quality branded wine, dry,
Innovative Wines ← p. 120

SLOVAK WINERIES FROM A TO Z

Rulandské šedé 2013
Sur Lie, grape selection, dry

Wine with protected indication of origin, VRoSS, Pribeta

The straw-yellow shade of this Pinot Gris has a golden hue, brilliant clarity and the pleasant smell of hazelnuts mixed with sweet tropical fruit, predominantly mango and dried pineapple. The modest residual sugar softens the taste of acids and the fullness of alcohol and complements the attractive oak barrel notes. The finish of this wine has a trace of butter brioche with apricot marmalade.

[750 l] • 0.75 l • €€ • L31 • 13.5 % vol. • ② • {6} • {1} • ★★★1/2

Alibernet 2013
quality wine, dry

Wine with protected indication of origin, VRoN, Santovka

This dark, purple-red wine has a smell of cranberries in contrast with the poppy seed mash with nuances of red paprika. The relatively distinctive green tannins and fiery tone of alcohol are present in the medium full taste. The lively, appropriately juicy acid along with the extract leaves the impression of red currants on the root of the tongue. The aftertaste offers a playful spicy finish.

[1,000 l] • 0.75 l • €€ • L35 • 13.8 % vol. • ① • ★★★1/2

VINÁRSTVO BLAHO

Igor Blaho
Hlavná 40, 919 21 Zeleneč
M: +421 905 489 009, +421 908 470 533
www.blaho.sk, vinarstvo@blaho.sk

VRoSC • 2004 • ☐ 17 ha • 70,000 l •

Igor Blaho farms on 17 ha of his own vineyards in the village of Zeleneč of the Trnava viticultural area and the Viticultural Region of the Small Carpathians. He cultivates red varieties and produces wines especially from new Slovak clones: Dunaj, Váh, Hron, Nitria, Rimava, Rudava, Torysa, Rosa. He also cultivates traditional red varieties of Pinot Noir, Blauer Portugieser and Saint Laurent; the newer German clones: Acolon [Lemberger (Blaufränkisch) x Dornfelder], Cabernet Dorsa (Dornfelder x Cabernet Sauvignon) and older new clones such as Zweigeltrebe, Dornfelder and Alibernet. He is also one of the few Slovak vinegrowers to cultivate the exotic Syrah. His white varieties are represented by Grüner Veltliner, Italian Riesling and Irsai Olivér; he also plans to plant Traminer. Growing quality grapes from one's own resources and the subsequent production of quality, naturally pure and mature wines with a minimum of technological intervention in the processing and production is the philosophy of this winery. He emphasizes adherence to an optimum bud load (1.0 – 1.5 kg) with the aim to achieve a healthy and ripe yield. He focuses on careful grape processing, proper maceration, and malolactic fermentation and maturing in oak barrels. The maturing process depends on the variety or nature of the wine and takes from 3 to 24 months. Afterwards, the wines are bottled stabilized and released for sale.

SIGNIFICANT WINE AWARDS

Nitria 2012 quality wine, dry
CH Valtické vínne trhy 2015

Hron 2012 quality wine, dry
SM Valtické vínne trhy 2015

Dunaj 2011 grape selection, dry
GM Valtické vínne trhy 2014
GM Celoslovenská výstava vín, Skalica 2014
GM Víno Hlohovec 2014
SM Víno Tirnavia 2014

SOMMELIER'S TIP

Rudava 2012 quality wine, dry,
Rudava ← p. 110

Hron 2012 quality wine, dry,
Hron ← p. 110

Dunaj 2011 grape selection, dry,
Dunaj ← p. 108

SLOVAK WINERIES FROM A TO Z

Modrý portugal 2013
quality wine, dry

Wine with protected indication of origin
VRoSC, Zeleneč, Pri Kríži Vineyard

This light, fruity Blauer Portugieser with a sparkly light red color and a garnet-red hint attracts with its smell of May cherries. Its pleasantly balanced taste with a delicious, sweetish tannin continues in a smooth aftertaste reminiscent of overripe sour cherries. Dark chocolate with undertones of bramble can also be detected.

[2,400 l] • 0.75 l • €€ • L-07 • 12.1 % vol. • 🍷 • ① • 🛢 • {6} • 🍾 • ★

Váh 2012
quality wine, dry

Wine with protected indication of origin
VRoSC, Zeleneč, Pri Kríži Vineyard

A dark, raspberry-red wine with a massive smell of overripe blackberries and sour cherries emphasized by a trace of spice. Its expressively rich and relatively long taste features a mixture of elderberries, currents and plums from a copper kettle. Slow maturing in an oak barrel added to its structured body elegance, which is also confirmed by the finish of sour cherries in chocolate with a pinch of black pepper.

[2,400 l] • 0.75 l • €€ • L-16 • 13.5 % vol. • 🍷 • ① • 🛢 • {16} • 🍴 • ★★★★

Nitria 2012
quality wine, dry

Wine with protected indication of origin
VRoSC, Zeleneč, Pri Kríži Vineyard

The dark, crimson shade and higher viscosity immediately attract attention, while the selection of berries with a sugar content of 26 °NM resulted in tones of candied cherries and cranberries in the aroma and emphasized the taste with a sweet velvet tannin and a marmalade note of chassis and high extract. The full taste with higher alcohol content is slightly bitter and fiery at the finish.

[1,500 l] • 0.75 l • €€ • L-08 • 14.0 % vol. • 🍷 • ① • 🛢 • {16} • 🍴 • ★★★1/2

Rosa 2012
quality wine, dry

Wine with protected indication of origin
VRoSC, Zeleneč, Pri Kríži Vineyard

The ink-violet shade, the intoxicating rose garden smell and harder tannin taste are unique for this red aromatic variety. Its heavy aromatic profile after opening is reminiscent of rose oil drops on a fading lily bouquet. The taste shows notes of anise, dark chocolate with grated dried orange peels and leaves a truly rough tannin tone on the palate, which eventually has a refreshing effect in combination with the fruit acid.

[500 l] • 0.75 l • €€ • L-10 • 12.5 % vol. • 🍷 • ① • ⬭ • 🍴 • ★★★1/2

SLOVAK WINERIES FROM A TO Z

VÍNKO KLIMKO MODRA

VÍNKO KLIMKO MODRA
Pod vinicami 6, 900 01 Modra
T: +421 908 732 125
www.vinkoklimko.sk, info@vinkoklimko.sk

VRoSC • 2012 • 1.5 ha • 7,000 l •

This young winery draws from a family viticultural tradition and the experience of Ing. Juraj Klimko, an enologist and graduate from the department of Biochemical Technology at the Faculty of Chemical and Food Technology of the Slovak University of Technology in Bratislava. He founded this family winery together with his brother Tomáš in 2012. Their wines come from Modra vineyard grapes. This is another reason for the originality, sincerity and joy of Klimko wines springing from various interesting locations in the unique Modra viticultural valley.

SIGNIFICANT WINE AWARDS

Veltlínske zelené 2013 straw wine, sweet
GM Austrian Wine Challenge, Vienna 2014

SOMMELIER'S TIP

Veltlínske zelené 2013 grape selection, dry, Grüner Veltliner ⟵ p. 74

Dievčie hrozno 2013
late harvest, dry

Wine with protected indication of origin
VRoSC, Modra, Šarkaperky Vineyard

This wine made from the rare Modra Mädchentraube variety has a light, green-yellow shade and brilliant clarity which are in pleasant harmony with its spicy-floral bouquet. It features the freshness of yellow grapefruit with the honey tones of the linden tree. The taste benefits from a higher acid content which enhances the overall impression and staying power of its juicy, fruity aftertaste.

[1,000 l] • 0.75 l • €€ • L0314 • 12.5 % vol. • ★★★

Tramín červený 2013
grape selection, dry

Wine with protected indication of origin
VRoSC, Modra, Grefty Vineyard

This Traminer has a fine, greenish color with a modest, golden sparkling shade. Its spicy-fruity smell features tones of dried fruit, predominately pineapple, against a background of basil, soap and a pinch of white pepper. The refreshing dry taste is medium full up to full and provides balance to an aroma with a firm acid which is just right.

[700 l] • 0.75 l • €€ • L0214 • 13.0 % vol. • ★★★1/2

VÍNO MATYŠÁK

Víno Matyšák s.r.o.
Glejovka 10/A, 902 01 Pezinok
T: +421 33 641 35 43
www.vinomatysak.sk, office@vinomatysak.sk

VRoSC / VRoSS • 1991 • purchase of grapes from contractual partners from an area 149 ha •
☐ 7 ha • 2,000,000 l •

Peter Matyšák is the pioneer and visionary of contemporary winemaking in Slovakia. In 1994, he was the first private winemaker to implement controlled alcoholic fermentation at regulated temperatures, and in 1997 he began to produce brandy. Since he doesn't own extensive winegrowing areas, since 1992 he has developed cooperation with four strategic partners regarding the provision of high quality wine grape varieties, thanks to which he has been able to offer a wide spectrum of varietal wines. Grapes supplied from viticultural cooperatives and private winegrowers from Grinava, Hlohovec, Mužla, Rúbaň and Búč form the traditional foundation for the quality of his future wine. His most important priorities in cooperation with the grape suppliers include optimizing the yield by vine pruning up to grape bunch selection in the ripening period, along with the integrated protection of plants, the stable bearing of plantings and selective processing at the proper agro-technical time according to the ripeness of the vintage. Víno Matyšák is a family brand. As the owner says, it is quite rare to have professionals working in a large company who not only become part of the family, but are able to work well and create a good working atmosphere. Peter Matyšák was the first wine maker to become a finalist in the Entrepreneur of the Year competition in Slovakia. In addition to building his own winery from scratch, he created his own brand with a vision for which he is rightfully proud. He is also successful in his original profession. As a passionate gastronome, hotelier and gourmet who supports the slow food movement, he opened a restaurant with the name Vinum Galeria Bozen, which is situated in the historical center of the town of Pezinok and the stylish Matyšák Hotel with one of the best thematic restaurants in Bratislava. When asked about the key to his success he stated, "Today I know that to build a brand is one thing, but it is equally important to maintain it, which requires great commitment. The better the brand, the greater the challenge for my team and me to improve its quality and value." This has also been confirmed by more significant investments in the largest processing facility for the controlled cooling of 900,000 l of grape juice and wine, the use of a pneumatic press for pressing grapes under an inert nitrogen atmosphere, the latest Gioiello type vinificators, and the successful production of their own grape juices and non-alcoholic beverages with a new bottling line at the plant in the Glejovka section of Pezinok.

SIGNIFICANT WINE AWARDS

Sekt Matyšák Brut 2011
Méthode Traditionelle,
GM Prague Wine Trophy 2015,
SM Finger Lakes International Wine Competition, New York 2015

Silvánske zelené 2013
Gold Prestige, grape selection, dry
GM Les Grands Concours du Monde, Strasburg 2014
GM Concours Mondial de Bruxelles, Brussels 2014
SM Mundus Vini, Berlin 2014
GM Vino Tirnavia, Trnava 2014

Irsai Oliver 2013 Vinum Galéria Bozen, quality wine, dry
GM Terravino Israel 2014

SLOVAK WINERIES FROM A TO Z

Müller Thurgau 2013 Prestige, late harvest, dry
GGM Bacchus Madrid 2014
GGM Concurso International de Vinos Madrid 204
GM Vínne thry Pezinok 2014

Sauvignon 2013 Prestige, late harvest, dry
SM Concours International du Vin, Thessaloniki 2014

Devín 2013 Gold Prestige,
selection of berries, medium sweet
Vinalies Internationales, Paris 2014
GGM Bacchus Madrid 2014
CH Vitis Aurea, Modra 2014

Cabernet Sauvignon 2013 Prestige,
late harvest, rosé, dry
SM Vinalies Internationales, Paris 2014
SM Le Mondial du Rosé 2014
GM Vienále Topoľčianky 2014

Frankovka modrá 2011 Oak Wood,
grape selection, dry
SM Concours Mondial Bruxelles, Brussles 2013
SM Mundus, Germany 2013
GM Košické slávnosti vína 2014
GM Medzinárodný festival Frankovky modrej a ružových vín, Rača 2014
Camerlon 2011 Oak Wood,
quality wine, red, dry
GM Mondial du Merlot et Assemblages, Switzerland 2014

Cabernet Franc 2011 Oak Wood,
quality wine, red, dry
GM Concours International de Lyon 2014
GM International Wine Challenge AWC, Vienna 2014
SM Concours International des Cabernets 2015
CH Vínne trhy Pezinok 2014
GM Berliner Wein Thophy 2013

SOMMELIER'S TIP

Sekt Matyšák Brut 2011 Méthode Traditionnelle, Sparkling Wines ⟵ p. 133

Irsai Oliver 2013 Vinum Galéria Bozen, quality wine, dry, Irsai Oliver ⟵ p. 82

Müller Thurgau 2013 Prestige, late harvest, dry, Müller Thurgau ⟵ p. 75

Silvánske zelené 2013 Gold Prestige, grape selection, dry, Grüner Silvaner ⟵ p. 86

Devín 2013 Gold Prestige, selection of berries, medium sweet, Devín ⟵ p. 100

Cabernet Sauvignon 2013 Prestige, late harvest, rosé, dry, Rosé Wines ⟵ p. 111

Frankovka modrá 2011 Oak Wood, grape selection, dry, Lemberger (Blaufränkisch) ⟵ p. 88

Camerlon 2011 Oak Wood, quality wine, red, dry, Cuvée ⟵ p. 122

Cabernet Franc 2011 Oak Wood, quality wine, dry, Terroir-respecting wines ⟵ p. 114

Merlot 2009 Oak Wood, dry, Innovative Wines ⟵ p. 119

Portito Rosso 4 years old, sweet, Innovative Wines ⟵ p. 119

SLOVAK WINERIES FROM A TO Z

Sekt Matyšák Rosé Brut 2011
Méthode Traditionnelle
Quality sparkling wine

This garnet-red and pink wine is accompanied by an intensive foaming of small sparkles which lasts for more than a day after opening the bottle. Its charming bouquet of red garden fruit is emphasized by dry citrus peels and a harmonious fruity taste with sufficient vital acids. A dosage slightly above the limit for Extra Brut helps to create the piquant aftertaste and encourages indulgence.

BF, FM • [2,250 l] • 0.75 l • €€ • L-87 • 13.0 % vol. • ♀ • ① • ⊙ {9} • ❄ • ✦
★★★1/2

Chardonnay – Sauvignon 2013
Prestige, late harvest, dry
Wine with protected indication of origin
VRoSC, Hlohovec, Šomoď Vineyard

This light greenish wine with golden hues originated in one vineyard and comes in two varieties. Its charming smell combines the ripeness of vineyard peaches of Sauvignon with the yellow melon tones of Chardonnay. The common genera of yeasts create the taste of a wonderful mixture of tones of yellow fruit and peach soap with a note of whipped cream whose finish is complemented by an aroma of forest strawberries.

CH, SB • [4,000 l] • 0.75 l • €€ • L 53 • 12.0 % vol. • ♀ • ① • ◯ • ✦ ★★★1/2

Sauvignon 2013
Prestige, late harvest, dry
Wine with protected indication of origin
VRoSS, Rúbaň, Kishegy allatti Vineyard

This wine has a watery appearance with a yellowish shade at its core, and an attractive herbal up to discreetly spicy smell of nettle leaves, elderberry flowers and pine needles. After swallowing, the taste is light and suited to its smell. The tones of freshly picked apples with an admixture of ripe peaches provide for an interesting combination. Fruit acids can also be found in the pure aftertaste where they leave a juicy trace of fresh citrus peels.

[7,500 l] • 0.75 l • €€ • L6 • 12.0 % vol. • ♀ • ① • ◯ • ✦ • ★★★★

Devín 2011
Prestige, selection of berries, sweet
Wine with protected indication of origin
VRoSS, Mužla, Malý Čipáň Vineyard

This sparkly, golden-yellow wine has an enchanting floral and fruity smell of roses and exotic fruit. Sweet tones of dried apricots, bananas and pineapple open up in the mouth. An elegant, naturally sweet wine with 116 g/l of residual sugar and a delicate fruity aftertaste featuring overripe grapes of this unique Slovak variety.

[3,000 l] • 0.50 l • €€ • L 55 • 9.5 % vol. • ♀ • ④ • ◯ • ✦ • ★★★★

SLOVAK WINERIES FROM A TO Z

Frankovka modrá 2014
Vinum Galéria Bozen, quality wine, rosé, dry
Wine with protected indication of origin, VRoSS

This ash-pink Lemberger (Blaufränkisch) with golden-yellow hues has the smell of forest fruit and overripe raspberries in equilibrium with a light, fruity taste featuring notes of dry citrus drops and the pulp of yellow grapefruit. A dry, pleasant, drinkable rosé from the most frequently cultivated red variety in Slovakia that will please but not only in daily gastronomy.

[60,000 l] • 0.75 l • € • L5 • 12.0 % vol. • ♀ • ① • ◯ • ♠ • ★

Cabernet Sauvignon 2013
Prestige, late harvest, rosé, dry
Wine with protected indication of origin
VRoSS, Búč, Vinohrady Vineyard

This attractive, garnet-red and pink wine has a crystal clear and intoxicating aroma of candied red fruit with a predominance of garden strawberries and sweet sour cherries. The marmalade notes of berries also appear in the taste. Its fruity structure is emphasized by a fresh acid and adequately rounded by residual sugar. The finishing impression belongs to red currents in white chocolate. A rosé in bloom, do not leave it in the bottle unnoticed.

[10,000 l] • 0.75 l • € € • L09 • 12.5 % vol. • ♀ • ①-② • ◯ • ♠ • ★★★★

Cabernet Sauvignon 2013
Vinum Galéria Bozen, quality wine, dry
Wine with protected indication of origin, VRoSS

A dark, claret-red wine with the smell of cassis and juniper with traces of tobacco leaves in the background. The medium-full taste of red currents hides young fruity tannins balanced out by the proper acid content and suitable alcohol level. Drinkable with a final aftertaste with marmalade and cocoa; medium with a lighter structure.

[55,000 l] • 0.75 l • € • L 68 • 12.5 % vol. • ♀ • ① • ◯ • ✎ • ★

Cabernet Franc 2011
Oak Wood, quality wine, red, dry
Wine with protected indication of origin
VRoSS, Rúbaň, Nový vrch Vineyard

A dark, claret-red wine with garnet, brick-red shades. Its full fruity aroma is dominated by an intensive note of cassis leaves. Thanks to longer maturing in oak casks, it has a noble smell of wood. The marmalade taste sensation is supported by tannin and an excellent development of bottle maturity. Traces of spices, tobacco, candied cherries in dark chocolate develop in the finish.

[7,950 l] • 0.75 l • € € € • L 89 • 14.5 % vol. • ♀ • ① • ▦ {30} • ✎ •
★★★★★

VÍNO MIROSLAV DUDO

Ing. Miroslav Dudo – VMD
Potočná 1, 900 01 Modra
T: +421 33 640 07 53, M: +421 903 451 534
www.vinodudo.sk, info@vinodudo.sk

VRoSC • 2001 • 11 ha • 50,000 l •

Miroslav Dudo's small winery cultivates grapevines in the viticultural area of Modra and makes quality varietal and branded wines of traditional varieties and new clones. His selection includes great Modra varieties such as Grüner Veltliner, Rhein Riesling and Saint Laurent. A smaller portion of production is comprised of wines made from grapes from the viticultural areas of Šintava and Strekov. Dudo enlarged his offer of red new clones in 2014 by the first fruit of the 2012 Dunaj variety. In addition to classical production methods, he employs various progressive elements such as the use of nitrogen (inert atmosphere), the maceration of skins in submerged pomace and the fermentation of clarified musts with the regulation of temperature. The branded white Naše cuvée and the branded red blend Móže byt mature in newer and older oak casks according to the winery's special formula. Fans of naturally sweet wines can try ice wine or straw wine, depending on the vintage, which are made from a selection of overripe grapes. The winery also has a tasting room where guests can attend wine tasting events guided by the winemaker himself, and accompanied by domestic culinary specialties and folk music from the village of Kraľovany.

SIGNIFICANT WINE AWARDS

Veltlínske zelené 2014 kabinett, dry
GM Vitis Aurea, Modra 2015

Naše cuvée zo starých viníc 2013
quality branded wine, dry
GM Víno Bojnice 2014

Cabernet Sauvignon 2013
grape selection, white, dry
GGM Benátecký hrozen,
Benátky nad Jizerou 2014
ZM Víno Tirnavia 2014

Móže byt 2012 quality branded wine, red, dry
GGM Benátecký hrozen,
Benátky nad Jizerou 2014
GM Víno Tirnavia 2014

SOMMELIER'S TIP

Sauvignon Blanc 2014 kabinett, dry,
Sauvignon ← p. 87

Tramín červený 2014 late harvest, medium dry,
Traminer ← p. 83

Devín 2014 late harvest, medium dry,
Devín ← p. 101

Naše cuvée zo starých viníc 2013 quality branded wine, white, dry, Cuvée ← p. 124

Cabernet Sauvignon 2013 grape selection, dry, Cabernet Sauvignon ← p. 92

Móže byt 2012 quality branded wine, red, dry, Cuvée ← p. 123

SLOVAK WINERIES FROM A TO Z

Veltlínske zelené 2014
kabinett, dry

Wine with protected indication of origin
VRoSC, Modra, Bolflajtna Vineyard

This is a yellow-green Grüner Veltliner with a graciously ripened fruity-Muscat smell with exotic tones of mango, spring primroses spiced, and up with a pinch of white pepper. The harmony of acids, alcohol and residual sugar in the taste creates a juicy, lively, up to medium-long sweet impression. The persistent fruity aftertaste is reminiscent of grapefruit pulp with a pleasantly tender bitterness in the finish.

[1,950 l] • 0.75 l • €€ • L186 • 12.0 % vol. • ♀ • ① - ② • ◯ • ▮ • ★★★

Cabernet Sauvignon ružové 2014
kabinett, medium dry

Wine with protected indication of origin
VRoSC, Doľany, Sexitále nad Krížom Vineyard

An elegant raspberry rosé that allures with its smell of forest strawberries and rhubarb. The pleasant fruity taste will impress with its tender equilibrium of acids and residual sugar. Its fruity notes are reminiscent of pieces of red water melon and elderberry. The aftertaste, with an undertone of ripened citruses and forest raspberries, has a shorter finish. With its piquant character and bouquet of summer fruit this wine is sure to please, especially in the first year after tasting.

[1,700 l] • 0.75 l • €€ • L189 • 11.5 % vol. • ♀ • ② • ◯ • ▮ • ★★★1/2

VÍNO MRVA & STANKO

VÍNO MRVA & STANKO, a. s.
Orešianska 7/A, 917 00 Trnava
T: +421 33 59 147 11
www.mrvastanko.sk, info@mrvastanko.sk

VRoSC • 1997 • purchase of grapes from contractual partners from an area of 70 ha • 300,000l

VÍNO MRVA & STANKO's annual production of 400 000 bottles makes it a medium-size company in terms of volume. Its assortment features quality wines with attribute, quality varietal wines and branded wines, of which approximately eighty percent are international varieties and 20 % are varieties typical for the Slovak viticultural country, including new, recently bred varieties. The new clones preserve their unique terroir. This winery's portfolio also includes sparkling wine and wine brandy. The limited collection branded Winemarker´s Cut comprises its top products. From the very beginning, this brand has been known for its originality and novelty, which is also expressed in the company logo - a wine leaf, which symbolizes the fact that a wine's fate is decided in the vineyard. The winery's stylish tasting premises with accommodations make it an attractive place for conferences and wine parties. The pension and wine shop are situated at the company seat.

SIGNIFICANT WINE AWARDS

Cuvée Brut 2011 Méthode Traditionnelle
GM Prague Wine Trophy, Prague 2014

Rizling vlašský 2013 late harvest, dry
SM Vinalies Internationales, Paris 2014
CH Vínne thry Pezinok 2014

Rulandské šedé 2013 grape selection, medium dry
GM International Wine Challenge AWC, Vienna 2014
GM Oenoforum 2014
Národný salón vín SR (Slovak National Wine Salon) 2014

Chardonnay 2012 grape selection, dry
GM Concours Mondial de Bruxelles, Brussels 2013
SM Chardonnay du Monde 2013
Národný salón vín SR (Slovak National Wine Salon) 2013

Chardonnay 2012 Winemaker´s Cut, grape selection, dry
SM Concours Mondial de Bruxelles, Brussles 2014

Rizling rýnsky 2013 late harvest, medium dry
GM International Wine Challenge AWC, Vienna 2014

Rizling rýnsky 2012 Winemaker´s Cut grape selection, dry
GM Vínne trhy Pezinok 2014
SM International Wine Challenge AWC, Vienna 2013
GM Národný salón vín SR (Slovak National Wine Salon) 2013

Tramín červený 2013
grape selection, medium sweet
GM Concours Mondial de Bruxelles, Brussles 2014
SM Vínne trhy Pezinok 2014

Devín 2013 selection of berries, sweet Devín 2013 selection of berries, sweet
GM Muvina Prešov 2014
SM International Wine Challenge AWC, Vienna 2014

Cabernet Sauvignon Rosé 2013 dry
SM Vinalies Internationales, Paris 2014
GM Bacchus Madrid 2014
GM Vínne thry Pezinok 2014

Pinot Noir 2012 grape selection, dry
SM International Wine Challenge AWC, Vienna 2014

SLOVAK WINERIES FROM A TO Z

Frankovka modrá 2012 Winemaker´s Cut, grape selection, dry
SM International Wine Challenge AWC, Vienna 2014
GM Vino Tirnavia 2014

Cabernet Sauvignon 2012 Winemaker´s Cut, grape selection, dry
SM Decanter World Wine Awards 2014
GM Vínne trhy Pezinok 2014

Cuvée Hron Váh Rimava Rudava 2011 Winemaker´s Cut, red, dry
GGM Concours Mondial de Bruxelles, Brussles 2014
Národný salón vín SR (Slovak National Wine Salon) 2014

SOMMELIER'S TIP

Cuvée Brut 2011 Méthode Traditionnelle, Sparkling Wines ⊢ p. 131

Rizling vlašský 2013 late harvest, dry, Italian Riesling ⊢ p. 75

Rulandské šedé 2013 grape selection, medium dry, Pinot Gris ⊢ p. 76

Rizling rýnsky 2013 late harvest, medium dry, Rhein Riesling ⊢ p. 80

Rizling rýnsky 2012 Winemaker´s Cut grape selection, dry, Terroir-respecting Wines ⊢ p. 114

Chardonnay 2012 grape selection, dry, Chardonnay ⊢ p. 84

Chardonnay 2012 Winemaker´s Cut, grape selection, dry, Terroir-respecting Wines ⊢ p. 113

Tramín červený 2013 grape selection, medium sweet, Traminer ⊢ p. 84

Devín 2013 selection of berries, sweet, Devín ⊢ p. 101

Cabernet Sauvignon Rosé 2013 dry, Rosé ⊢ p. 111

Modrý Portugal 2013 dry, Blauer Portugieser ⊢ p. 96

Pinot Noir 2012 grape selection, dry, Pinot Noir ⊢ p. 95

Frankovka modrá 2012 Winemaker´s Cut, grape selection, dry, Innovative Wines ⊢ p. 118

Cabernet Sauvignon 2012 barique Winemaker´s Cut, grape selection, dry, Cabernet Sauvignon ⊢ p. 91

Cuvée Hron Váh Rimava Rudava 2011 Winemaker´s Cut, red, dry, Wines made of red new clones ⊢ p. 110

VÍNO NITRA

Víno Nitra, spol. s r.o.
Dolnozoborská 14, 949 01 Nitra
M: +421 903 901 061
www.vinonitra.sk, vinonitra@vinonitra.sk

VRoN • 1960 • ☐ 780 ha • 4,500,000 l

Vino Nitra is a Slovak wine producer with a half century tradition and which can base its production on its own vineyards in three viticultural regions of Slovakia – Nitra, Southern Slovakia and the Small Carpathians. The grapes are cultivated within an integrated production system and then processed under the supervision of master winemakers while using the most up-to-date technology. The quality is guaranteed by Ing. Jozef Adamovič, PhD., the production manager for almost a decade; he can be proud of the numerous domestic and foreign awards he has won during this period. In addition to non-sparkling wines, the winery produces Sekt Pálffy premium sparkling wines, which garnered the highest award in the history of Slovak sparkling wines – the gold medal from the Effervescents du Monde competition in Dijon, France.

Nitra wines are exported to the Czech Republic, Japan, the USA, Poland and China, where this winery closely cooperates with its Chinese partner under the joint project entitled Zhongjie Nitra Winery, Ltd. Wines from the Nitra cellar won 5 silver medals in 2015.

SIGNIFICANT WINE AWARDS

Veltlínske zelené 2013 Exclusive Collection, grape selection, dry
SM Výstava vín Viničné 2014

Sahara 2012 Exclusive Collection, quality branded wine, red, dry
SM Víno Bojnice 2014
SM Výstava vín Limbach 2014

SOMMELIER'S TIP

Sekt Pálffy Brut Méthode Classique, dry, Sparkling Wines ⊢ p. 131

Sekt Pálffy Rosé Méthode Classique, extra dry, Sparkling Wines ⊢ p. 132

Sekt Pálffy Brut
Méthode Classique
Sparkling wine from the Slovak Republic

A sparkling wine made by the traditional method of fermentation in bottles from the basic wine combination of Pinot Blanc and Chardonnay. Its brilliant yellow and greenish appearance is accompanied by the creation of foam with an intensive sparkling of small bubbles of carbon dioxide. The smell of overripe fruit with a trace of lime biscuit is harmoniously balanced out by a fresh, medium-long taste. The lively sparkling of CO_2 heightens the overall feeling of refreshment with a sour citrus aftertaste.

PB, CH • [2,625 l] • 0.75 l • € € • L662 • 12.0 % vol. • ★★★★

SLOVAK WINERIES FROM A TO Z

Sekt Pálffy Extra Dry
Méthode Classique

Sparkling wine from the Slovak Republic

A Cuvée made from a combination of basic wines of Pinot Blanc and Chardonnay varieties after secondary fermentation and clarification with a dosage of 16 grams of residual sugar per liter. It has a golden-yellow shade, brilliant clarity and the fine persistent sparkling of carbon dioxide bubbles. The smell of dried honey pears with an herbal note shows longer yeasts contact after fermentation.

PB, CH • [4,500 l] • 0.75 l • €€ • L661 • 12.0 % vol. • 🍷 • ❄ • ② • ✒ • ★★★★

Veltlínske zelené 2013
Exclusive Collection, grape selection, dry

Wine with protected indication of origin D.S.C.
VRoN, Nitra viticultural area

A yellow-greenish wine with golden hues. Its spicy, fruity smell features a combination of citrus and nutmeg, while traces of linden blossoms appear after opening. The medium-long taste is emphasized by fruit acid with tones of grapefruit and green apples and the spicy character of its aftertaste is stressed by a pleasant fruit bitterness.

[15,000 l] • 0.75 l • €€ • L-14 • 12.0 % vol. • 🍷 • ① • ⌒ {7} • 🍾 • ★★★

Rulandské modré 2012
Exclusive Collection, grape selection, dry

Wine with protected indication of origin D.S.C.
VRoSS, Galanta viticultural area

This ruby-red Pinot Noir has a velvety bouquet of blackberries and dried plums with an interesting and delicious medium-long taste. The well-balanced content of smooth tannins and alcohol is properly refreshed by decent acid which, thanks to the mature vintage, leaves a juicy aftertaste that is slightly reminiscent of sour cherries in chocolate. A drinkable partner for dining and discussions.

[10,000 l] • 0.75 l • €€ • L-7 • 12.0 % vol. • 🍷 • ① • ◐ • 🍴 {17} • 🍾 • ★★★1/2

Sahara 2012
Exclusive Collection, quality branded wine, red, dry

Wine with protected indication of origin D.S.C., VRoSC

The non-transparent crimson color with dark violet edges is attractively complemented by the sweet spicy aroma of cherries in chocolate and blueberries. The fuller tannin taste with a trace of bitter almonds, blackberries and roasted coffee is supported by a higher alcohol content. The mature taste profile concentrates balsamic notes of wood with candied sour cherries on the root of tongue.

DO • [6,500 l] • 0.75 l • €€ • L-15 • 13.0 % vol. • 🍷 • ① • ◐ • 🍴 {17} • ✒ • ★★★1/2

VÍNO-MASARYK

VÍNO-MASARYK s.r.o.
Sasinkova 2333/18A, 909 01 Skalica
T: +421 34 664 69 60
www.vino-masaryk.sk
vino-masaryk@vino-masaryk.sk

VRoSC • 1996 • ☐ 10 ha • 100,000 l •

VÍNO-MASARYK was founded by Alojz Masaryk in 1996 in Skalica in Western Slovakia, which has been famous for winegrowing since the 15th century. Masaryk, a pioneer of winegrowing and winemaking and a Slovak and Záhorie patriot, has taken care of the vineyards and made wine with love for over 40 years. He utilizes his knowledge and experience to make the highest quality wine exclusively from Slovak grapes. As he says: "We should not poison ourselves with wine, but enjoy its purity, fullness, freshness and bouquet." The family company farms on approximately 11 ha of vineyards under an integrated production system that complies with conditions for cross compliance. Wines from the Skalica region are harder and more diverse due to the increased concentration of iron in the soil. Lemberger (Blaufränkisch) is the flagship of cultivated varieties and known here as Skalický rubín (Ruby of Skalica). Its taste is excellent, and thanks to the high antioxidant and flavonoid content, it is extremely beneficial to the health. Its positive effect has been proven by university researchers in Spain, Portugal, Moravia and the Slovak University of Agriculture in Nitra thanks to samples from the winery of Alojz Masaryk. The company's annual production is approximately 100,000 l. In addition to the grapes from its own vineyards, the company uses grapes from vineyards in Southern Slovakia. The company uses top modern technology which preserves the high content of the natural substances in the wine. VÍNO-MASARYK has cooperated with Ing. Ondrej Korpás, the internationally renowned Slovak grapevine breeder, for many years. He also deserves credit for making the Devín, Dunaj, Milia, Váh popular. The quality of this wine is confirmed by fans and experts alike. VÍNO-MASARYK annually wins many awards at prestigious exhibitions at home and abroad. Customers gladly return to the company seat, either to get a bottle of good wine or for wine tasting in the pleasant company of Alojz Masaryk. VÍNO-MASARYK wines can be purchased at the company shop or at the company website. They annually offer 25 to 30 types of white, red and rosé wines and naturally sweet wines such as nobly rotten raisin wine, raisin selection and ice wine.

SIGNIFICANT WINE AWARDS

Milia 2013, grape selection, dry
GM Linčanský džbánek, Zeleneč 2014
GM Radošovce 2014
SM Celoslovenská výstava vín, Skalica 2014
GM Vinum Zoborensis, Komjatice 2014

Sauvignon 2012 late harvest, medium sweet
GM Vinum Pistensis, Piešťany 2013
SM Linčanský džbánek, Zeleneč 2013

Noria 2013, late harvest, medium sweet
GM Medzinárodná súťaž vín,
Veľké Pavlovice 2015
SM Celoslovenská výstava vín, Skalica 2014
GGM Cortona Cru, Neded 2014
GM Radošovce 2014

Dunaj 2011, selection of berries, dry
GM Valtické vínne trhy, Valtice 2012
SM WEINparade Poysdorf 2013, Austria
GM VinFest, Vinica 2012
GM Víno Bojnice 2012
SM Tokaj, Viničky 2013

SOMMELIER'S TIP

Milia 2013, grape selection, dry,
Milia ⊢ p. 104

Noria 2013, late harvest, medium sweet,
Noria ⊢ p. 104

Enem 2014 red quality branded wine, dry,
Cuvée ⊢ p. 124

Dunaj 2011, selection of berries, dry,
Dunaj ⊢ p. 109

SLOVAK WINERIES FROM A TO Z

Müller Thurgau 2014
quality varietal wine, dry
Wine with protected indication of origin, VRoSS

A light, yellow-green wine with brilliant sparkles and a tender, spicy and fruity bouquet with a hint of Muscat, ripened peaches and elderberry blossoms. The taste is well balanced with the smell. It is interesting because of its soft, fruity taste and tones of quince and its harmonious content of acids with discreet residual sugar. The pure aftertaste of this wine features a delicate drop of tropical fruit enhanced by a pleasant overall impression.

[6,000 l] • 0.75 l • € • L 4 • 11.0 % vol. • ⚲ • ② • ◯ • ▯ • ★★★1/2

Sauvignon 2012
late harvest, medium sweet
Wine with protected indication of origin, VRoSS

A light, yellow-green wine with a fine honey up to fruity bouquet of elderberry blossoms and ripe peaches and a herbal trace of nettle leaves in the background. Its medium-full body taste is typical of the harmony of its smell and soft fruitiness. The taste is well matured, and pure wine with a delicate acid content and pleasant residual sugar. The finish is reminiscent of a mixture of gooseberries and rhubarb with a drop of citrus juice. This vintage is at its peak.

[3,500 l] • 0.75 l • €€ • L 4 • 12.0 % vol. • ⚲ • ③ • ◯ • ▯ • ★★★★

Frankovka modrá ružové 2014
quality varietal wine, medium dry
Wine with protected indication of origin, VRoSC, Skalica

This violet-pink rosé Lemberger (Blaufränkisch) has a ripe, fruity smell reminiscent of raspberries with an admixture of garden strawberries, lilacs in blossom and sweet cherries. This mixture of summer red fruit is accompanied by a juicy, acid taste refreshed by drops of citrus juice. It is a rosé with a direct smell and an open lively taste. The qualities of this wine will stand out best within one year from bottling.

[6,000 l] • 0.75 l • € • L 24 • 11.0 % vol. • ⚲ • ② • ◯ • ▯ • ★

Skalický rubín 2014
red quality branded wine, dry
Wine with protected indication of origin, VRoSC, Skalica

An intensive spectrum of garnet-red up to ruby-red colors, a piquant smell of dark stone fruit and cinnamon and a medium-long fruity taste with higher tannin content. The clay soil and a humid and sunny autumn with a colder finish left the wine from this 55 year old vineyard an impressive extract and a typical fruit acidity with a blackberry aftertaste.

BF • [1,500 l] • 0.75 l • €€ • L 25 • 13.0 % vol. • ⚲ • ① • ◯ • + • 🛢 • ✦ • ★★★1/2

VPS – VINOHRADNÍCTVO PAVELKA A SYN

VPS – Vinohradníctvo Pavelka a syn, s.r.o.
Šenkvická 14/L, 902 01 Pezinok
T: +421 33 645 10 64
www.pavelkavino.sk, vino@pavelkavino.sk

VRoSC • 1995 • 50 ha • 300,000 l •

Bottles with the Pavelka label first appeared on the Slovak market in 1995. Two years later, its late harvest 1997 Pinot Blanc was the first wine to receive the official strip stamp and became the first Slovak wine with attribute from controlled production. In 2000, wine lovers had the first opportunity to be enchanted by the strong barrique wines from the Paves brand. In 2005, the winery introduced the Chateau Zumberg brand for consumers preferring lighter drinks. Despite the French and German sound of the title, the wine from the Chateau Zumberg collection has a local identity. For wine lovers with a good memory for taste, the company prepared the Premium collection with the best archive vintages of wines from their own production. The Pavelka a syn winery is the leading brand on the Slovak market. It offers the possibility to get to know the genuine terroir of the best of the Small Carpathians – a unique combination of location, soil and climate conditions which gives the wines a unique character.

SIGNIFICANT WINE AWARDS

Sekt Pavelka Blanc de Blancs, Brut
GM Vino Ljubljana 2015
SM Finger Lakes International Wine Competition 2015
GM Prague Wine Trophy 2015
SM Agrovíno, Nitra 2015
Národný salón vín SR (Slovak national Wine Salon) 2015

ROSÉ Cuvée 2014 late harvest, dry
SM Finger Lakes International Wine Competition 2015
GM Vienále Topoľčianky 2015

Chardonnay 2014 grape selection, dry
GM Prague Wine Trophy 2015

Národný salón vín SR (Slovak national Wine Salon) 2015

Rizling rýnsky 2014 grape selection, dry
Národný salón vín SR (Slovak national Wine Salon) 2015

Alibernet 2013 grape selection, dry
Národný salón vín SR (Slovak national Wine Salon) 2015

Alibernet 2011 barrique, grape selection, dry
GM International Wine Challenge AWC, Vienna 2014
Národný salón vín SR (Slovak national Wine Salon) 2013

SOMMELIER'S TIP

Sekt Pavelka Blanc de Blancs, Brut,
Sparkling Wines ⊢ p. 133

ROSÉ Cuvée 2014 late harvest, dry,
Rosé Wines ⊢ p. 111

Pinot Blanc 2014 grape selection, dry,
Pinot Blanc ⊢ p. 85

Chardonnay 2014 grape selection, dry,
Chardonnay ⊢ p. 84

Rizling rýnsky 2014 grape selection, dry,
Rhein Riesling ⊢ p. 79

PAVES CUVÉE 2011 quality branded wine, dry,
Cuvée ⊢ p. 124

Pinot noir 2013 grape selection, dry,
Pinot Noir ⊢ p. 94

Frankovka modrá 2013 grape selection, dry,
Lemberger (Blaufränkisch) ⊢ p. 89

Alibernet 2013 grape selection, dry,
Alibernet ⊢ p. 108

PAVES CUVÉE 2012 quality branded wine, red, dry,
Cuvée ⊢ p. 123

Alibernet 2011 barrique, grape selection, dry,
Alibernet ⊢ p. 106

SLOVAK WINERIES FROM A TO Z

Müller Thurgau 2014

Chateau Zumberg, quality varietal wine, dry

Slovak Wine D.S.C., VRoSC, Pezinok

This citrus-green wine with yellow up to golden hues has a light, spicy fruity smell that reveals traces of summer fruit with a predominance of gooseberries, apples and a fine hint of linden tree blossoms. The taste is more distinctive than the smell. A wine nicely combining decent acids with a tender bouquet reminiscent of a tropical fruit cocktail finished with a peel of pome fruit.

[7,500 l] • 0.75 l • € • L-1 • 11.0 % vol. • ♀ • ① • ◯ • ♠ • ★

Veltlínske zelené 2014

Chateau Zumberg, quality varietal wine, dry

Slovak Wine D.S.C., VRoSC, Pezinok

A bright green and yellow Grüner Veltliner with a pleasantly fresh fruity smell and a taste which features traces of Muscat and freshly ground apples with green almond undertones. Its lower alcohol content in combination with a soft and less distinctive aftertaste creates a delicious overall impression. The refreshing and bitter traces of grapefruit and lemon peel on the palate are interesting.

[7,500 l] • 0.75 l • € • L-2 • 11.5 % vol. • ♀ • ① • ◯ • ✦ • ★

Iršai Oliver 2014

Chateau Zumberg, quality varietal wine, dry

Slovak Wine D.S.C., VRoSC, Pezinok

This Irsai Oliver with a distinctive, golden-yellow shade and nutmeg tones is complemented by a smell of hazelnuts and freshly picked forest strawberries. It has a fragile, juicy taste with delicate velvet grapefruit acid and pleasant floral and fruity finish. The last drops are emphasized on the tongue by acids in addition to a trace of residual sugar, typical for this vintage which was wisely left by master winemakers after fermentation.

[7,500 l] • 0.75 l • € • L-7 • 11.0 % vol. • ♀ • ① • ◯ • ✦ • ★

Rizling vlašský 2014

late harvest, dry

Wine with protected indication of origin D.S.C.
VRoSC, Pezinok, Stará hora Vineyard

A light, golden-yellow Italian Riesling with a nice greenish shade and viscosity. The smell is fruity and distinctive, affected by the reduction of the yield before harvesting and pure modern processing. In addition to tons of green apples, butter pear and gooseberries it features traces of almond and fern emphasized by a citrus drop. Lively fruity acids are at the core of this excellent tasting experience of simple perfection based on the Sur lie method.

[1,000 l] • 0.75 l • €€ • L0102 • 12.0 % vol. • ♀ • ① • ◯ {1} • ◯ • ✦ • ★★★1/2

Tramín červený 2014

grape selection, dry

Wine with protected indication of origin D.S.C.
VRoSC, Pezinok, Grefty Vineyard

A greenish-yellow Traminer with golden hues. The pleasant aromatic structure of this wine features traces of overripe summer fruit, while the mixture of peaches and pineapple with cloves and the spicy note on the tongue brings about an intensive powder smell of coconut soap and rose petals. The distinctive, fresh fruity up to bitter-spicy aftertaste of this wine leaves traces of citrus peels and carnations on the tongue.

[1,000 l] • 0.75 l • € € • L0107 • 12.5 % vol. • ♈ • ① • ☐ • ✦ • ★★★1/2

Trojka 2013

quality branded wine, red, dry

Wine with protected indication of origin D.S.C.
VRoSC, Pezinok

A blend of the dark, violet-red up to ruby color with a rich bouquet of forest fruit which features tones of elderberry and late blackberries. The full, robust velvet taste of bitter almonds with distinctive tannin content is refreshed by relatively distinctive acids combined with higher alcohol. A fiery and effective combination of three dominant varieties with long spicy finish.

OR, BF, DO • [1,000 l] • 0.75 l • € € • L-2222 • 13.0 % vol. • ♈ • ① • ◎ • ☐ • ✦ • ★★★1/2

VVD

VVD – Vinohradnícko vinárske družstvo
Branovská cesta 1926, 941 31
Dvory nad Žitavou
T: +421 35 648 48 21
www.vinodvory.sk, info@vinodvory.sk,
obchod@vinodvory.sk

VRoSS • 1972 • ☐ 145 ha • 700,000 l •

The modern history of this company began in 2004. Located in Dvory nad Žitavou, VVD farms on 145 hectares of vineyards; they process a significant portion of the yield on their own with an average annual production of 700,000 liters of quality varietal wines and quality varietal wines with attribute. They offer the remaining grapes for sale to famous winemakers throughout Slovakia. They produce quality varietal wines from healthy and high quality grapes. Care for the vineyards is under the control of integrated production which is a guarantee of quality and ecological winegrowing. The use of careful protective substances for grapevines, which easily decompose in a natural ecosystem, is reflected in the quality of the wine and the sensitive impact of the winery on the environment. The exemplarily farmed vineyards in Viničný vrch produce the white grape wine varieties of Devín, Chardonnay, Irsai Oliver, Müller-Thurgau, Pinot Blanc, Pinot Gris, Italian and Rhein Riesling, Sauvignon, Traminer and Grüner Veltliner. Red varieties are represented by Alibernet, Cabernet Sauvignon, Lemberger (Blaufränkisch), Pinot Noir, Saint Laurent and Zweigeltrebe. In addition to wine tasting in the company's stylish cellar and purchasing wine directly, visitors can stop by the Chapel of St. Urban which dates back to the days of the reign of Maria Theresa and is situated in the heart of the vineyards.

SIGNIFICANT WINE AWARDS

Rizling vlašský 2013 Vinitory Premium,
late harvest, dry
SM Danube Wine, Komárno 2014

Sauvignon 2014 Vinitory Premium, late harvest, dry
SM Vitis Aurea, Modra 2015
SM Mun-Dus, Dunajská Streda 2015

Rulandské šedé 2014 Vinitory Premium,
grape selection, dry
GM Mun-Dus, Dunajská Streda 2015
SM Vitis Aurea, Modra 2015
SM Linčanský džbánek, Zeleneč 2015

Chardonnay 2014 Vinitory Premium,
grape selection, dry
SM Vitis Aurea, Modra 2015

Rulandské biele 2014 Vinitory Premium,
late harvest, dry
GM Linčanský džbánek, Zeleneč 2015
SM Danube Wine, Komárno 2015

Tramín červený 2014 Vinitory Premium,
grape selection, dry
SM Mun-Dus, Dunajská Streda 2015
SM Linčanský džbánek, Zeleneč 2015

Alibernet 2013 Vinitory Premium, late harvest, dry
SM Vienále Topoľčianky 2015
SM Linčanský džbánek, Zeleneč 2014
SM Tokaj, Viničky 2014

Cabernet Sauvignon 2013 Vinitory Premium,
grape selection, dry
GM Vinum Pistiensis, Piešťany 2014
SM Linčanský džbánek, Zeleneč 2014
SM Danube Wine, Komárno 2015

Frankovka modrá 2013 Vinitory Premium,
late harvest, dry
SM Linčanský džbánek, Zeleneč 2015

SOMMELIER'S TIP

Rulandské šedé 2014 Vinitory Premium,
grape selection, dry, Pinot Gris ⊢ p. 77

Rulandské biele 2014 Vinitory Premium,
late harvest, dry, Pinot Blanc ⊢ p. 86

SLOVAK WINERIES FROM A TO Z

Rizling vlašský 2013

Vinitory Premium, late harvest, dry

Wine with protected indication of origin D.S.C. VRoSS, Dvory nad Žitavou, Viničný vrch Vineyard

A light green Italian Riesling with straw-yellow hues. The piquantly fruity smell of summer green apples and greengages is pleasant and refreshing and reminiscent of garden gooseberries in the finish. The clear and pure structure of the medium-long taste is enriched by a higher acid content and a final tone of dry citrus peels.

[5,000 l] • 0.75 l • €€ • L-08 • 12.5 % vol. • ⚟ • ① • ○ • ✦ • ★★★1/2

Sauvignon 2014

Vinitory Premium, late harvest, dry

Wine with protected indication of origin D.S.C. VRoSS, Dvory nad Žitavou, Viničný vrch Vineyard

This green-yellow wine has a herbal smell of nettles complemented by tones of current buds with a hint of white pepper. The taste shows traces of piquant fruit acids while its fresh and spicy character in the medium-long finish is complemented by tones of fresh limes and forest raspberries against a background of yellow grapefruit peels.

[5,000 l] • 0.75 l • €€ • L-35 • 12.5 % vol. • ⚟ • ① • ○ • ✦ • ★★★1/2

Chardonnay 2014

Vinitory Premium, grape selection, dry

Wine with protected indication of origin D.S.C. VRoSS, Dvory nad Žitavou, Viničný vrch Vineyard

This yellowish wine with green hues has a fruity-honey smell that features traces of ripening apricots and vineyard peaches refined by beeswax after opening. Elegant tones of lemon balm and dried apricots also appear in the bouquet after swallowing. The higher acid content and proper extract, which complement the overall fresh impression of this vintage, are the basis for the medium-long fruity structure of the taste.

[5,000 l] • 0.75 l • €€ • L-43 • 13.5 % vol. • ⚟ • ① • ○ • ✦ • ★★★1/2

Tramín červený 2014

Vinitory Premium, grape selection, dry

Wine with protected indication of origin D.S.C. VRoSS, Dvory nad Žitavou, Viničný vrch Vineyard

This yellow and green Traminer with golden hues will enchant you with its attractive and intensive smell of dried pears with drops of honey and a pinch of white pepper. Floral tones of rose petals complemented by a trace of carnation appear in the goblet after opening. The taste is similar to the smell and its intensity is emphasized by juicy acids and extract with a stronger trace of cinnamon and alcohol.

[5,000 l] • 0.75 l • €€ • L-36 • 13.0 % vol. • ⚟ • ① • ○ • ✦ • ★★★1/2

SLOVAK WINERIES FROM A TO Z

Zweigeltrebe ružové 2014

Vinitory Premium, medium dry

Wine with protected indication of origin D.S.C.
VRoSS, Dvory nad Žitavou, Viničný vrch Vineyard

A bright, claret-red rosé with a juicy fruity aroma. The tones of May cherries and a pleasant citrus note in the taste are supported by fresh fruit acid. Fermentation left 12 g/l of residual sugar in this wine, which along with the piquant tannins released from skins, create a pleasant overall taste.

[5,000 l] • 0.75 l • €€ • L-26 • 11.5 % vol. • ♀ • ② • ◯ • ♣ • ★★★

Alibernet 2013

Vinitory Premium, late harvest, dry

Wine with protected indication of origin D.S.C.
VRoSS, Dvory nad Žitavou, Viničný vrch Vineyard

This dark violet wine with purple hues has a persistent aroma with tones of cranberries, cassis and juniper. The full-bodied taste with rich tannin content is well-balanced with the smell by tones of blueberries, green poppies, mowed grass and plums and supported in the finish by delicious fresh acid. Its pure reductive style represents the varietal characteristics of the vintage from this tannin variety.

[5,000 l] • 0.75 l • €€ • L-27 • 12.5 % vol. • ♀ • ① • ◎ • ◯ • ♣ • ★★★

Cabernet Sauvignon 2013

Vinitory Premium, grape selection, dry

Wine with protected indication of origin D.S.C.
VRoSS, Dvory nad Žitavou, Viničný vrch Vineyard

A ruby-red wine accompanied by claret hues on the edges and a pleasant, intensive smell of red currents and mulberries which promises a pleasant taste experience. The lively fruity taste with traces of forest strawberries and juniper is a result of careful fermentation and the right acid and extract content. Its finish has a coffee-spicy note with a light gooseberry skin aftertaste.

[5,000 l] • 0.75 l • €€ • L-28 • 12.5 % vol. • ♀ • ① • ◎ • ◯ • ♣ • ★★★1/2

Frankovka modrá 2013

Vinitory Premium, late harvest, dry

Wine with protected indication of origin D.S.C.
VRoSS, Dvory nad Žitavou, Viničný vrch Vineyard

A dark violet-red Lemberger (Blaufränkisch) with ruby hues. Tones of plum marmalade on butter toast briefly appear in a fuller smell after pouring. The bouquet then develops in a spicy-cinnamon up to bitter almond taste with medium-long fading on the tongue. It has a well-balanced and provocative aftertaste with cherry acid and lively tannin traces.

[5,000 l] • 0.75 l • €€ • L-29 • 13.5 % vol. • ♀ • ① • ◎ • ◯ • ♣ • ★★★1/2

ŽITAVSKÉ VINICE

Žitavské vinice
Hlavná 204, 941 03 Úľany nad Žitavou
T: +421 905 536 399
www.zitavskevinice.sk, info@zitavskevinice.sk

VRoN · 2008 · ☐ 3.5 ha · 5,000 l ·

The philosophy of the brand is sincere and open. Jozef Teplan and Tomáš Strelinger are ambitiously building this young winery. While respecting Mother Nature, they convert the best possible grapes cultivated in their own vineyards in the vicinity of village of Černík into beautifully full and perfect varietal wines ranging from naturally sweet wines, which are their greatest passion, up to dry whites and reds. Just as every human being is different and exceptional in certain respects, they use the same approach with individual varieties. They try to avoid their weaknesses and take advantage of their potential. The wine that you taste is of a distinctive varietal character and frequently the essence of a given variety; moreover it contains the unmistakable signature of its origin from the vineyards of Žitava.

SIGNIFICANT WINE AWARDS

Pinot Gris 44 2012 wine without geographical indication, sweet
GM International Wine Challenge AWC, Vienna 2014

SOMMELIER'S TIP

Devín 2013 wine without geographical indication, dry, Devín ⊢ p. 102

Pinot Gris 44 2012 wine without geographical indication, sweet, Terroir-respecting wine ⊢ p. 114

Dunaj 2013 wine without geographical indication, dry, Dunaj ⊢ p. 109

INDEX

Adamovič, Jozef 230
André, Christian Karl 35
Bel, Matej 188
Béla IV 20
Benedict V 20
Blaho, Igor 219
 see Vinárstvo Blaho
Bobeková, V. 41
BOTT FRIGYES 81, 90, 94, 125, **144 – 145**
Čajkovič, Marián 146
Čajkovič Winery 87, **146 – 147**
Catherine I 20
Catherine II 20
Charmat, Eugen 54
Château Belá 78, 79, 91 – 94, 106, 108, **160 – 161**
Chateau Modra 78, 82, 85, 105, **162 – 163**
Château Rúbaň 73, 101, 104, **164 – 165**
Château Topolčianky 74, 75, 90, 97, 109, 132, **166 – 167**
Csernus, Karol 184
 see Pivnica Csernus
Elizabeth I 20
Elizabeth II 20, 188
Dudo, Miroslav 226
Ďuríková, Jana 196
 see Rodinné vinárstvo Ďurík
ELESKO 77, 103, 108, 110, 122, **150 – 152**
ELESKO TOKAY 98, 99, 132, **148 – 149**
Euro-Agro
 see BOTT FRIGYES
FEDOR MALÍK & SYN. 74, 84, 114, **153**
Foltánová, A. 41
Francis II Rákóczi 20
Franz Josef I 157
Fries, von Johann 36
GEORGINA – RODINNÉ VINÁRSTVO 120, 125, **154 – 155**
HACAJ 132, 133, **156**
Hečko, František 36, 197
Hubert J.E. 131, 133, **157 – 159**
J. & J. Ostrožovič 98, 99, 115, 123, 127, **168 – 170**
KARPATSKÁ PERLA 73, 76, 79, 100, 103, 107, 115, 118, 122, 123, **171 – 173**
Kasnyik rodinné vinárstvo 80, 89, **174 – 175**
Kasnyik, Gabriel 174
Kasnyik, Tomáš 174
Korpás, Ondrej 39, 42 – 43
Kraus, V. 44
Křivánek, V. 39

Krockow, Ilona von 160
Louis XIV 20
Malík, Fedor 153
Maria Theresa 20
Martin Pomfy – Mavín 74, 80, 85, 86, 92, 93, 94, 101, 112, **176 – 178**
Masaryk, Alojz 232
 see VÍNO-MASARYK
Máté, Ladislav Sepši 20
Máťuš, Miloš 180
 see Vinohradníctvo a vinárstvo Miloš Máťuš
Mátyás – Rodinné vinárstvo 129, **179**
Matyšák, Peter 222
 see Víno Matyšák
Melecsky, Tibor 208
MOVINO 83, 93, 102, **181 – 182**
Mrva, Vladimír 228
Müller, Egon 27, 160
Nagy, Gejza 154
Nagy Veronika 154
Natural Domin & Kušický 129, 130, **183**
Novák, I. 41
Ostrožovič, Jaroslav 168
 see J. & J. Ostrožovič
Parker, Robert 160
Pavelka a syn
 see VPS – Vinohradníctvo Pavelka a syn
Peter the Great 20
Petrech, Miroslav 27, 160
Pivnica Csernus 116, 126, **184**
Pivnica Orechová 73, 76, 77, 81, 91, 100, 109, **185 – 187**
Pivnica Radošina 95, 107, 115, 117, **188 – 190**
Pivnica Tibava 82, 102, 107, **191 – 192**
Pivnica Zsigmond 77, 81, 93, **193 – 194**
Pomfy, Martin
 see Martin Pomfy – Mavín
Pospíšilová, Dorota 39, 42 – 44, 46 – 47, 195
REGIA TT
 see Pivnica Orechová
repa winery 90, 119, 120, 124, **195**
Repa, Jozef 195
Rodinné vinárstvo Ďurík 75, 80, 95, 126, **196**
Rodinné vinárstvo Magula 89, 96, 113, **197**
Ruland, Johann Segner 31
Šebo, Eduard 162
 see CHATEAU MODRA
Šebo, Margita and Ladislav 171
 see KARPATSKÁ PERLA
Slobodné vinárstvo 115, 126, **198 – 199**
SOŠVO Modra 87, **200 – 201**

INDEX

Stredná odborná škola vinársko-ovocinárska Modra
  see SOŠVO Modra
Strekov 1075 90, 96, 116, 120, **202**
SVV VINANZA 78, 82, 104, **203 – 204**
Tajna Vineyards and Winery 85, 86, 92, 95, 125, **205 – 206**
TERRA PARNA 96, 106, 107, **207**
Tibor Melecsky 117, **208**
TOKAJ & CO 127, 128, **209 – 210**
TOKAJ MACIK WINERY 116, 119, 125, 128, **211 – 212**
Velkeer 76, 83, 102, 103, **213 – 214**
Vienna DC
  see Château Rúbaň
VILLA VINO RAČA 83, 88, 89, 91, **215 – 216**
Vinárstvo Berta 81, 120, **217 – 218**
Vinárstvo Blaho 108, 110, **219 – 220**
VÍNKO KLIMKO MODRA 74, **221**
VINO MAGULA
  see Rodinné vinárstvo Magula
Víno Matyšák 75, 82, 86, 88, 100, 111, 114, 119, 122, 133, **222 – 225**
Víno Miroslav Dudo 83, 87, 92, 101, 123, 124, **226 – 227**
VÍNO MRVA & STANKO 75, 76, 80, 84, 91, 95, 96, 101, 113, 110, 111, 114, 118, 131, **228 – 229**
Víno Nitra 131, 132, **230 – 231**
Vinohradníctvo a vinárstvo Miloš Máťuš 88, 113, **180**
VÍNO-MASARYK 104, 109, 124, **232 – 233**
VPS – Vinohradníctvo Pavelka a syn 79, 84, 85, 89, 94, 106, 108, 111, 123, 124, 133, **234 – 236**
VVD 77, 86, **237 – 239**
Warhol, Andy 150
Zatloukal, F. 40
Zenagro
  see TERRA PARNA
Žitavské vinice 102, 109, 114, **240**
Zsigmond, Gabriel 193
Zvolenský, Jozef 207
  see TERRA PARNA

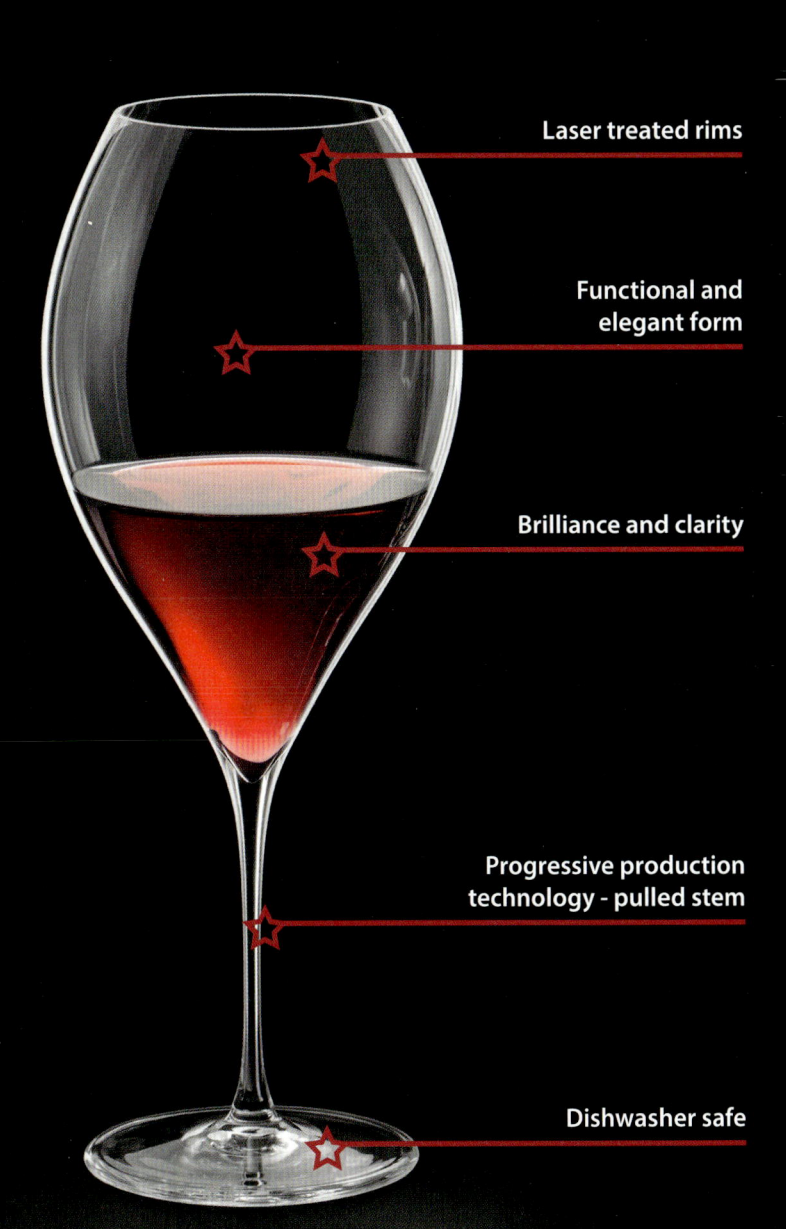

RONA
5 STAR GLASS

Made to serve
www.rona.sk

- ★ Laser treated rims
- ★ Functional and elegant form
- ★ Brilliance and clarity
- ★ Progressive production technology - pulled stem
- ★ Dishwasher safe

medusa
restaurant & club

WIEN

MEDUSA RESTAURANT & CLUB A 3-STOREY RESTAURANT IN THE VERY CITY CENTRE OF VIENNA, NEAR THE OPERA HOUSE. UNIQUELY DESIGNED CONNECTION OF A RESTAURANT WITH AN OPEN-VIEW KITCHEN THAT OFFERS A SELECTION OF EXCELLENT INTERNATIONAL CUISINE.

NEUER MARKT 8, 1010 WIEN, WWW.MEDUSARESTAURANT.AT

RIO IS A BEAUTIFUL AND SPACIOUS BRAZILIAN RESTAURANT DEFINED BY A SOUTH AMERICAN INTERIOR WITH COLONIAL FURNISHINGS, WITH A SEPARATE NIGHT CLUB AND BAR IN THE BASEMENT. FUSION OF BRAZILIAN AND INTERNATIONAL CUISINE AND PREMIUM WINES.

HVIEZDOSLAVOVO NÁM. 15, PANSKÁ 31, 811 01 BRATISLAVA – CENTRE, WWW.RIORESTAURANT.SK

BRATISLAVA

KOŠICE

THE LEGENDARY PRIMI IS ALSO IN KOŠICE NOW, ON KOVÁČSKA STREET. GREAT MEDITERRANEAN CUISINE, BEAUTIFUL INTERIOR AND LAID BACK ATMOSPHERE.

KOVÁČSKA 2 – HISTORICAL DOWNTOWN, 040 01 KOŠICE, WWW.PRIMIKOSICE.SK

WE OPENED BARROCK IN PRAGUE IN SEPTEMBER 2015. THE BEST ROCK MUSIC OF ALL TIMES, DJS, LIVE ROCK CONCERTS, BURGERS, RIBS, BURRITOS AND, OF COURSE, BEER, SHOTS AND COCKTAILS.

VÁCLAVSKÉ NÁMĚSTÍ 48, 110 00 PRAHA – CENTRE, WWW.BARROCKPRAHA.CZ

PRAGUE

www.facebook.com/BratislavaRegionTourism

Taste
the region

www.gob.sk

BRATISLAVA REGION

ELESKO WINE PARK

In Slovakia in the centre of Europe on the foothills of the Small Carpathians on a space spanning 110 hectares we find the vineyards from which the noble and unique ELESKO wine stems. In the vineyards we place great emphasis on quality and uniqueness, our wine is made exclusively from the fruits of our vineyards – all of which are arranged in integrated production – which is sparing to the environment and minimises the use of chemical treatment in favour of biological protection and environmental protection. The Winery is one of the most modern in Europe.

ELESKO RESTAURANT

In the ELESKO restaurant you can taste the most homely "plain" meals of extraordinary quality as well as, of course, ELESKO wine. Here you will find traditional gastronomy with modern twist and excellent game dishes, prepared from game that comes exclusively from Slovak forests.

ELESKO FOREST

ELESKO Forest which focuses its activities chiefly on the management of forest land and breeding ungulates with a valuable gene pool and high-value trophy hunting and farming - has prepared unique hunting on a hunting range for you in the forests of the Small Carpathians with an area encompassing more than 2800 hectares, of which 420 hectares is made up by the Balunky game reserve. Balunky was founded in 1997 and high quality trophy mouflon, fallow deer and red deer can be found there.

ZOYA MUSEUM

In the middle of the vineyards, on premises with a developed area of more than 1,000 square meters, you can find a museum of contemporary international modern art. ZOYA MUSEUM is one of the largest private museums in Europe. The museum collection hosts dozens of original works of the King of pop art, the artist with Slovak roots, Andy Warhol.

ELESKO
WINE PARK MODRA

www.elesko.sk

Malokarpatské
múzeum
v Pezinku

EXPERIENCE WINE

Color and light wine tasting

Wine tasting in the dark

www.muzeumpezinok.sk